THE TRANSFORMERS
HEROES & VILLAINS

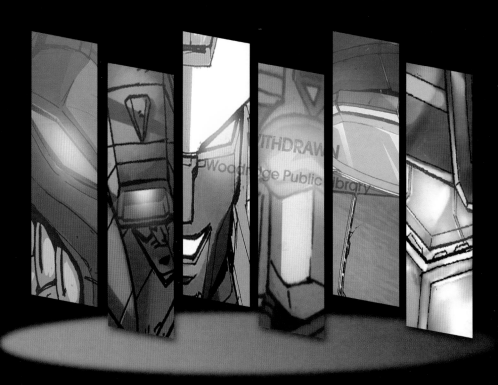

Special thanks to Hasbro's Aaron Archer,
Michael Kelly, Amie Lozanski, Val Roca,
Ed Lane, Michael Provost, Erin Hillman,
Samantha Lomow, and Michael Verrecchia
for their invaluable assistance.

Cover by
Guido Guidi

Cover Colors by
Joana Lafuente

Collection Edits by
Justin Eisinger

Collection Design by
Tom B. Long

IDW Publishing is:
Operations:
Ted Adams, Chief Executive Officer
Greg Goldstein, Chief Operating Officer
Matthew Ruzicka, CPA, Chief Financial Officer
Alan Payne, VP of Sales
Lorelei Bunjes, Dir. of Digital Services
AnnaMaria White, Marketing & PR Manager
Marci Hubbard, Executive Assistant
Alonzo Simon, Shipping Manager
Editorial:
Chris Ryall, Publisher/Editor-in-Chief
Scott Dunbier, Editor, Special Projects
Andy Schmidt, Senior Editor
Justin Eisinger, Editor
Kris Oprisko, Editor/Foreign Lic.
Denton J. Tipton, Editor
Tom Waltz, Editor
Mariah Huehner, Associate Editor
Design:
Robbie Robbins, EVP/Sr. Graphic Artist
Ben Templesmith, Artist/Designer
Neil Uyetake, Art Director
Chris Mowry, Graphic Artist
Amauri Osorio, Graphic Artist
Gilberto Lazcano, Production Assistant

ISBN 978-1-60010-634-7
12 11 10 09 1 2 3 4 5

To discuss this issue of *Transformers*, or join
the IDW Insiders, or to check out exclusive Web
offers, check out our site:

WWW.IDWPUBLISHING.com

Originally published as THE TRANSFORMERS: SPOTLIGHTS: OPTIMUS PRIME,
ULTRA MAGNUS, GRIMLOCK, SHOCKWAVE, RAMJET, and SOUNDWAVE.

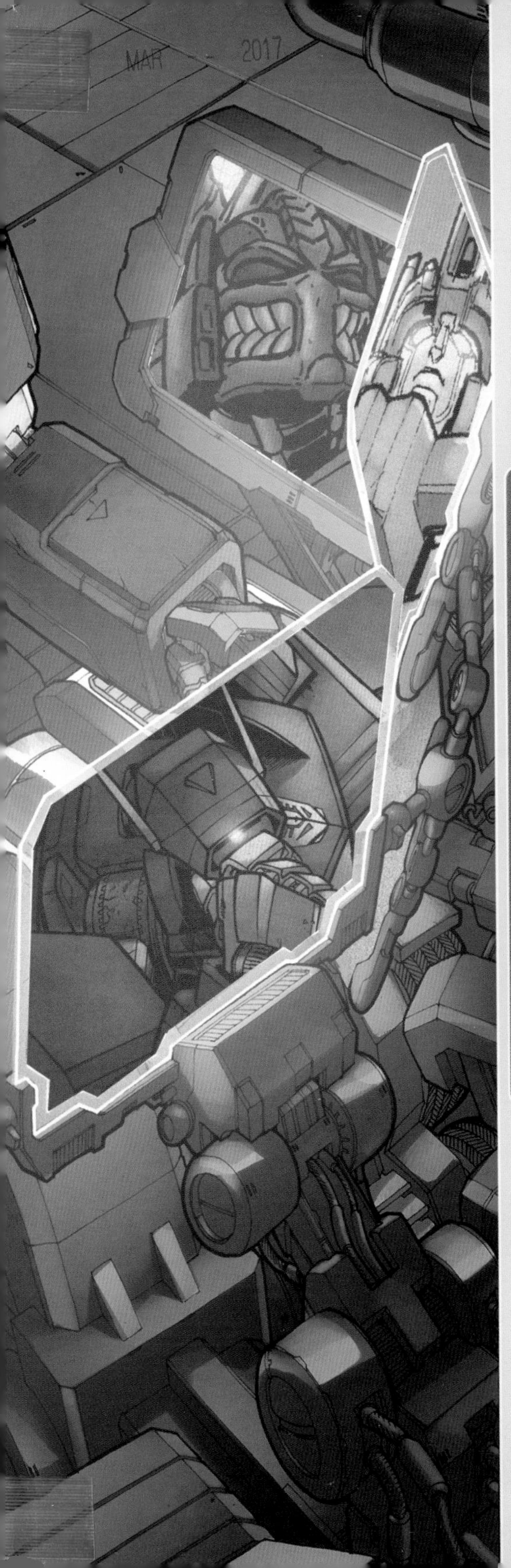

Table of Contents

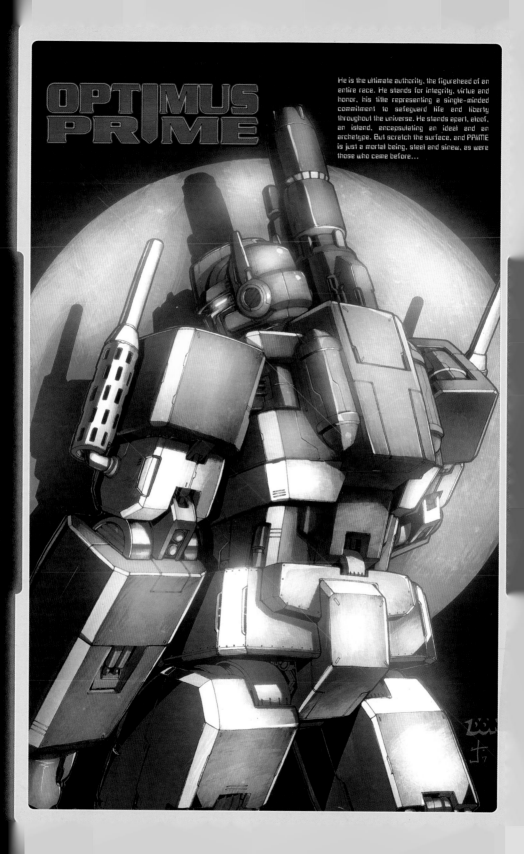

OPTIMUS PRIME

He is the ultimate authority, the figurehead of an entire race. He stands for integrity, virtue and honor, his title representing a single-minded commitment to safeguard life and liberty throughout the universe. He stands apart, aloof, an island, encapsulating an ideal and an archetype. But scratch the surface, and PRIME is just a mortal being, steel and sinew, as were those who came before...

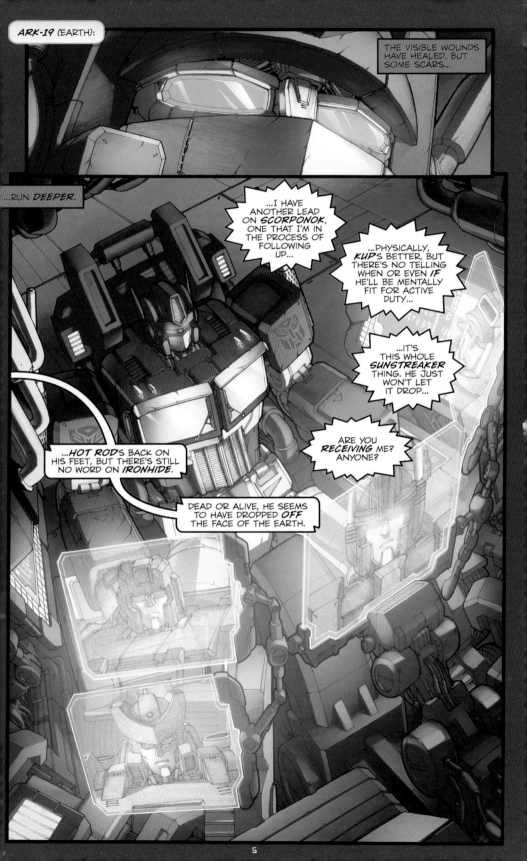

THE VISIBLE WOUNDS HAVE HEALED, BUT SOME SCARS...

...RUN *DEEPER.*

...I HAVE ANOTHER LEAD ON *SCORPONOK,* ONE THAT I'M IN THE PROCESS OF FOLLOWING UP...

...PHYSICALLY, *KUP'S* BETTER, BUT THERE'S NO TELLING WHEN OR EVEN *IF* HE'LL BE MENTALLY FIT FOR ACTIVE DUTY...

...IT'S THIS WHOLE *SUNSTREAKER* THING. HE JUST WON'T LET IT DROP...

ARE YOU *RECEIVING* ME? ANYONE?

...*HOT ROD'S* BACK ON HIS FEET, BUT THERE'S STILL NO WORD ON *IRONHIDE.*

DEAD OR ALIVE, HE SEEMS TO HAVE DROPPED *OFF* THE FACE OF THE EARTH.

5

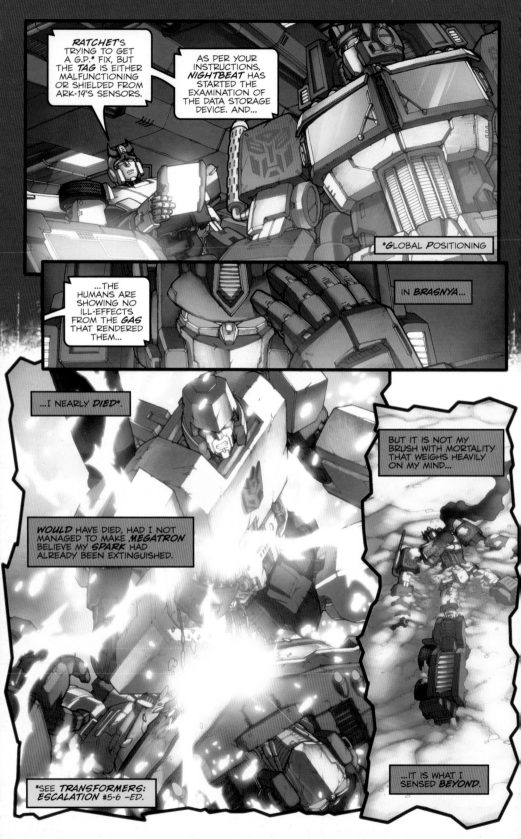

RATCHET'S TRYING TO GET A G.P.* FIX, BUT THE TAG IS EITHER MALFUNCTIONING OR SHIELDED FROM ARK-19'S SENSORS.

AS PER YOUR INSTRUCTIONS, NIGHTBEAT HAS STARTED THE EXAMINATION OF THE DATA STORAGE DEVICE. AND...

*GLOBAL POSITIONING

...THE HUMANS ARE SHOWING NO ILL-EFFECTS FROM THE GAS THAT RENDERED THEM...

IN BRASNYA...

...I NEARLY DIED*.

BUT IT IS NOT MY BRUSH WITH MORTALITY THAT WEIGHS HEAVILY ON MY MIND...

WOULD HAVE DIED, HAD I NOT MANAGED TO MAKE MEGATRON BELIEVE MY SPARK HAD ALREADY BEEN EXTINGUISHED.

*SEE TRANSFORMERS: ESCALATION #5-6 —ED.

...IT IS WHAT I SENSED BEYOND.

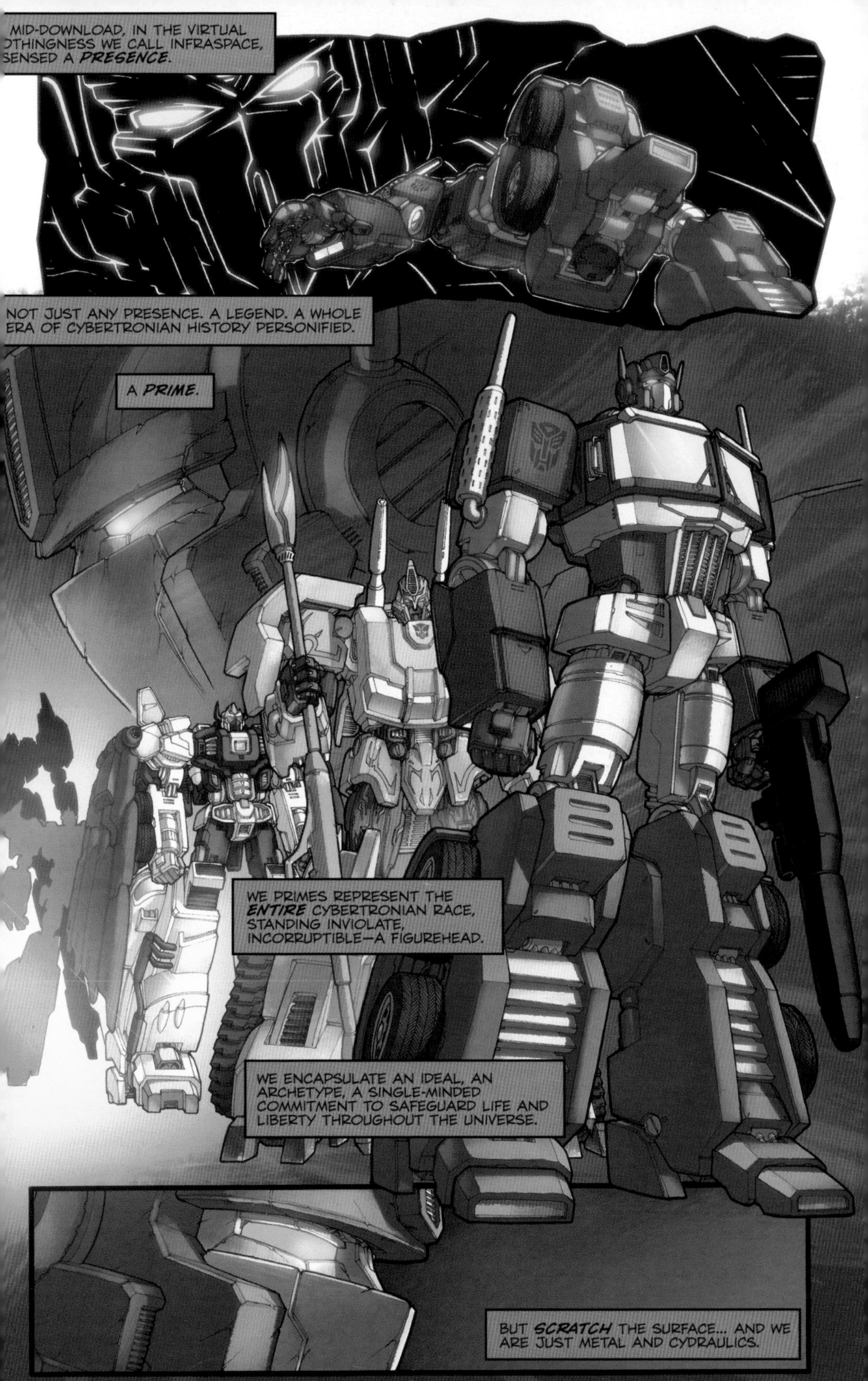
MID-DOWNLOAD, IN THE VIRTUAL OTHINGNESS WE CALL INFRASPACE, SENSED A *PRESENCE*.
NOT JUST ANY PRESENCE. A LEGEND. A WHOLE ERA OF CYBERTRONIAN HISTORY PERSONIFIED.
A *PRIME*.
WE PRIMES REPRESENT THE *ENTIRE* CYBERTRONIAN RACE, STANDING INVIOLATE, INCORRUPTIBLE—A FIGUREHEAD.
WE ENCAPSULATE AN IDEAL, AN ARCHETYPE, A SINGLE-MINDED COMMITMENT TO SAFEGUARD LIFE AND LIBERTY THROUGHOUT THE UNIVERSE.
BUT *SCRATCH* THE SURFACE... AND WE ARE JUST METAL AND CYDRAULICS.

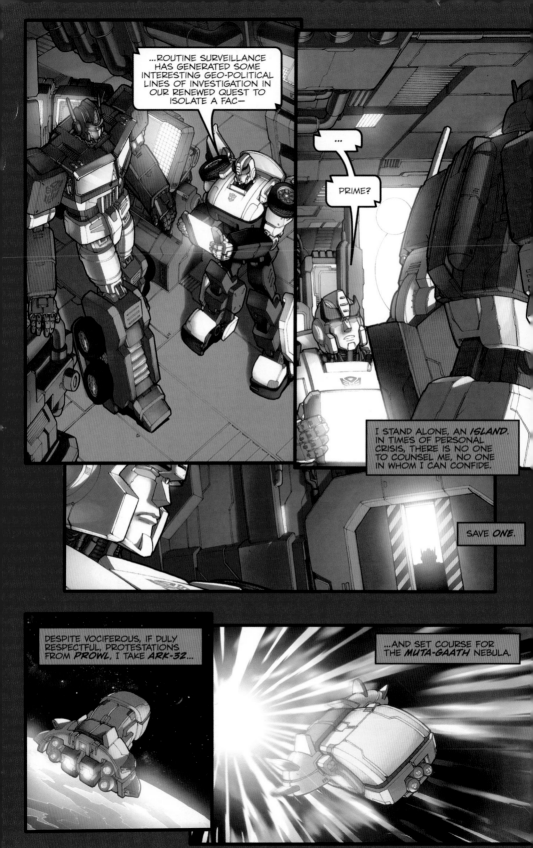

...ROUTINE SURVEILLANCE HAS GENERATED SOME INTERESTING GEO-POLITICAL LINES OF INVESTIGATION IN OUR RENEWED QUEST TO ISOLATE A FAC—

...

PRIME?

I STAND ALONE, AN *ISLAND*. IN TIMES OF PERSONAL CRISIS, THERE IS NO ONE TO COUNSEL ME, NO ONE IN WHOM I CAN CONFIDE.

SAVE *ONE*.

DESPITE VOCIFEROUS, IF DULY RESPECTFUL, PROTESTATIONS FROM *PROWL*, I TAKE *ARK-32*...

...AND SET COURSE FOR THE *MUTA-GAATH* NEBULA.

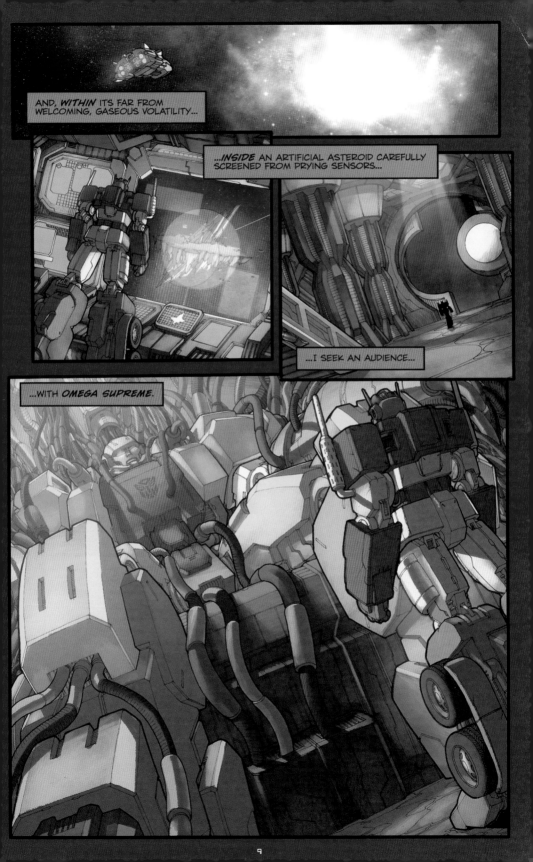

AND, *WITHIN* ITS FAR FROM WELCOMING, GASEOUS VOLATILITY...

...*INSIDE* AN ARTIFICIAL ASTEROID CAREFULLY SCREENED FROM PRYING SENSORS...

...I SEEK AN AUDIENCE...

...WITH *OMEGA SUPREME.*

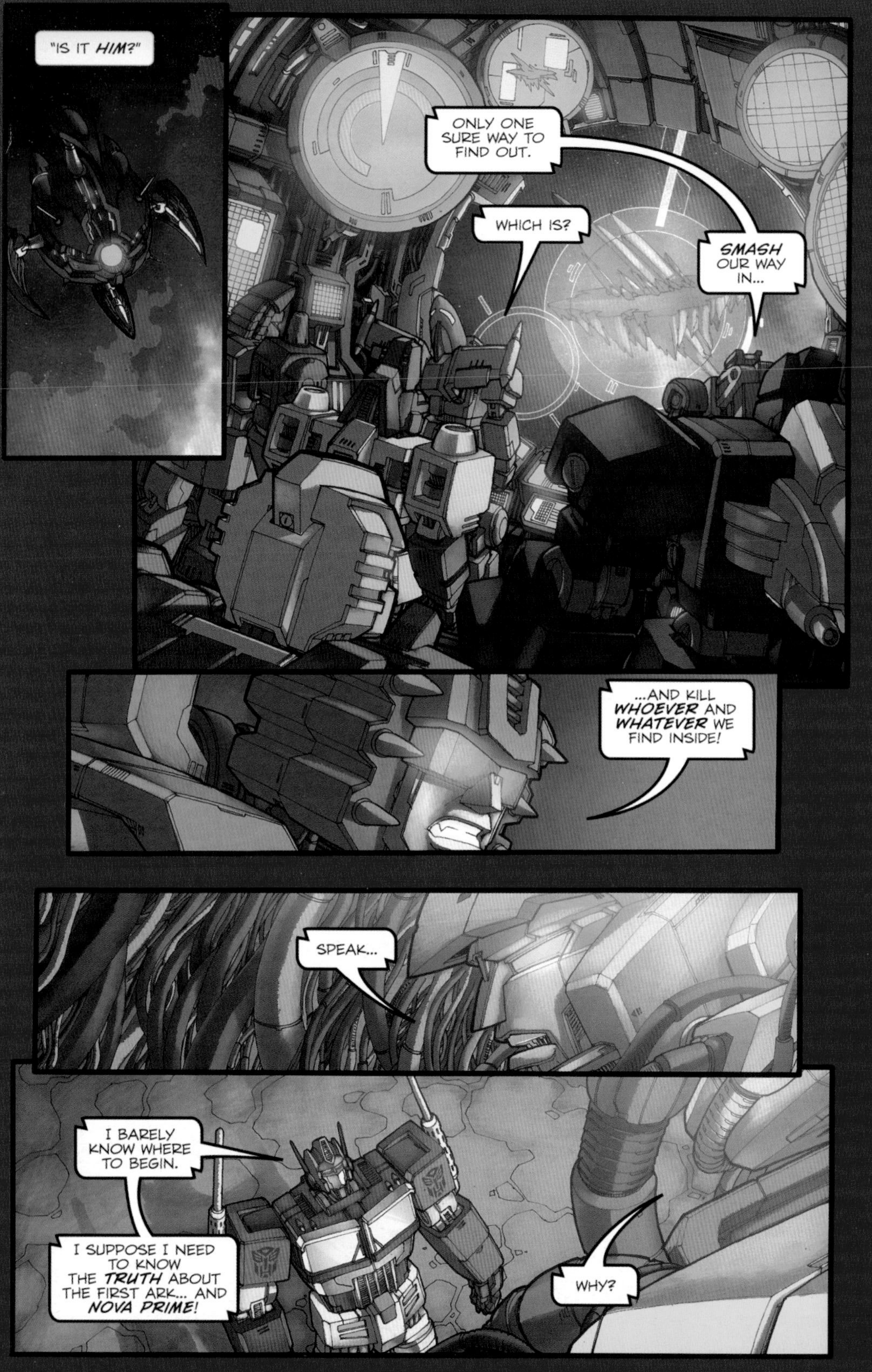
"IS IT HIM?"
ONLY ONE SURE WAY TO FIND OUT.
WHICH IS?
SMASH OUR WAY IN...
...AND KILL WHOEVER AND WHATEVER WE FIND INSIDE!
SPEAK...
I BARELY KNOW WHERE TO BEGIN.
I SUPPOSE I NEED TO KNOW THE TRUTH ABOUT THE FIRST ARK... AND NOVA PRIME!
WHY?

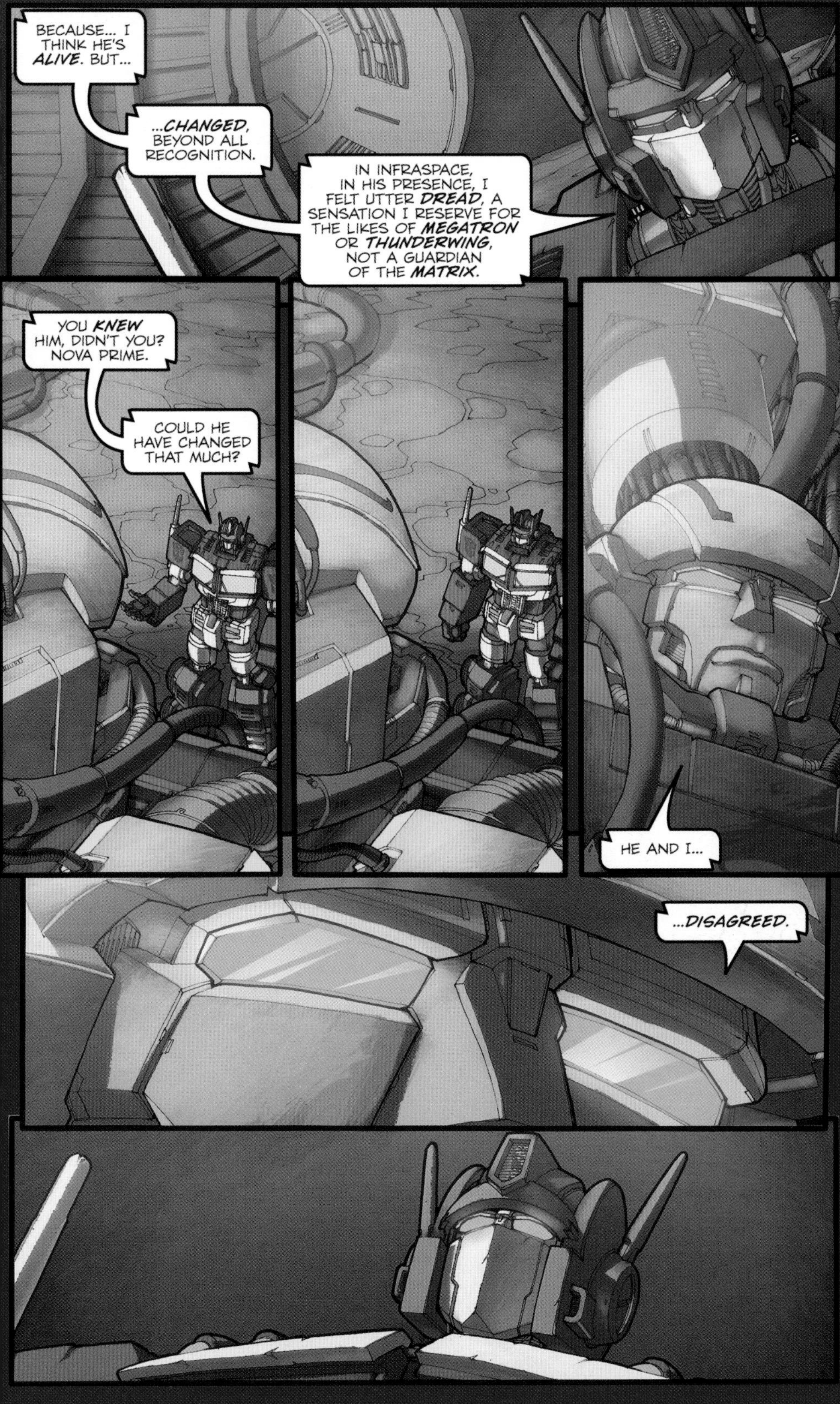
BECAUSE... I THINK HE'S ALIVE. BUT...
...CHANGED, BEYOND ALL RECOGNITION.
IN INFRASPACE, IN HIS PRESENCE, I FELT UTTER DREAD, A SENSATION I RESERVE FOR THE LIKES OF MEGATRON OR THUNDERWING, NOT A GUARDIAN OF THE MATRIX.
YOU KNEW HIM, DIDN'T YOU? NOVA PRIME.
COULD HE HAVE CHANGED THAT MUCH?
HE AND I...
...DISAGREED.

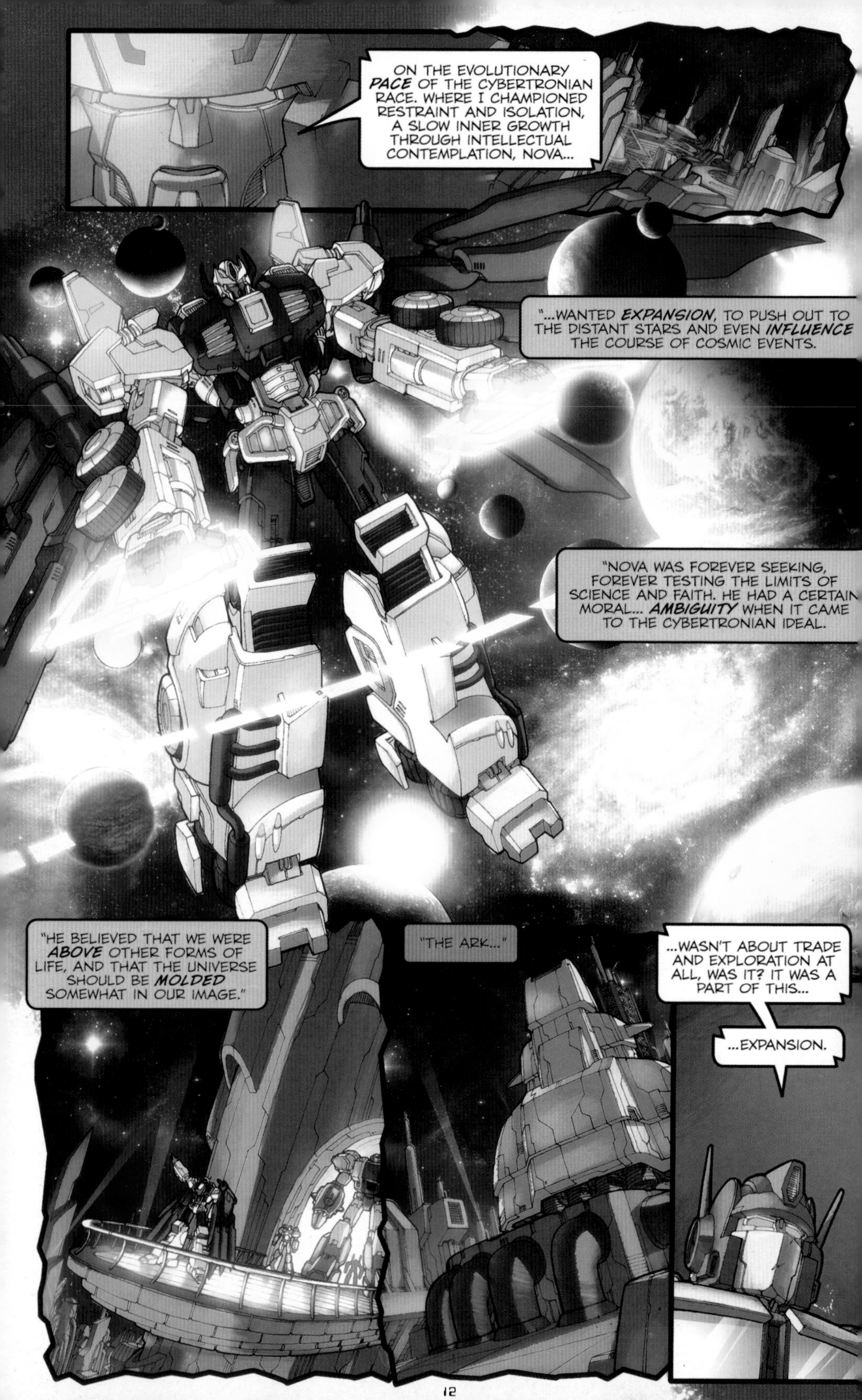
ON THE EVOLUTIONARY *PACE* OF THE CYBERTRONIAN RACE. WHERE I CHAMPIONED RESTRAINT AND ISOLATION, A SLOW INNER GROWTH THROUGH INTELLECTUAL CONTEMPLATION, NOVA...
"...WANTED *EXPANSION*, TO PUSH OUT TO THE DISTANT STARS AND EVEN *INFLUENCE* THE COURSE OF COSMIC EVENTS.
"NOVA WAS FOREVER SEEKING, FOREVER TESTING THE LIMITS OF SCIENCE AND FAITH. HE HAD A CERTAIN MORAL... *AMBIGUITY* WHEN IT CAME TO THE CYBERTRONIAN IDEAL.
"HE BELIEVED THAT WE WERE *ABOVE* OTHER FORMS OF LIFE, AND THAT THE UNIVERSE SHOULD BE *MOLDED* SOMEWHAT IN OUR IMAGE."
"THE ARK..."
...WASN'T ABOUT TRADE AND EXPLORATION AT ALL, WAS IT? IT WAS A PART OF THIS...
...EXPANSION.

I SUSPECT AS MUCH, YES. AS TO WHETHER HE MIGHT STILL BE ALIVE... IT IS *POSSIBLE*. THE ULTIMATE FATE OF THE ARK AND ITS CREW HAS NEVER BEEN DETERMINED.

BUT—

KALUNNNNG!

WHAT—?

KALUNNNNG!

BA-
TTANKK!

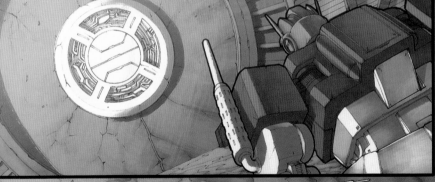

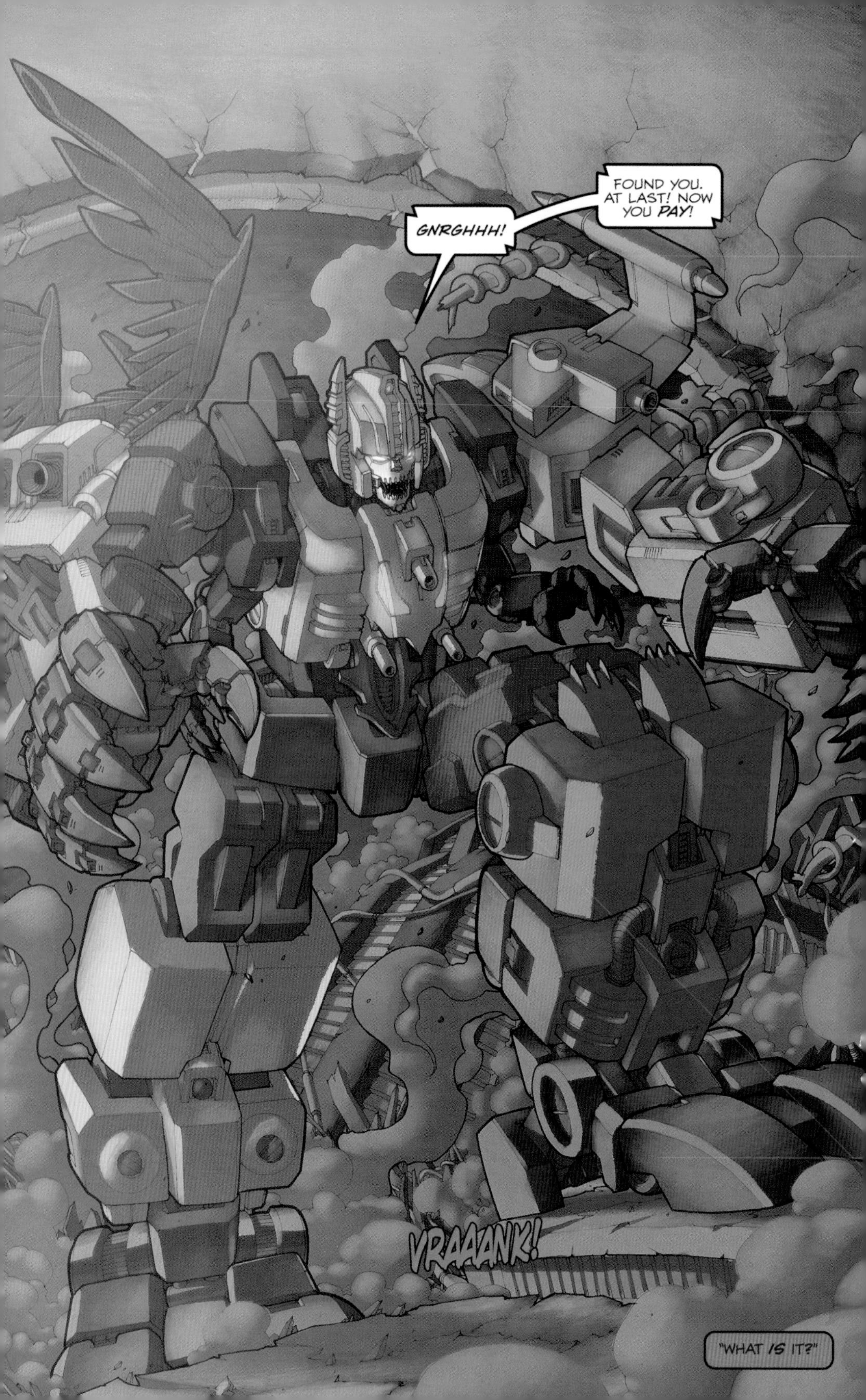
FOUND YOU. AT LAST! NOW YOU PAY!
GNRGHHH!
VRAAANK!
"WHAT IS IT?"

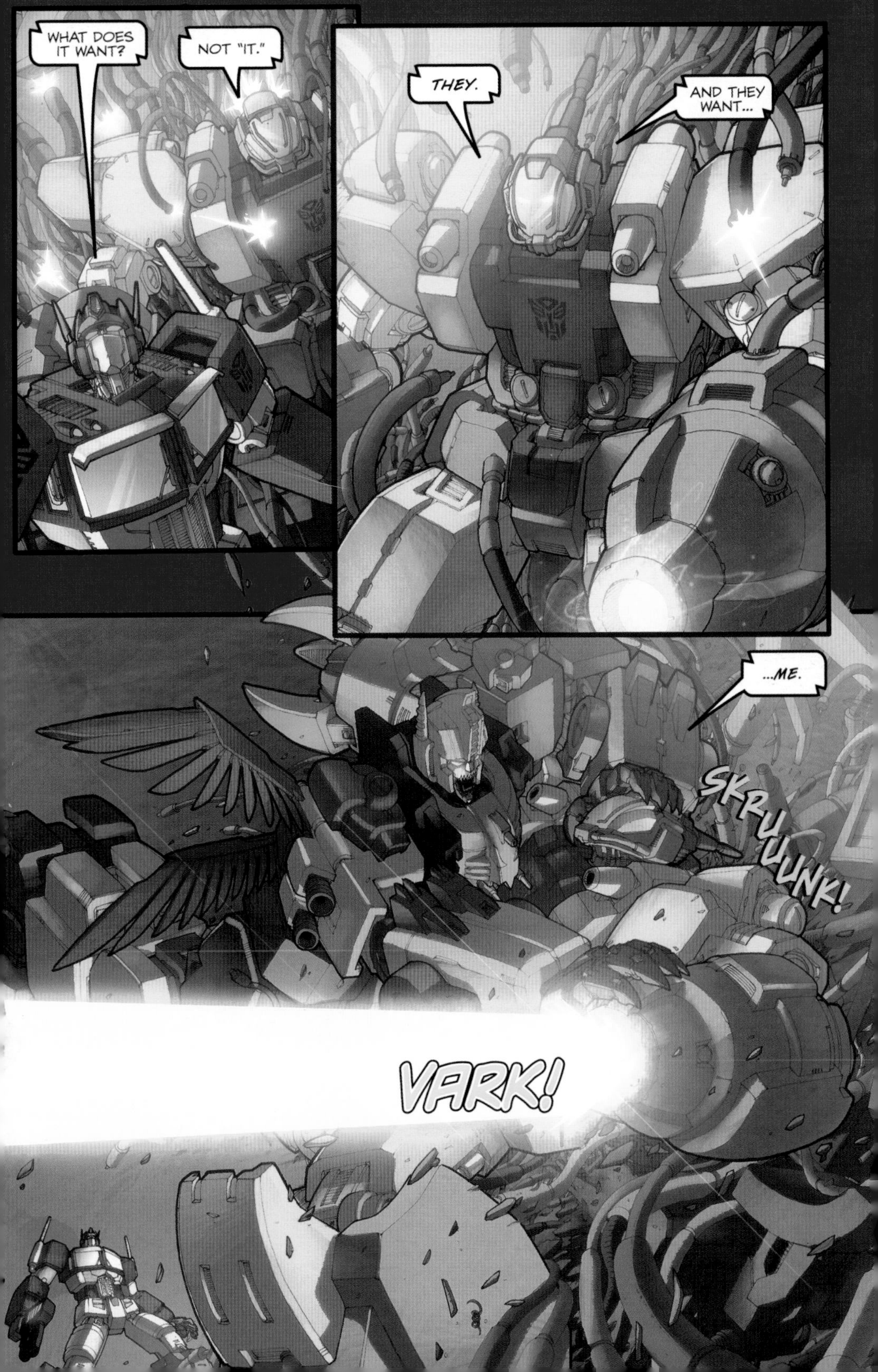
WHAT DOES IT WANT?
NOT "IT."
THEY.
AND THEY WANT...
...ME.
SKRUUUNK!
VARK!

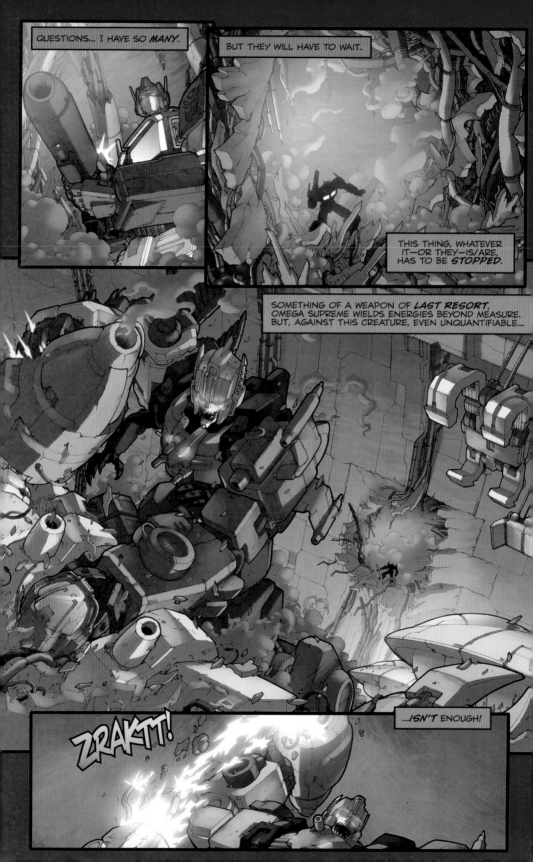

QUESTIONS... I HAVE SO *MANY*.

BUT THEY WILL HAVE TO WAIT.

THIS THING, WHATEVER IT—OR THEY—IS/ARE, HAS TO BE *STOPPED*.

SOMETHING OF A WEAPON OF *LAST RESORT*, OMEGA SUPREME WIELDS ENERGIES BEYOND MEASURE. BUT, AGAINST THIS CREATURE, EVEN UNQUANTIFIABLE...

...*ISN'T* ENOUGH!

ZRAKTT!

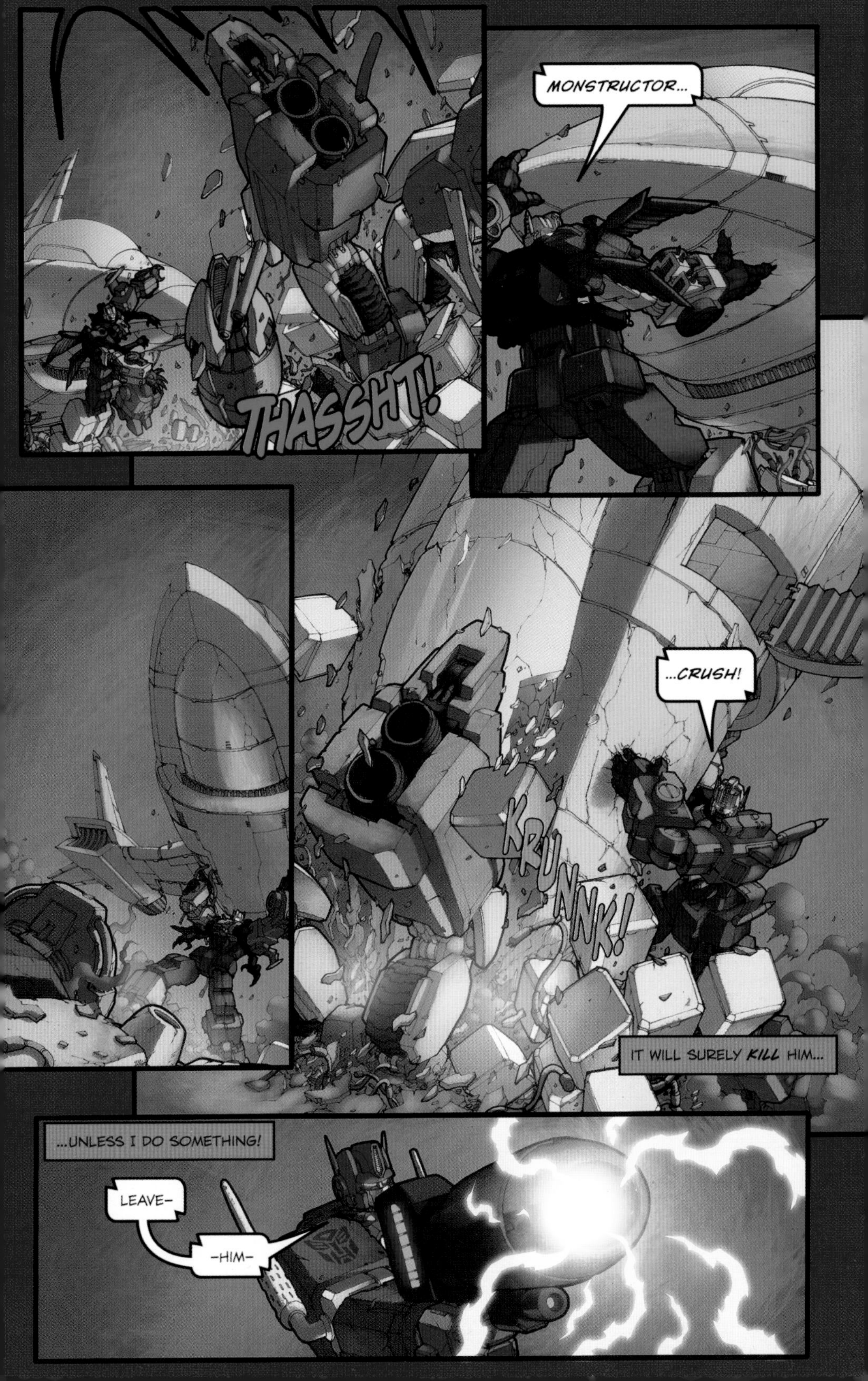
THASSHT!
MONSTRUCTOR...
...CRUSH!
KRUNNNK!
IT WILL SURELY KILL HIM...
...UNLESS I DO SOMETHING!
LEAVE-
-HIM-

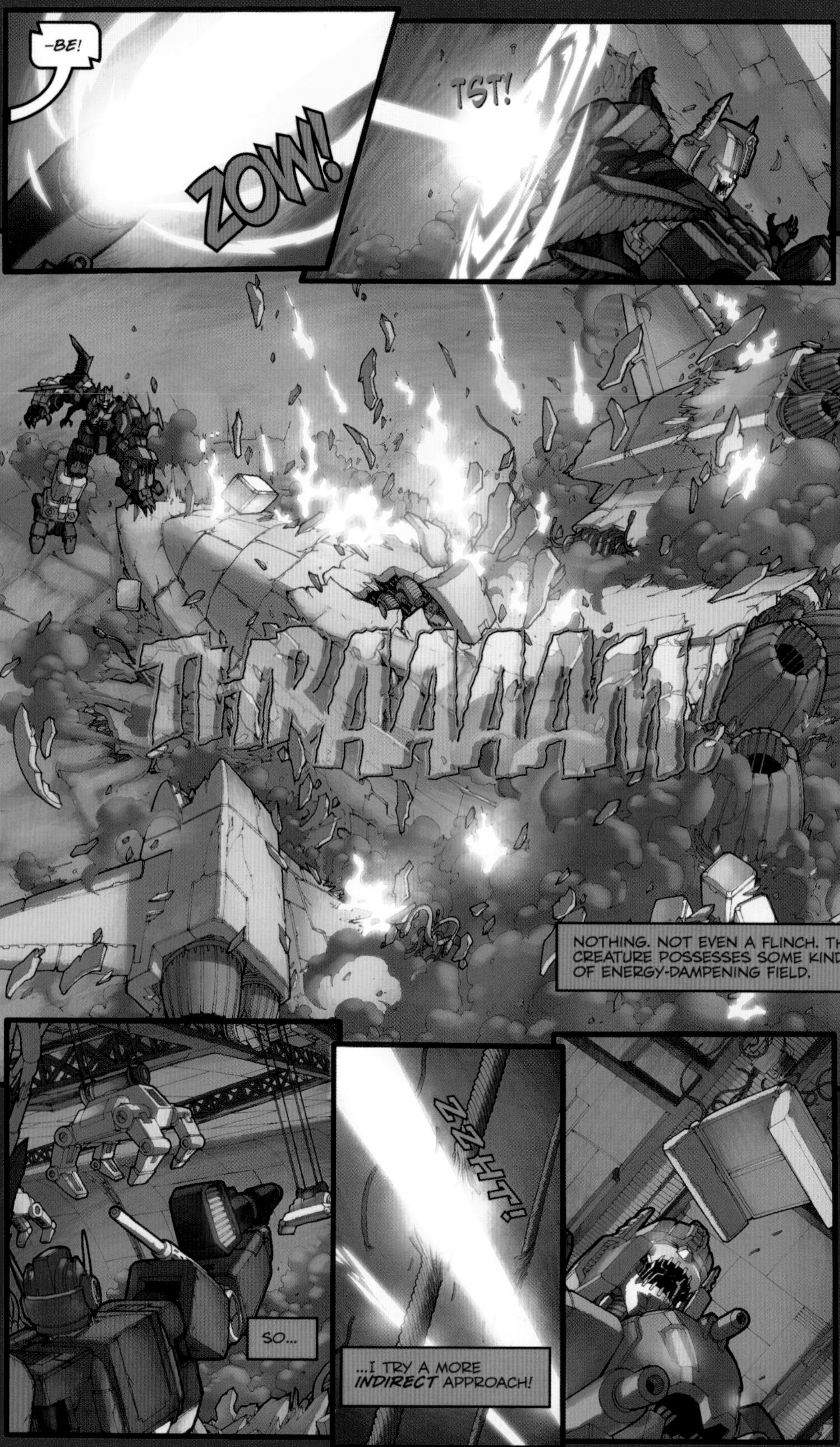
-BE!
ZOW!
TST!
THRAAAM!!
NOTHING. NOT EVEN A FLINCH. THE CREATURE POSSESSES SOME KIND OF ENERGY-DAMPENING FIELD.
SO...
ZZHT!
...I TRY A MORE *INDIRECT* APPROACH!

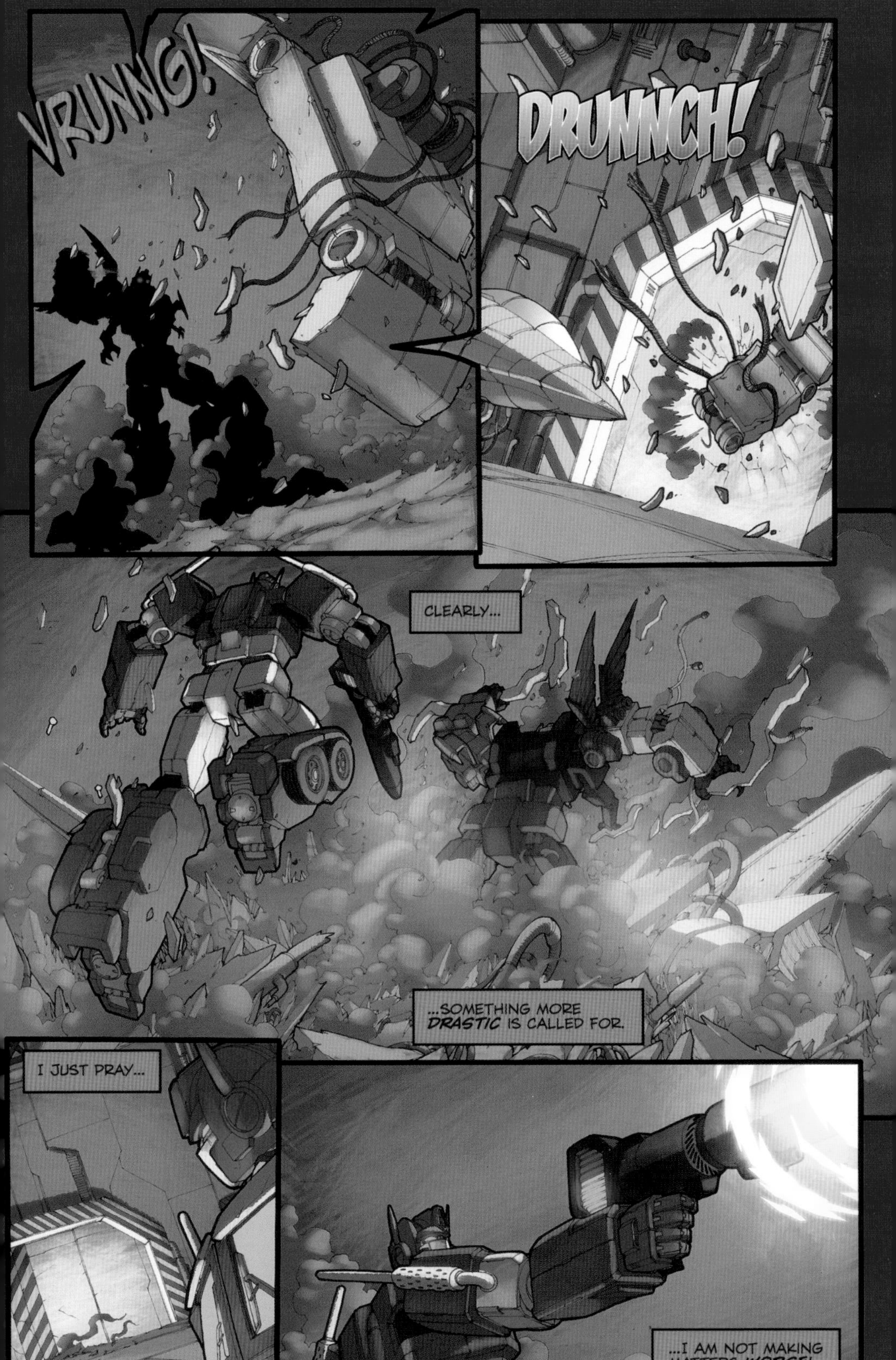
VRUNNG!
DRUNNCH!
CLEARLY...
...SOMETHING MORE DRASTIC IS CALLED FOR.
I JUST PRAY...
...I AM NOT MAKING MATTERS WORSE!

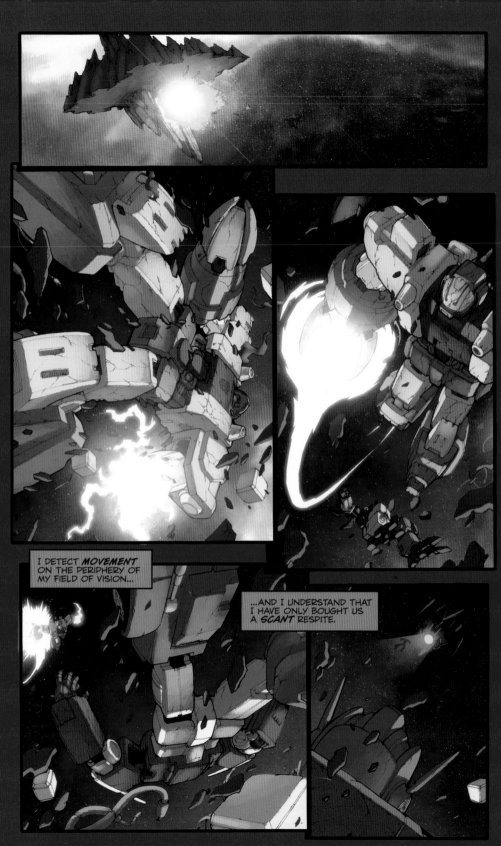

I DETECT *MOVEMENT* ON THE PERIPHERY OF MY FIELD OF VISION...

...AND I UNDERSTAND THAT I HAVE ONLY BOUGHT US A *SCANT* RESPITE.

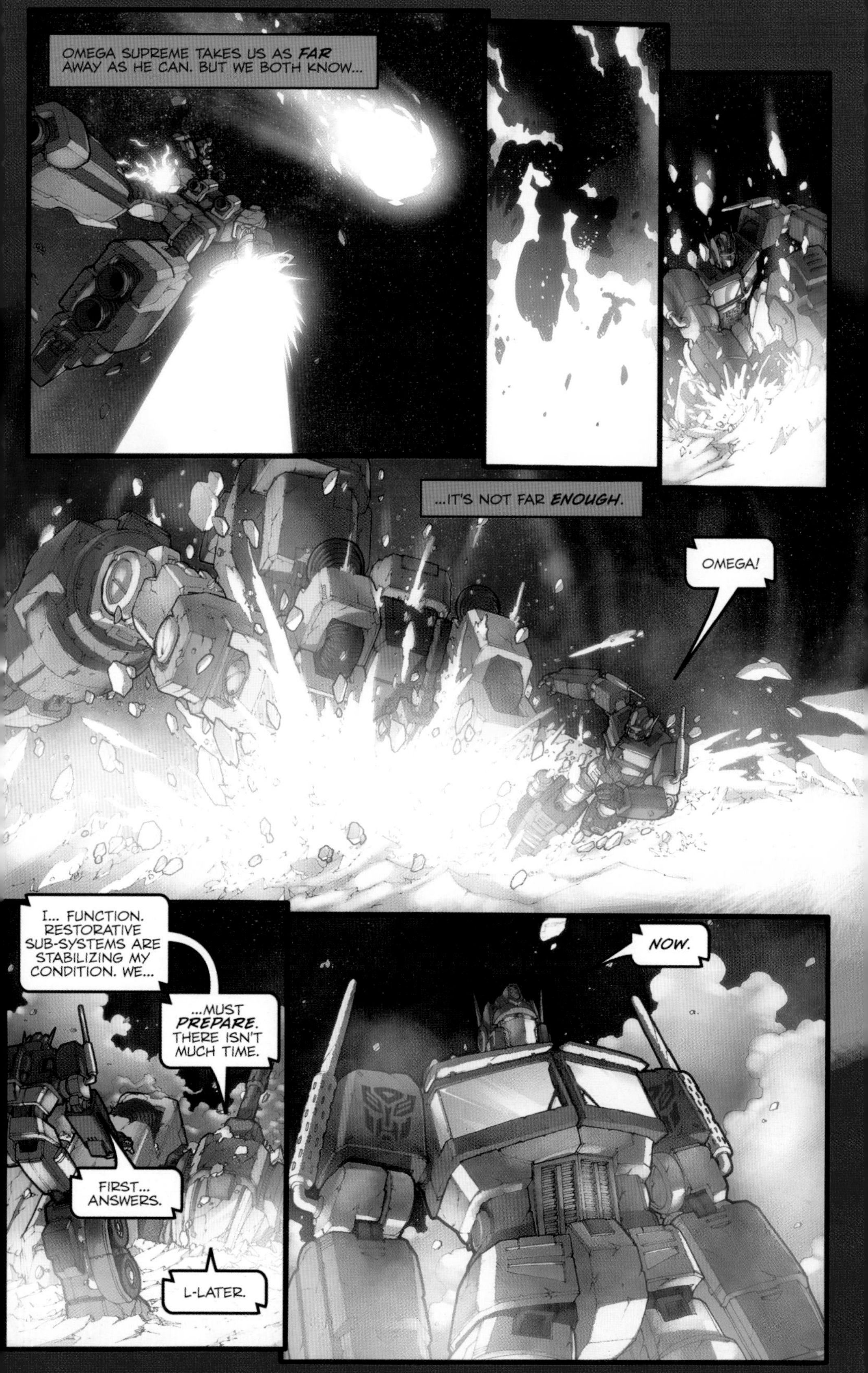
OMEGA SUPREME TAKES US AS FAR AWAY AS HE CAN. BUT WE BOTH KNOW...
...IT'S NOT FAR ENOUGH.
OMEGA!
I... FUNCTION. RESTORATIVE SUB-SYSTEMS ARE STABILIZING MY CONDITION. WE...
...MUST PREPARE. THERE ISN'T MUCH TIME.
FIRST... ANSWERS.
L-LATER.
NOW.

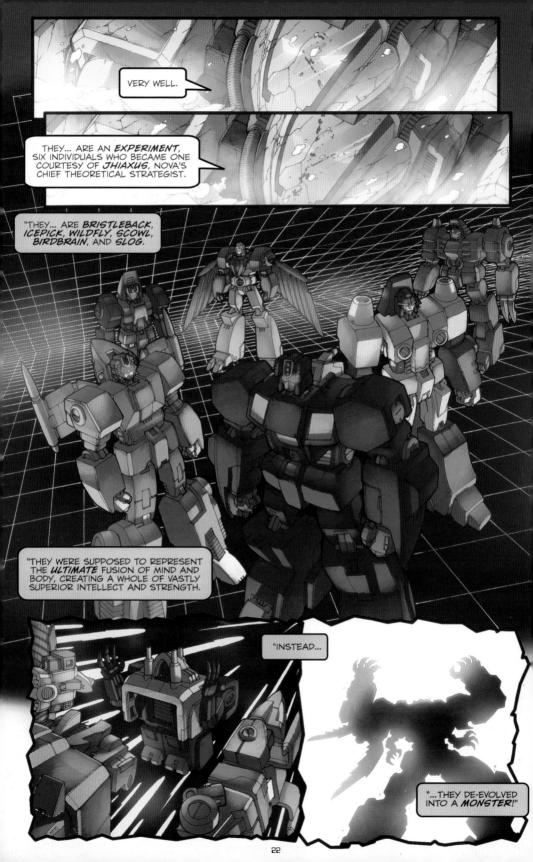

VERY WELL.

THEY... ARE AN *EXPERIMENT*, SIX INDIVIDUALS WHO BECAME ONE COURTESY OF *JHIAXUS*, NOVA'S CHIEF THEORETICAL STRATEGIST.

"THEY... ARE *BRISTLEBACK*, *ICEPICK*, *WILDFLY*, *SCOWL*, *BIRDBRAIN*, AND *SLOG*.

"THEY WERE SUPPOSED TO REPRESENT THE *ULTIMATE* FUSION OF MIND AND BODY, CREATING A WHOLE OF VASTLY SUPERIOR INTELLECT AND STRENGTH.

"INSTEAD...

"...THEY DE-EVOLVED INTO A *MONSTER!*"

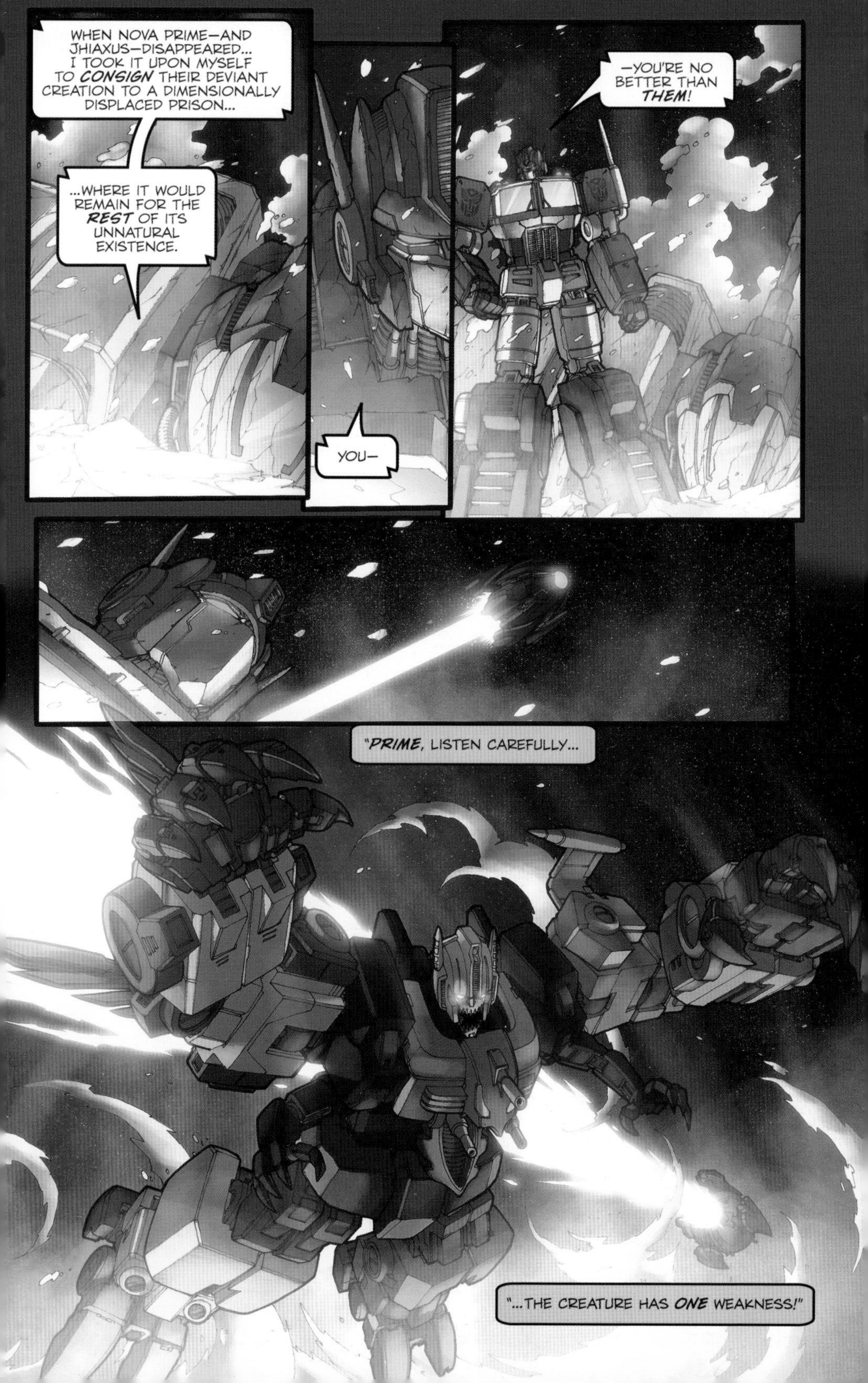
WHEN NOVA PRIME—AND JHIAXUS—DISAPPEARED... I TOOK IT UPON MYSELF TO CONSIGN THEIR DEVIANT CREATION TO A DIMENSIONALLY DISPLACED PRISON...
...WHERE IT WOULD REMAIN FOR THE REST OF ITS UNNATURAL EXISTENCE.
YOU—
—YOU'RE NO BETTER THAN THEM!
"PRIME, LISTEN CAREFULLY...
"...THE CREATURE HAS ONE WEAKNESS!"

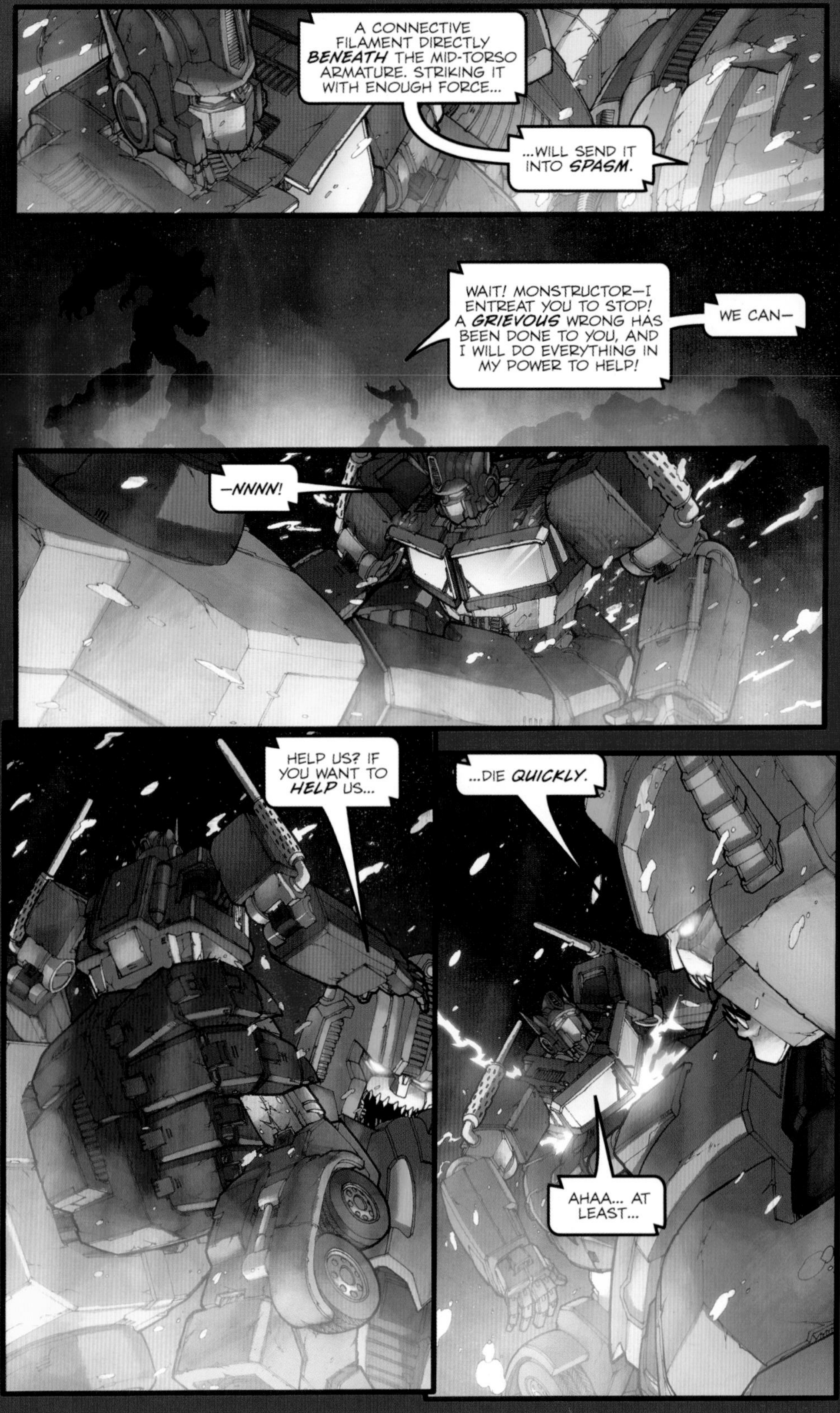
A CONNECTIVE FILAMENT DIRECTLY BENEATH THE MID-TORSO ARMATURE. STRIKING IT WITH ENOUGH FORCE...
...WILL SEND IT INTO SPASM.
WAIT! MONSTRUCTOR—I ENTREAT YOU TO STOP! A GRIEVOUS WRONG HAS BEEN DONE TO YOU, AND I WILL DO EVERYTHING IN MY POWER TO HELP!
WE CAN—
—NNNN!
HELP US? IF YOU WANT TO HELP US...
...DIE QUICKLY.
AHAA... AT LEAST...

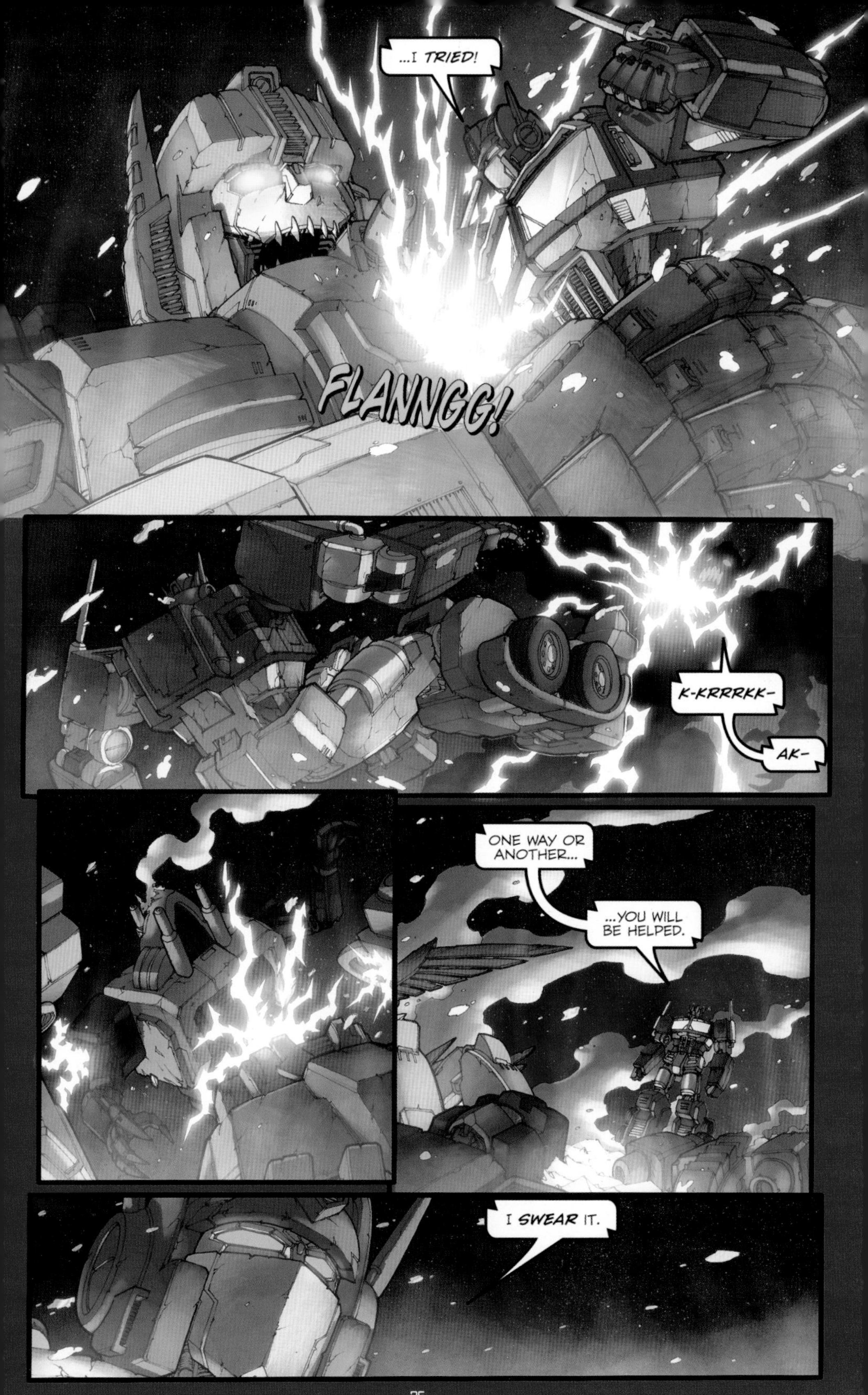
...I TRIED!
FLANNGG!
K-KRRRKK-
AK-
ONE WAY OR ANOTHER...
...YOU WILL BE HELPED.
I SWEAR IT.

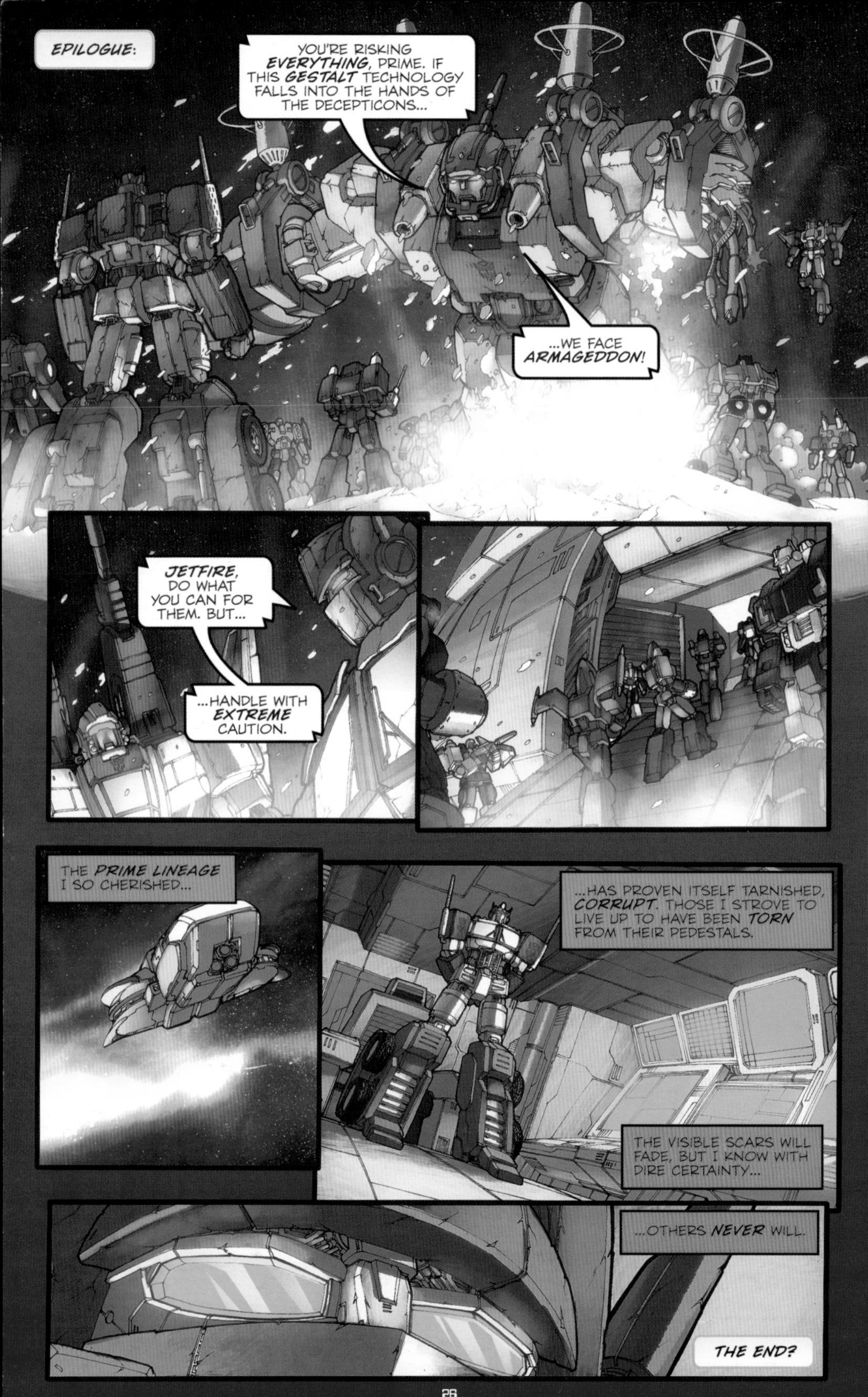
EPILOGUE:
YOU'RE RISKING EVERYTHING, PRIME. IF THIS GESTALT TECHNOLOGY FALLS INTO THE HANDS OF THE DECEPTICONS...
...WE FACE ARMAGEDDON!
JETFIRE, DO WHAT YOU CAN FOR THEM. BUT...
...HANDLE WITH EXTREME CAUTION.
THE PRIME LINEAGE I SO CHERISHED...
...HAS PROVEN ITSELF TARNISHED, CORRUPT. THOSE I STROVE TO LIVE UP TO HAVE BEEN TORN FROM THEIR PEDESTALS.
THE VISIBLE SCARS WILL FADE, BUT I KNOW WITH DIRE CERTAINTY...
...OTHERS NEVER WILL.
THE END?

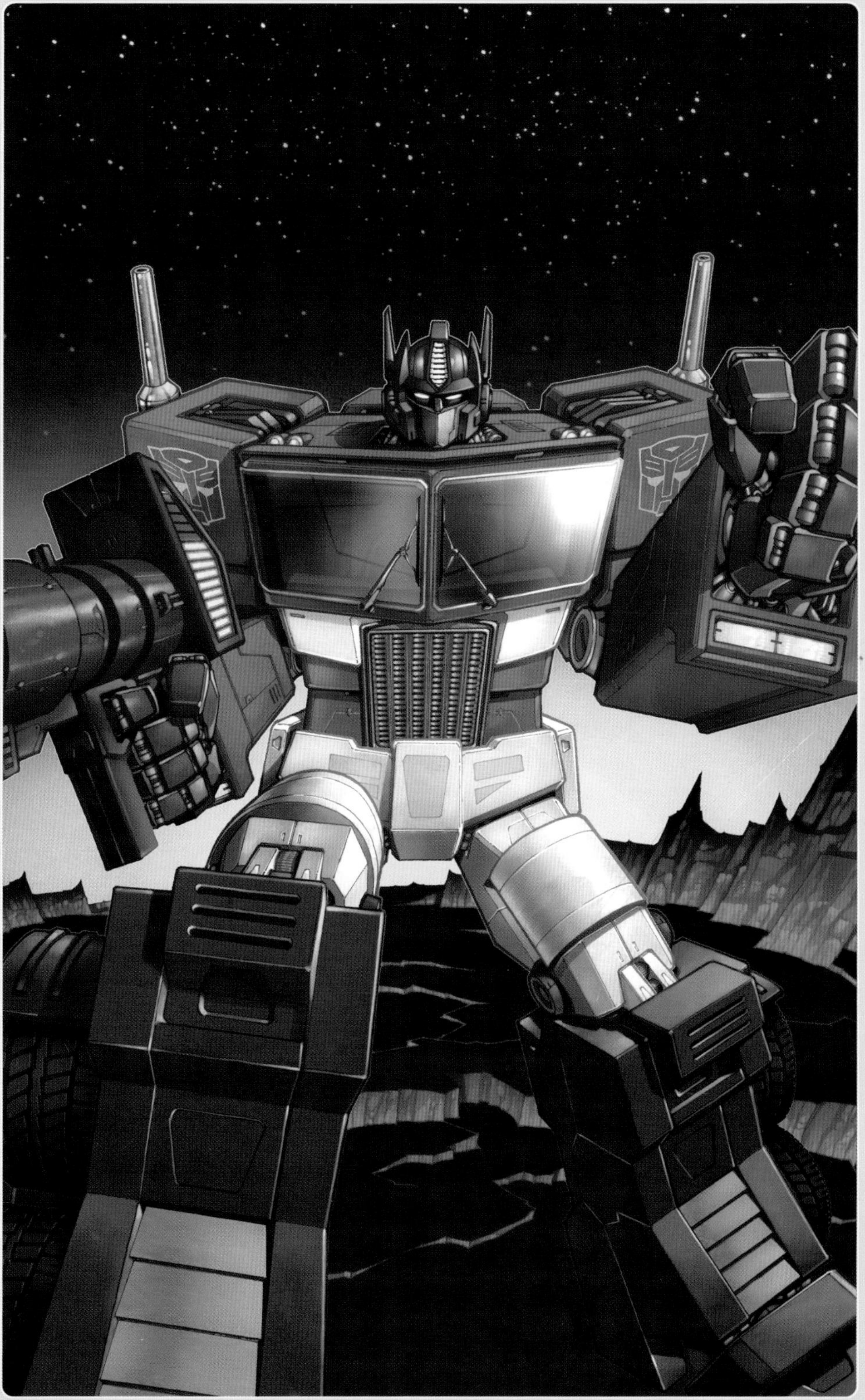

Even in war, there are codes of conduct that must be abided by and, when there are transgressions, enforced. In this respect, ULTRA MAGNUS is the law. Though an AUTOBOT by allegiance, he fulfills a largely autonomous role, investigating, assessing and — if necessary — punishing those who cross the line drawn in the sand...

ULTRA MAGNUS

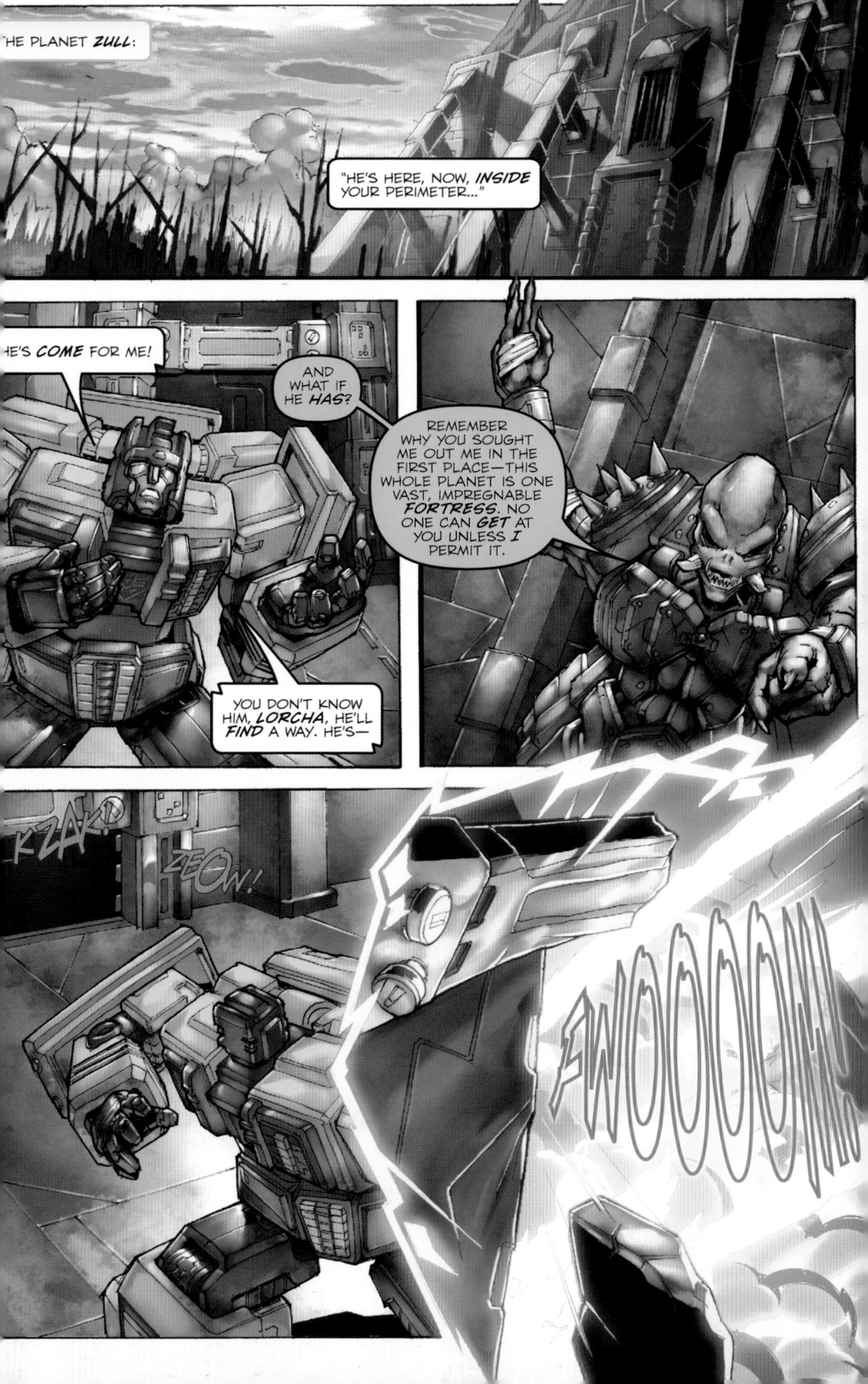

THE PLANET ZULL:
"HE'S HERE, NOW, INSIDE YOUR PERIMETER..."
HE'S COME FOR ME!
AND WHAT IF HE HAS?
REMEMBER WHY YOU SOUGHT ME OUT ME IN THE FIRST PLACE—THIS WHOLE PLANET IS ONE VAST, IMPREGNABLE FORTRESS. NO ONE CAN GET AT YOU UNLESS I PERMIT IT.
YOU DON'T KNOW HIM, LORCHA, HE'LL FIND A WAY. HE'S—
KZAK!
ZEOW!
FWOOOOM!

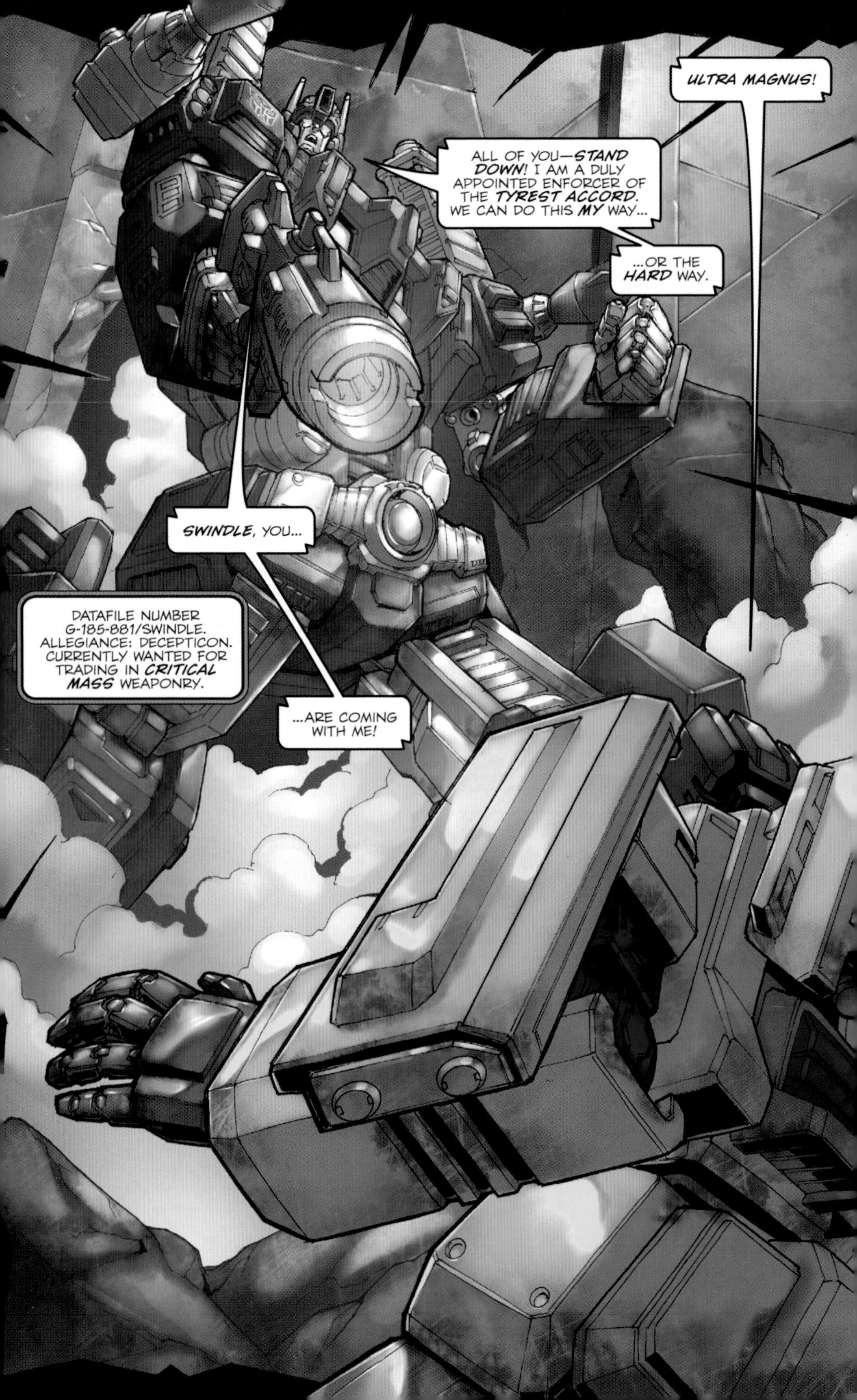
ULTRA MAGNUS!
ALL OF YOU—STAND DOWN! I AM A DULY APPOINTED ENFORCER OF THE TYREST ACCORD. WE CAN DO THIS MY WAY...
...OR THE HARD WAY.
SWINDLE, YOU...
DATAFILE NUMBER G-185-881/SWINDLE. ALLEGIANCE: DECEPTICON. CURRENTLY WANTED FOR TRADING IN CRITICAL MASS WEAPONRY.
...ARE COMING WITH ME!

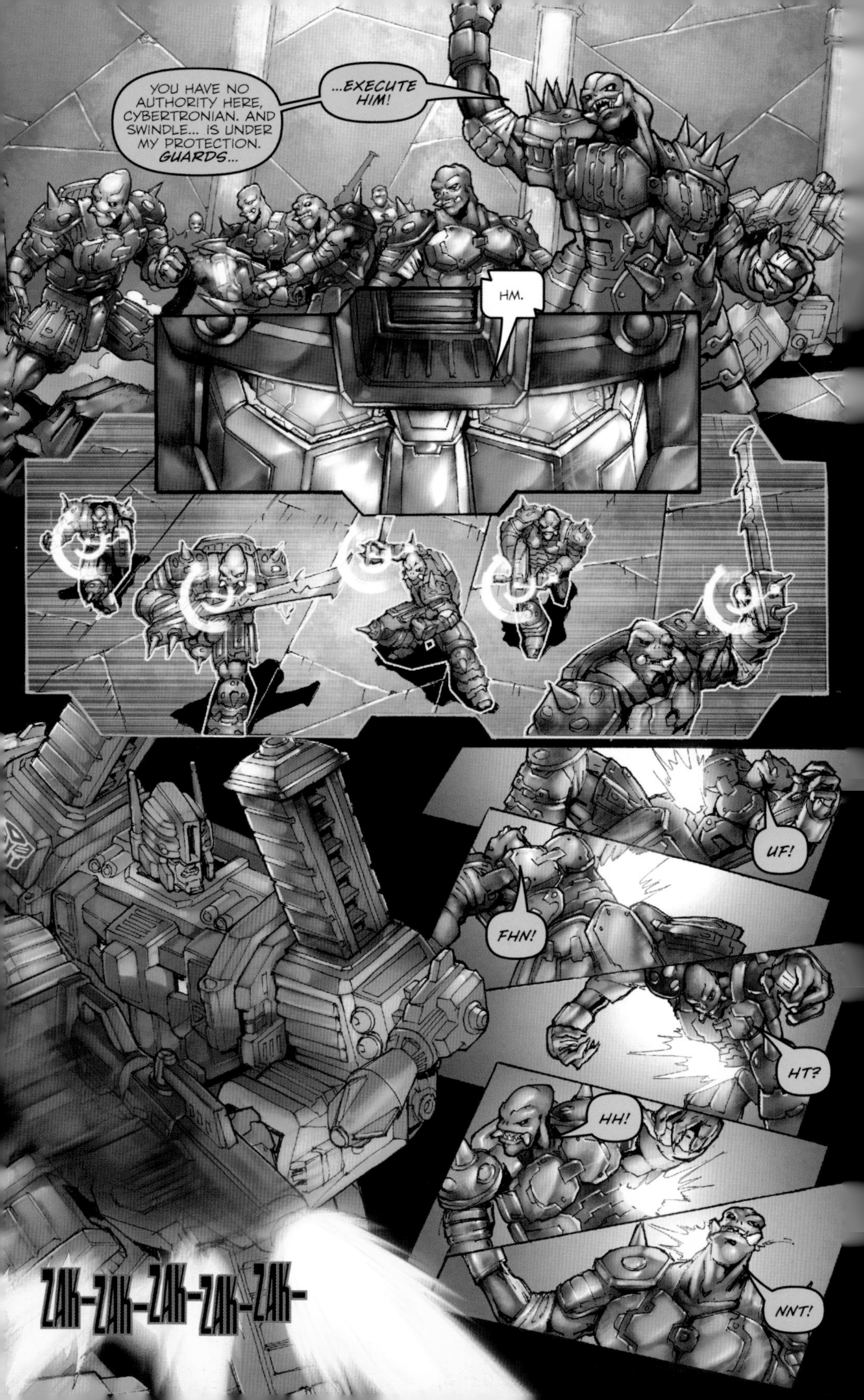
YOU HAVE NO AUTHORITY HERE, CYBERTRONIAN. AND SWINDLE... IS UNDER MY PROTECTION. GUARDS...
...EXECUTE HIM!
HM.
UF!
FHN!
HT?
HH!
NNT!
ZAK-ZAK-ZAK-ZAK-ZAK-

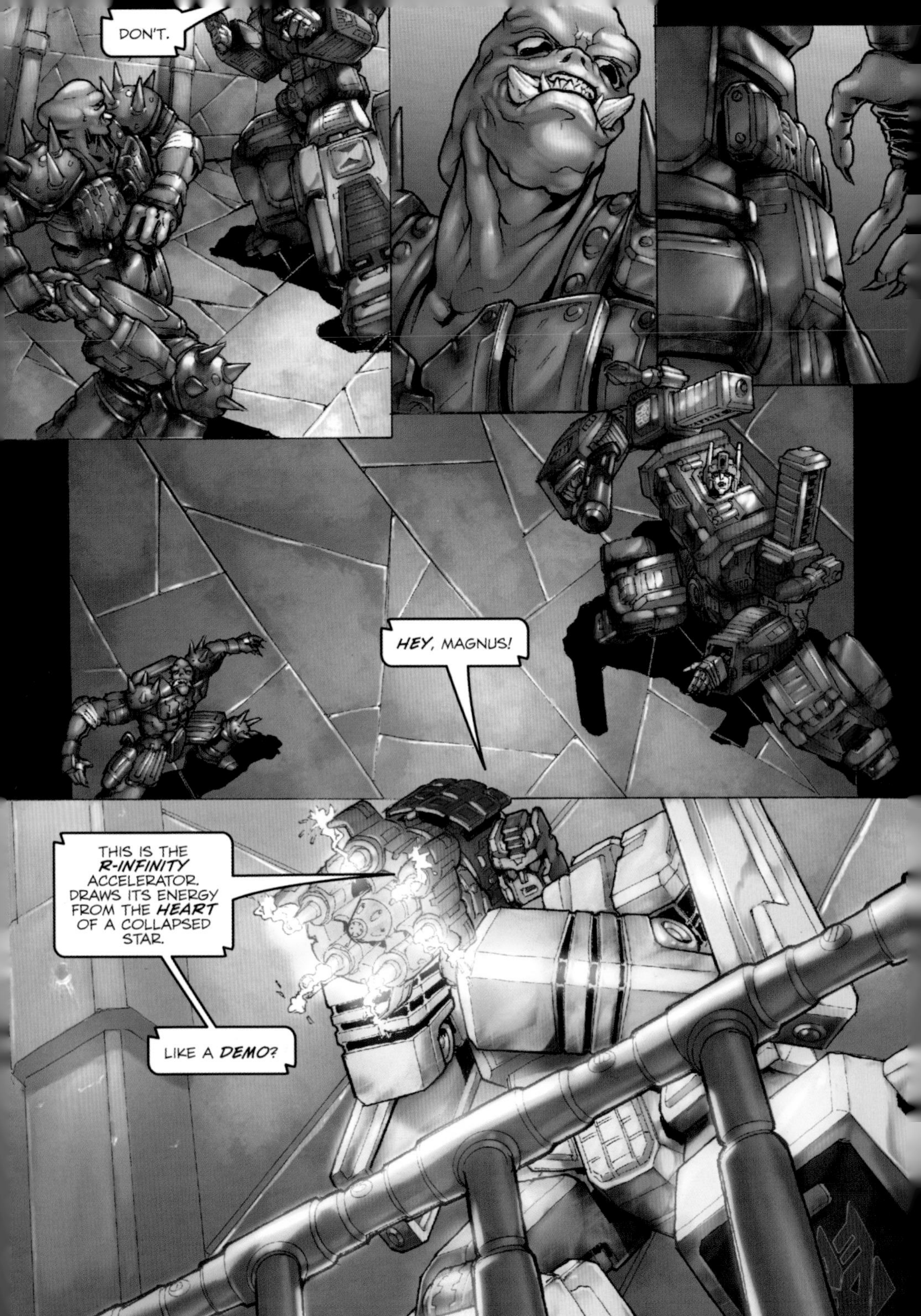
DON'T.
HEY, MAGNUS!
THIS IS THE R-INFINITY ACCELERATOR. DRAWS ITS ENERGY FROM THE HEART OF A COLLAPSED STAR.
LIKE A DEMO?

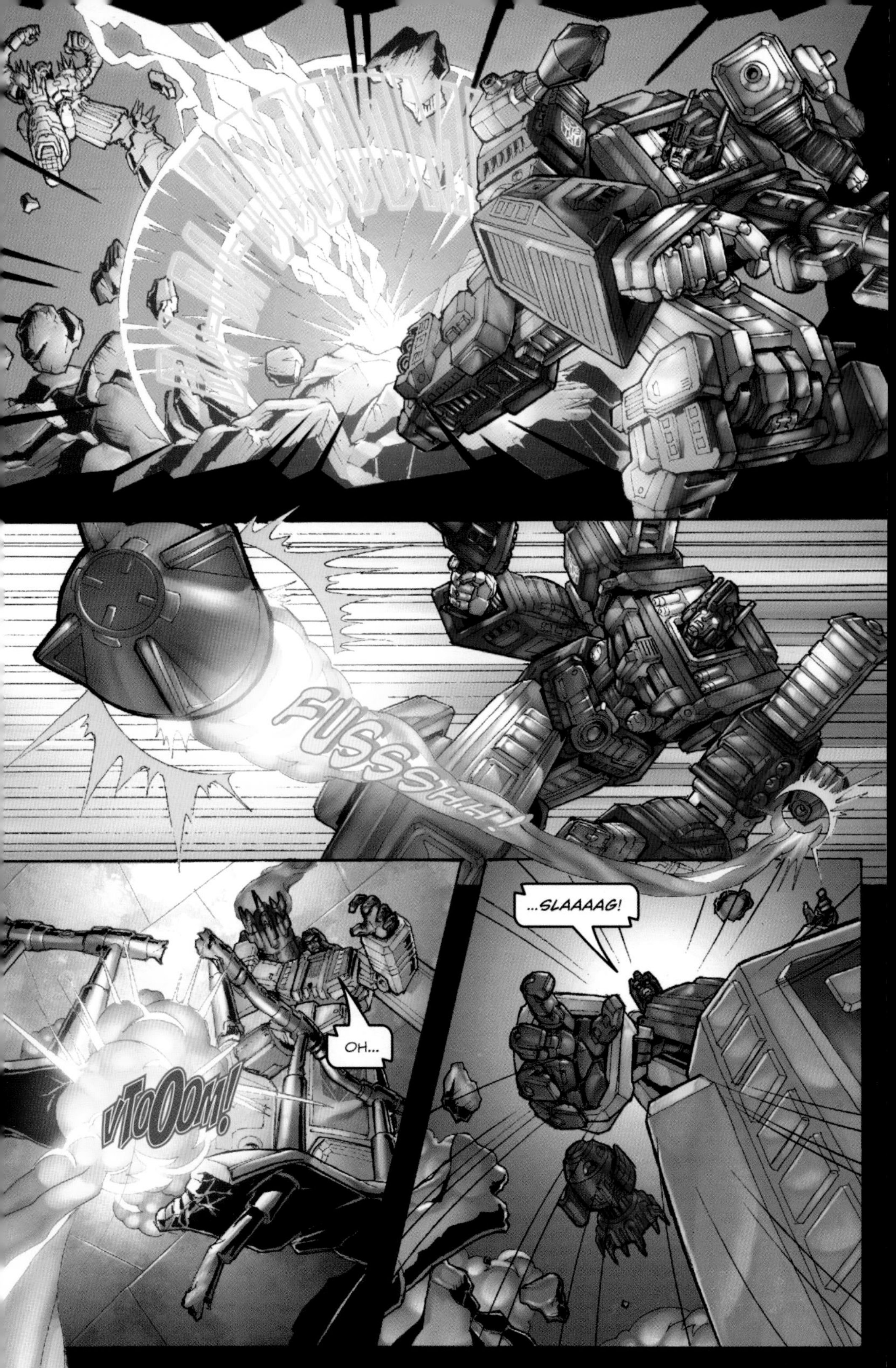
FUSSSHH!
OH...
VTOOOM!
...SLAAAAG!

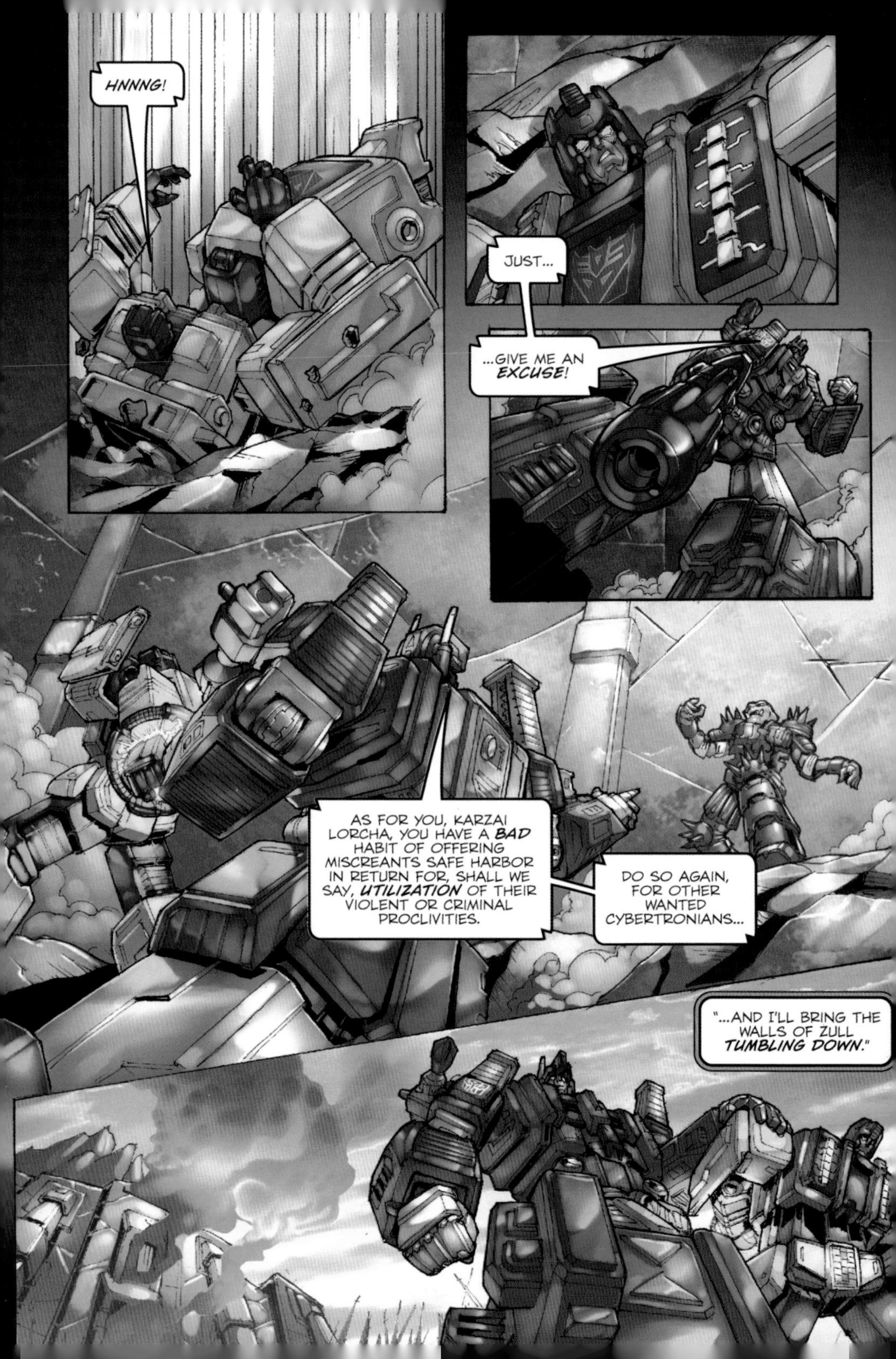
HNNNG!
JUST...
...GIVE ME AN EXCUSE!
AS FOR YOU, KARZAI LORCHA, YOU HAVE A BAD HABIT OF OFFERING MISCREANTS SAFE HARBOR IN RETURN FOR, SHALL WE SAY, UTILIZATION OF THEIR VIOLENT OR CRIMINAL PROCLIVITIES.
DO SO AGAIN, FOR OTHER WANTED CYBERTRONIANS...
"...AND I'LL BRING THE WALLS OF ZULL TUMBLING DOWN."

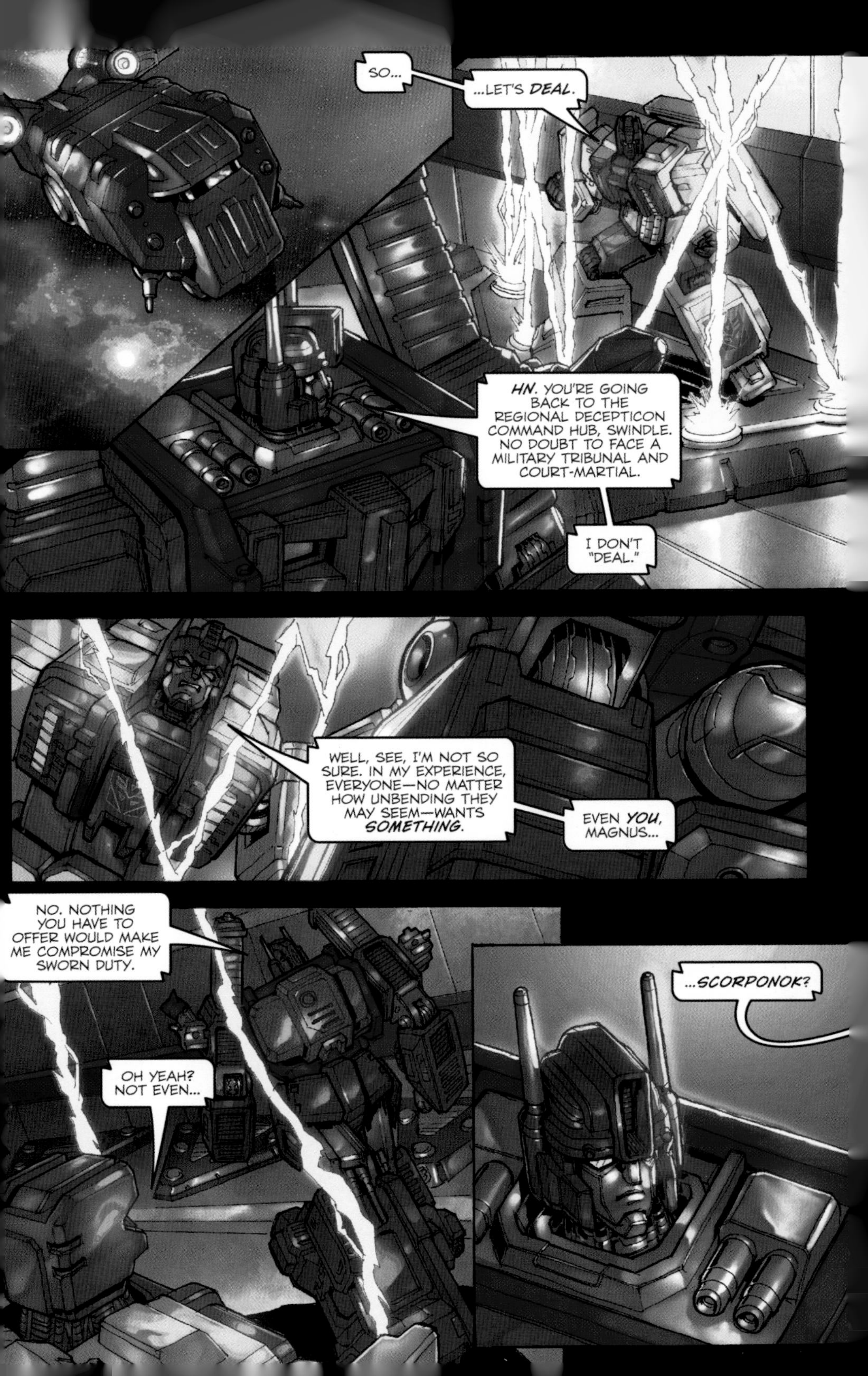
SO...
...LET'S DEAL.
HN. YOU'RE GOING BACK TO THE REGIONAL DECEPTICON COMMAND HUB, SWINDLE. NO DOUBT TO FACE A MILITARY TRIBUNAL AND COURT-MARTIAL.
I DON'T "DEAL."
WELL, SEE, I'M NOT SO SURE. IN MY EXPERIENCE, EVERYONE—NO MATTER HOW UNBENDING THEY MAY SEEM—WANTS SOMETHING.
EVEN YOU, MAGNUS...
NO. NOTHING YOU HAVE TO OFFER WOULD MAKE ME COMPROMISE MY SWORN DUTY.
OH YEAH? NOT EVEN...
...SCORPONOK?

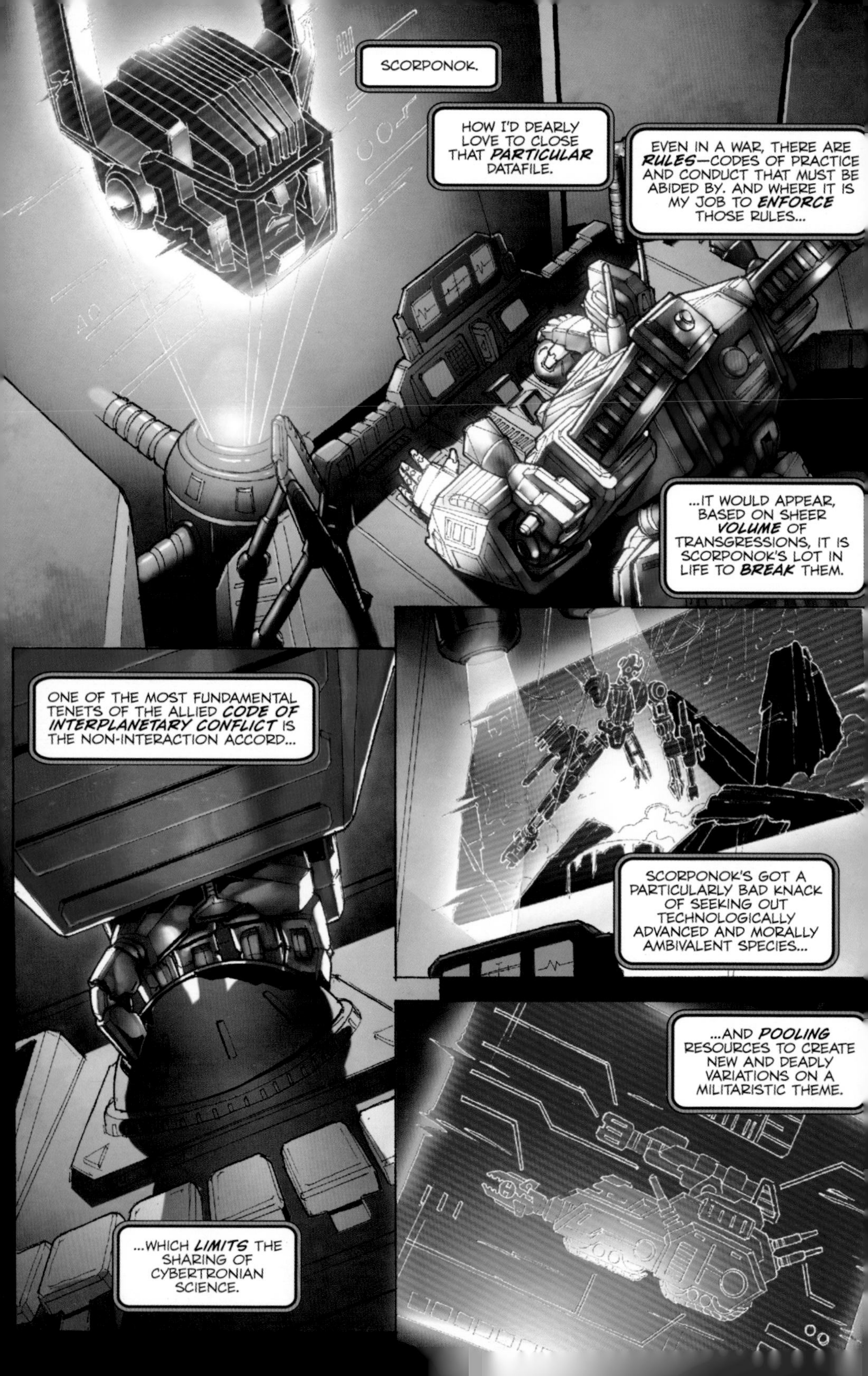
SCORPONOK.
HOW I'D DEARLY LOVE TO CLOSE THAT PARTICULAR DATAFILE.
EVEN IN A WAR, THERE ARE RULES—CODES OF PRACTICE AND CONDUCT THAT MUST BE ABIDED BY. AND WHERE IT IS MY JOB TO ENFORCE THOSE RULES...
...IT WOULD APPEAR, BASED ON SHEER VOLUME OF TRANSGRESSIONS, IT IS SCORPONOK'S LOT IN LIFE TO BREAK THEM.
ONE OF THE MOST FUNDAMENTAL TENETS OF THE ALLIED CODE OF INTERPLANETARY CONFLICT IS THE NON-INTERACTION ACCORD...
...WHICH LIMITS THE SHARING OF CYBERTRONIAN SCIENCE.
SCORPONOK'S GOT A PARTICULARLY BAD KNACK OF SEEKING OUT TECHNOLOGICALLY ADVANCED AND MORALLY AMBIVALENT SPECIES...
...AND POOLING RESOURCES TO CREATE NEW AND DEADLY VARIATIONS ON A MILITARISTIC THEME.

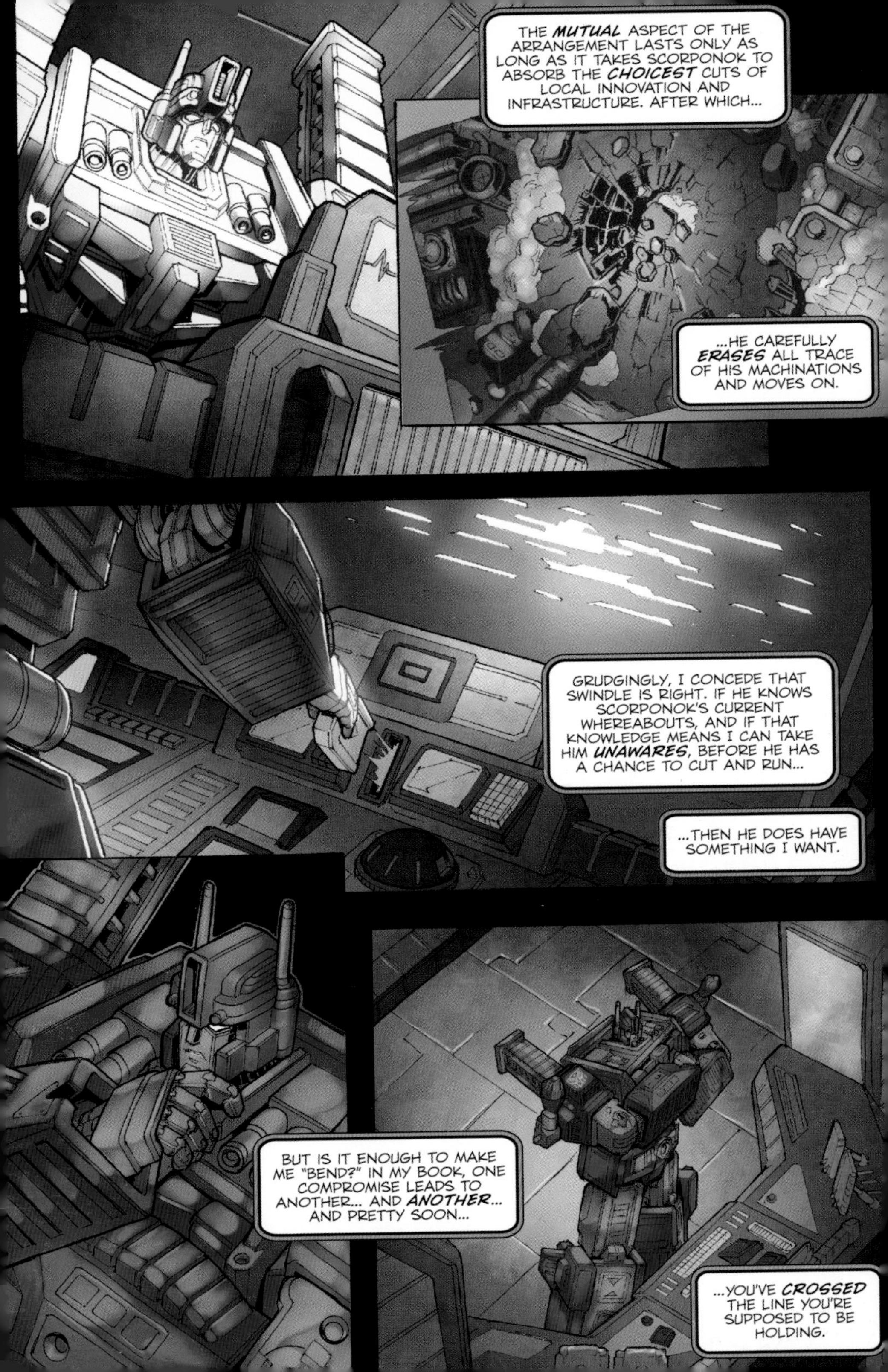
THE MUTUAL ASPECT OF THE ARRANGEMENT LASTS ONLY AS LONG AS IT TAKES SCORPONOK TO ABSORB THE CHOICEST CUTS OF LOCAL INNOVATION AND INFRASTRUCTURE. AFTER WHICH...
...HE CAREFULLY ERASES ALL TRACE OF HIS MACHINATIONS AND MOVES ON.
GRUDGINGLY, I CONCEDE THAT SWINDLE IS RIGHT. IF HE KNOWS SCORPONOK'S CURRENT WHEREABOUTS, AND IF THAT KNOWLEDGE MEANS I CAN TAKE HIM UNAWARES, BEFORE HE HAS A CHANCE TO CUT AND RUN...
...THEN HE DOES HAVE SOMETHING I WANT.
BUT IS IT ENOUGH TO MAKE ME "BEND?" IN MY BOOK, ONE COMPROMISE LEADS TO ANOTHER... AND ANOTHER... AND PRETTY SOON...
...YOU'VE CROSSED THE LINE YOU'RE SUPPOSED TO BE HOLDING.

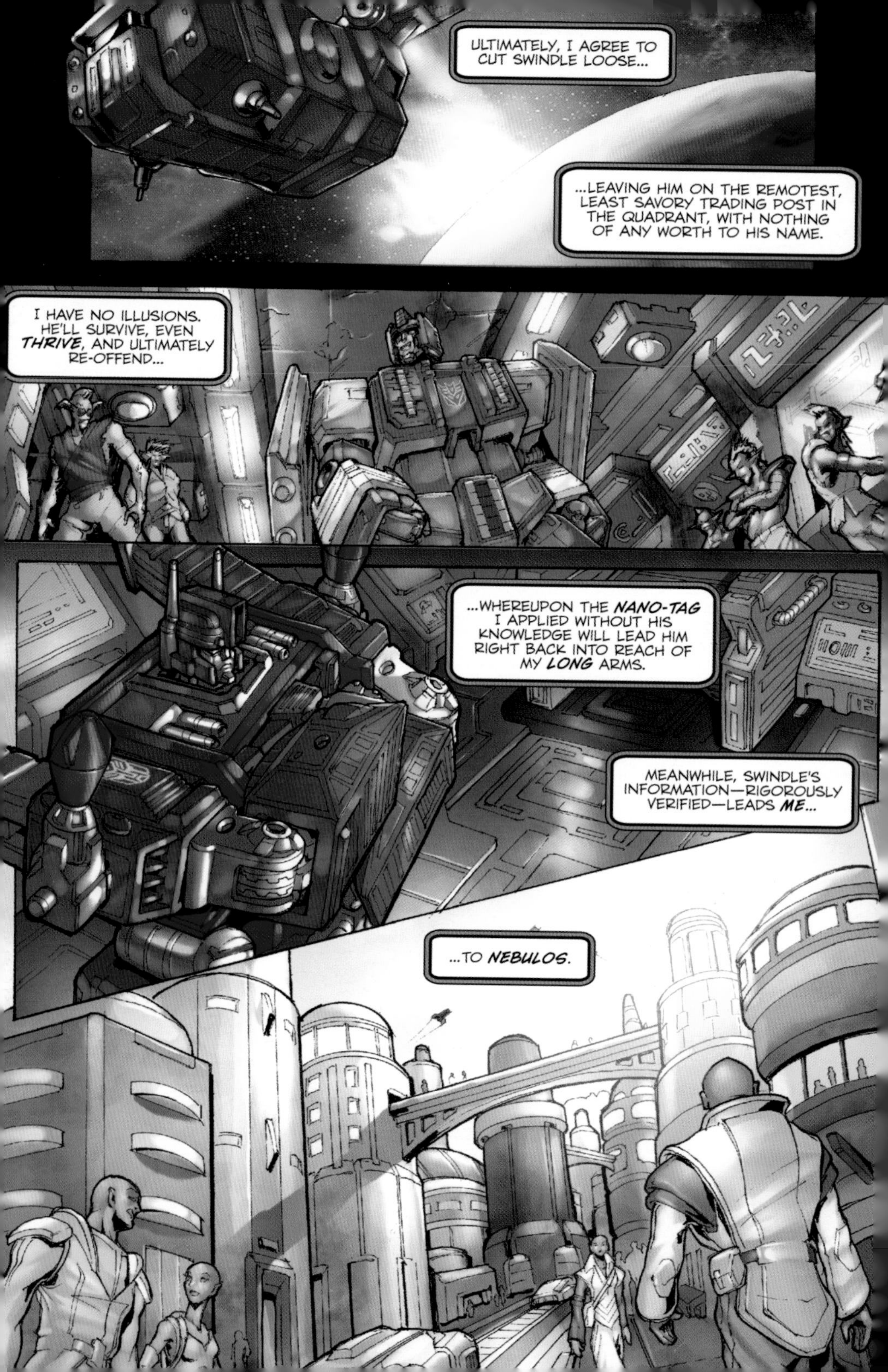
ULTIMATELY, I AGREE TO CUT SWINDLE LOOSE...
...LEAVING HIM ON THE REMOTEST, LEAST SAVORY TRADING POST IN THE QUADRANT, WITH NOTHING OF ANY WORTH TO HIS NAME.
I HAVE NO ILLUSIONS. HE'LL SURVIVE, EVEN THRIVE, AND ULTIMATELY RE-OFFEND...
...WHEREUPON THE NANO-TAG I APPLIED WITHOUT HIS KNOWLEDGE WILL LEAD HIM RIGHT BACK INTO REACH OF MY LONG ARMS.
MEANWHILE, SWINDLE'S INFORMATION—RIGOROUSLY VERIFIED—LEADS ME...
...TO NEBULOS.

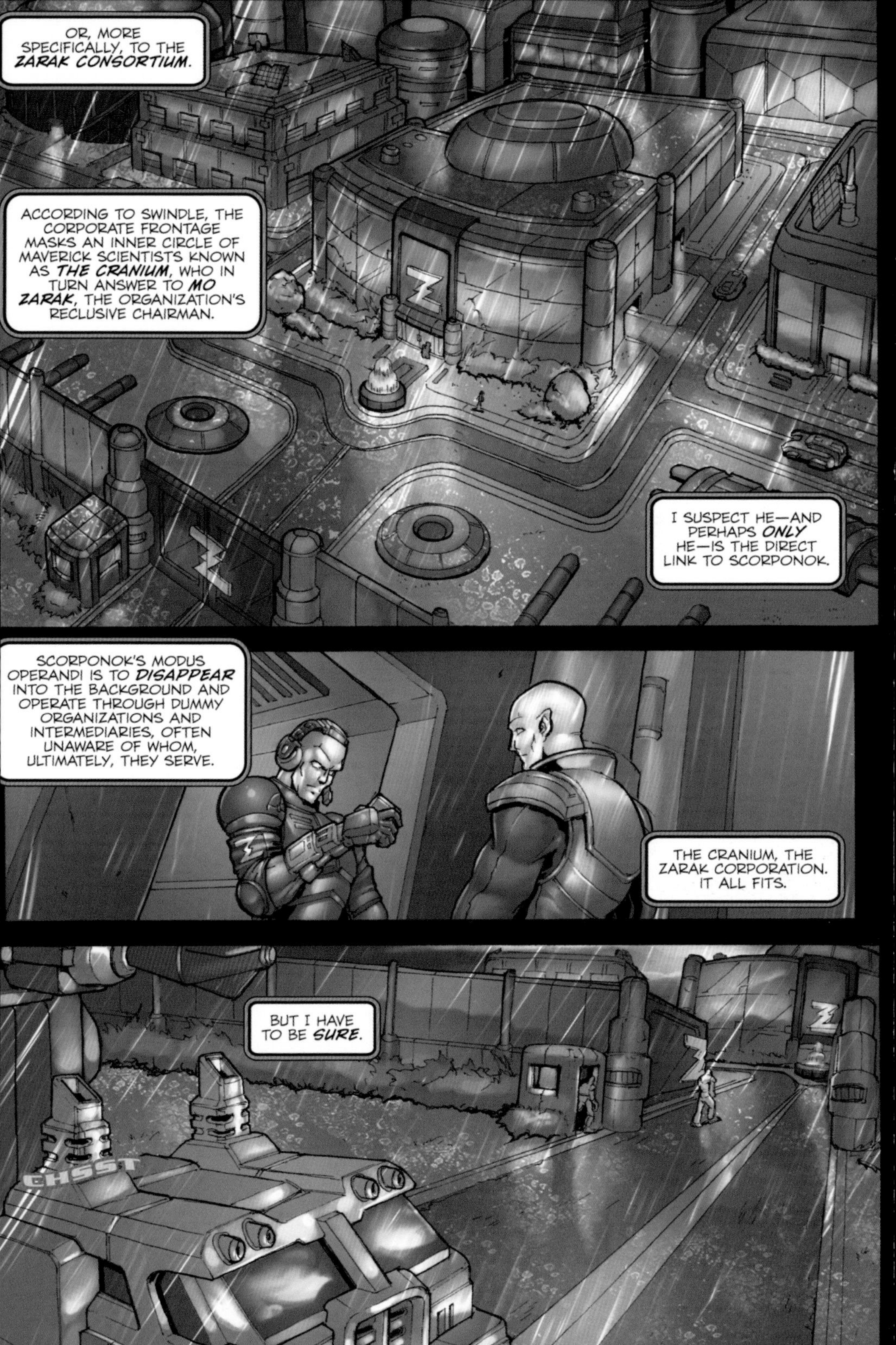
OR, MORE SPECIFICALLY, TO THE ZARAK CONSORTIUM.
ACCORDING TO SWINDLE, THE CORPORATE FRONTAGE MASKS AN INNER CIRCLE OF MAVERICK SCIENTISTS KNOWN AS THE CRANIUM, WHO IN TURN ANSWER TO MO ZARAK, THE ORGANIZATION'S RECLUSIVE CHAIRMAN.
I SUSPECT HE—AND PERHAPS ONLY HE—IS THE DIRECT LINK TO SCORPONOK.
SCORPONOK'S MODUS OPERANDI IS TO DISAPPEAR INTO THE BACKGROUND AND OPERATE THROUGH DUMMY ORGANIZATIONS AND INTERMEDIARIES, OFTEN UNAWARE OF WHOM, ULTIMATELY, THEY SERVE.
THE CRANIUM, THE ZARAK CORPORATION. IT ALL FITS.
BUT I HAVE TO BE SURE.

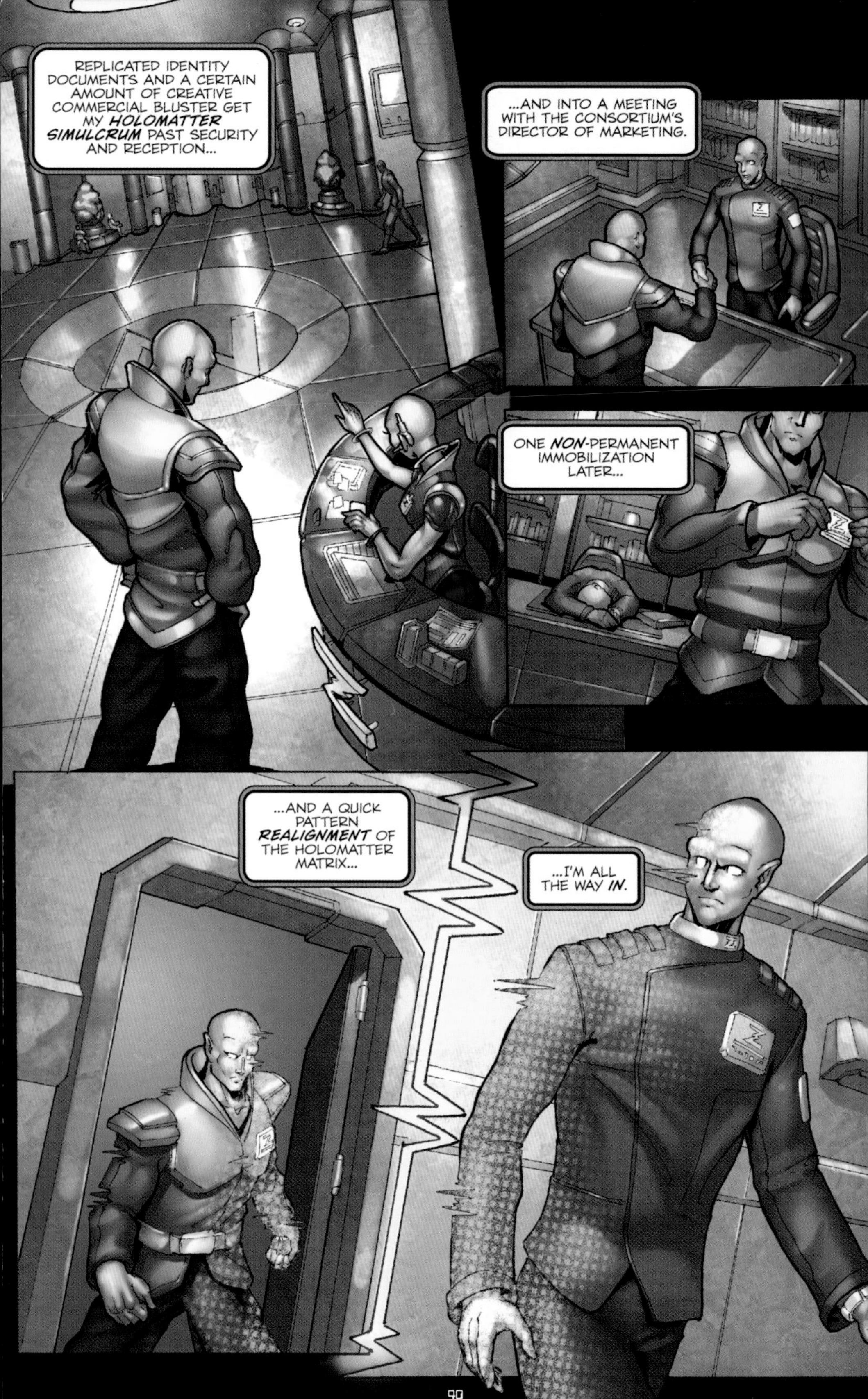
REPLICATED IDENTITY DOCUMENTS AND A CERTAIN AMOUNT OF CREATIVE COMMERCIAL BLUSTER GET MY *HOLOMATTER SIMULCRUM* PAST SECURITY AND RECEPTION...
...AND INTO A MEETING WITH THE CONSORTIUM'S DIRECTOR OF MARKETING.
ONE *NON*-PERMANENT IMMOBILIZATION LATER...
...AND A QUICK PATTERN *REALIGNMENT* OF THE HOLOMATTER MATRIX...
...I'M ALL THE WAY *IN*.

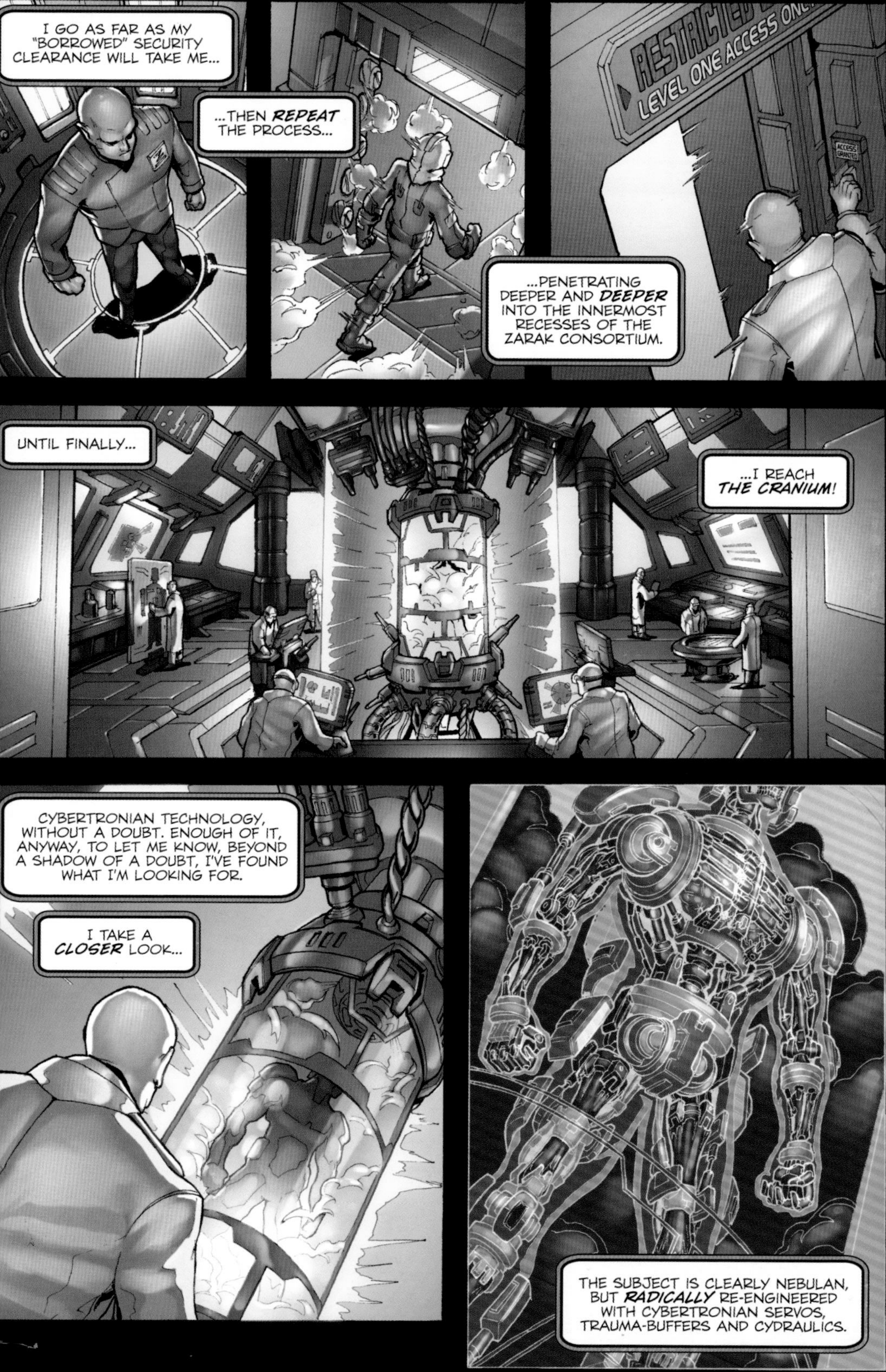
I GO AS FAR AS MY "BORROWED" SECURITY CLEARANCE WILL TAKE ME...
...THEN REPEAT THE PROCESS...
RESTRICTED
LEVEL ONE ACCESS ONLY
ACCESS GRANTED
...PENETRATING DEEPER AND DEEPER INTO THE INNERMOST RECESSES OF THE ZARAK CONSORTIUM.
UNTIL FINALLY...
...I REACH THE CRANIUM!
CYBERTRONIAN TECHNOLOGY, WITHOUT A DOUBT. ENOUGH OF IT, ANYWAY, TO LET ME KNOW, BEYOND A SHADOW OF A DOUBT, I'VE FOUND WHAT I'M LOOKING FOR.
I TAKE A CLOSER LOOK...
THE SUBJECT IS CLEARLY NEBULAN, BUT RADICALLY RE-ENGINEERED WITH CYBERTRONIAN SERVOS, TRAUMA-BUFFERS AND CYDRAULICS.

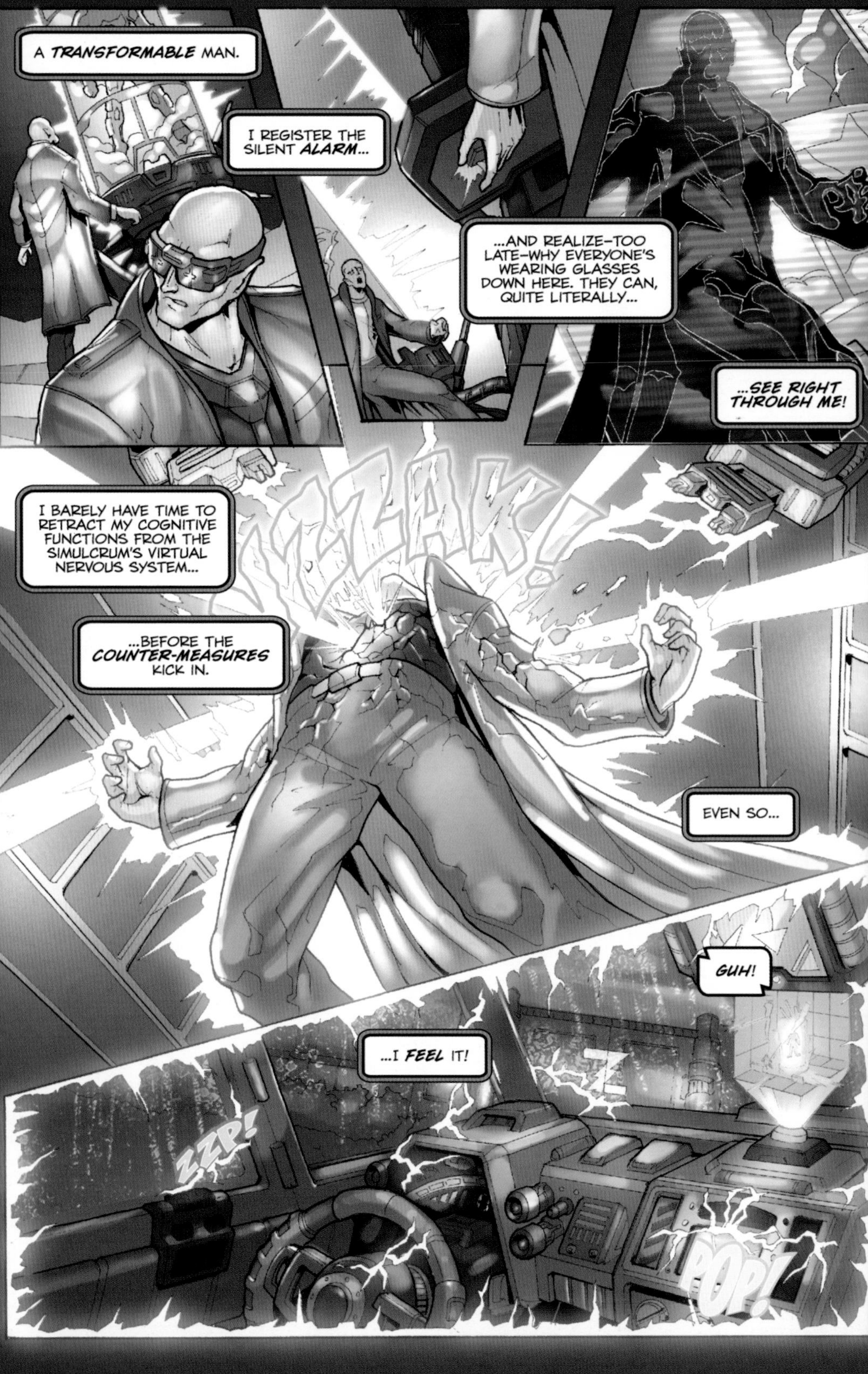
A TRANSFORMABLE MAN.
I REGISTER THE SILENT ALARM...
...AND REALIZE—TOO LATE—WHY EVERYONE'S WEARING GLASSES DOWN HERE. THEY CAN, QUITE LITERALLY...
...SEE RIGHT THROUGH ME!
I BARELY HAVE TIME TO RETRACT MY COGNITIVE FUNCTIONS FROM THE SIMULCRUM'S VIRTUAL NERVOUS SYSTEM...
...BEFORE THE COUNTER-MEASURES KICK IN.
EVEN SO...
GUH!
...I FEEL IT!
ZZZP!
POP!

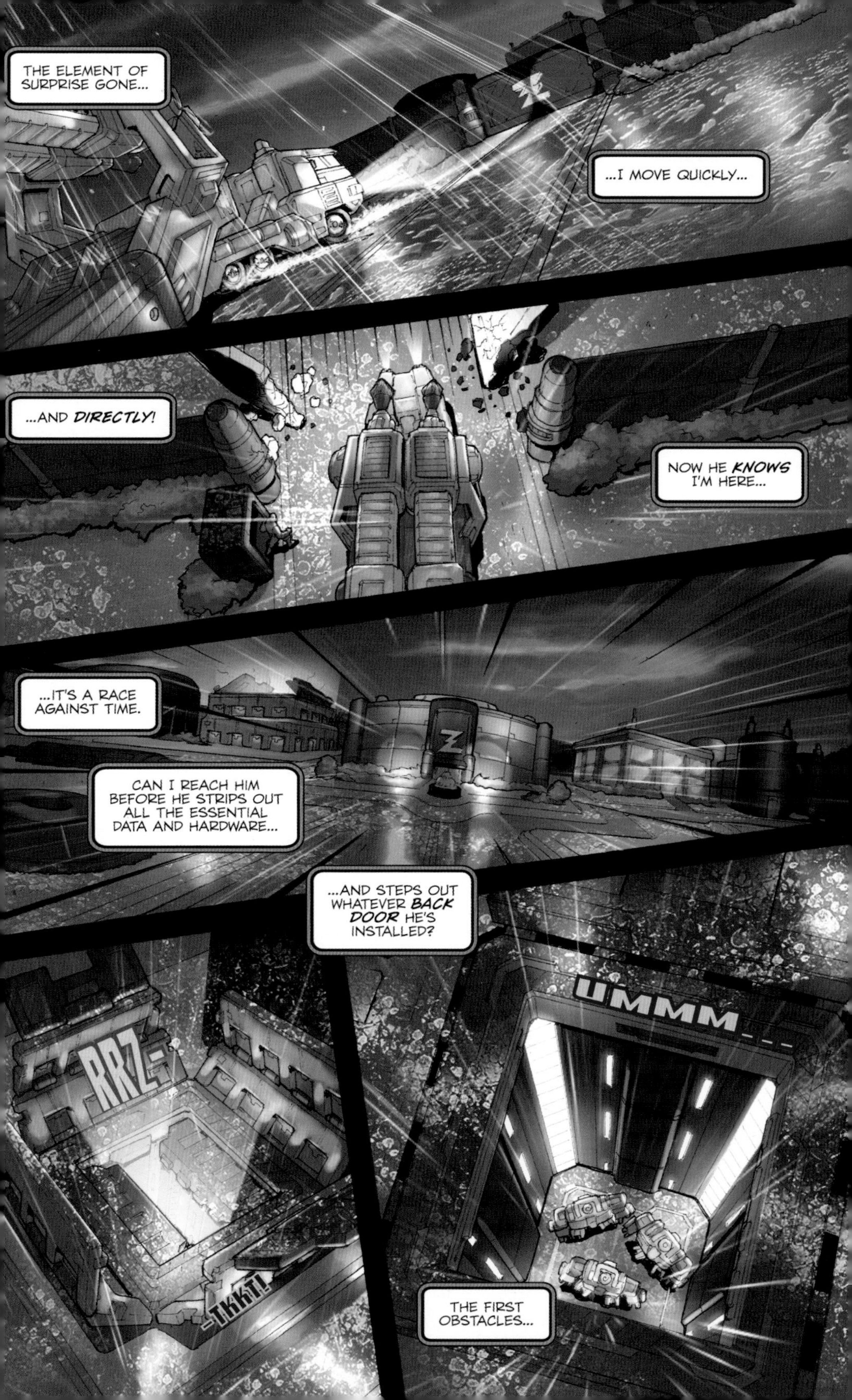
THE ELEMENT OF SURPRISE GONE...
...I MOVE QUICKLY...
...AND DIRECTLY!
NOW HE KNOWS I'M HERE...
...IT'S A RACE AGAINST TIME.
CAN I REACH HIM BEFORE HE STRIPS OUT ALL THE ESSENTIAL DATA AND HARDWARE...
...AND STEPS OUT WHATEVER BACK DOOR HE'S INSTALLED?
RRZ
-TKKT!
UMMM...
THE FIRST OBSTACLES...

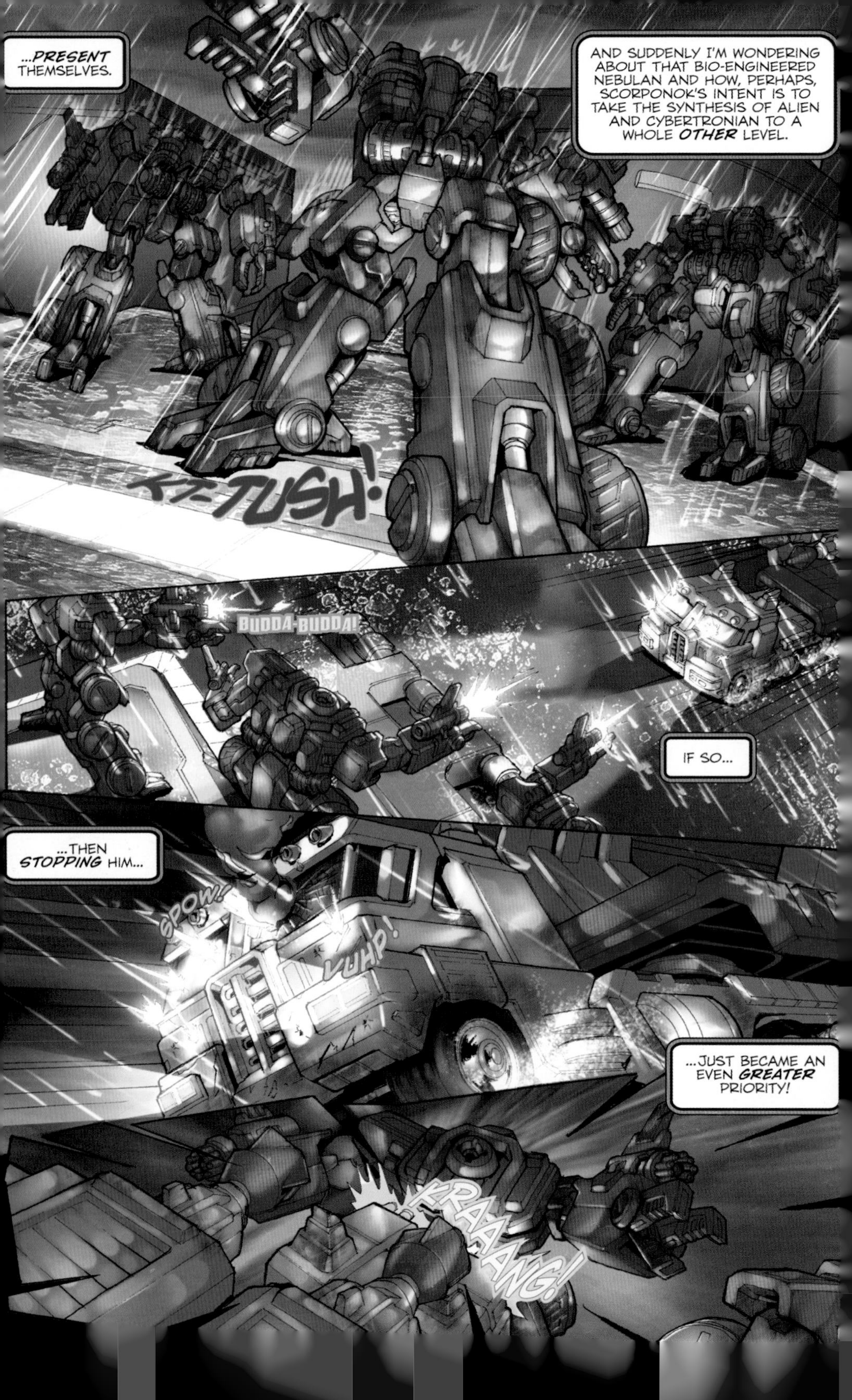
...PRESENT THEMSELVES.
AND SUDDENLY I'M WONDERING ABOUT THAT BIO-ENGINEERED NEBULAN AND HOW, PERHAPS, SCORPONOK'S INTENT IS TO TAKE THE SYNTHESIS OF ALIEN AND CYBERTRONIAN TO A WHOLE OTHER LEVEL.
KT-TUSH!
BUDDA-BUDDA!
IF SO...
...THEN STOPPING HIM...
SPOW!
VUHP!
...JUST BECAME AN EVEN GREATER PRIORITY!
KRAAANG!

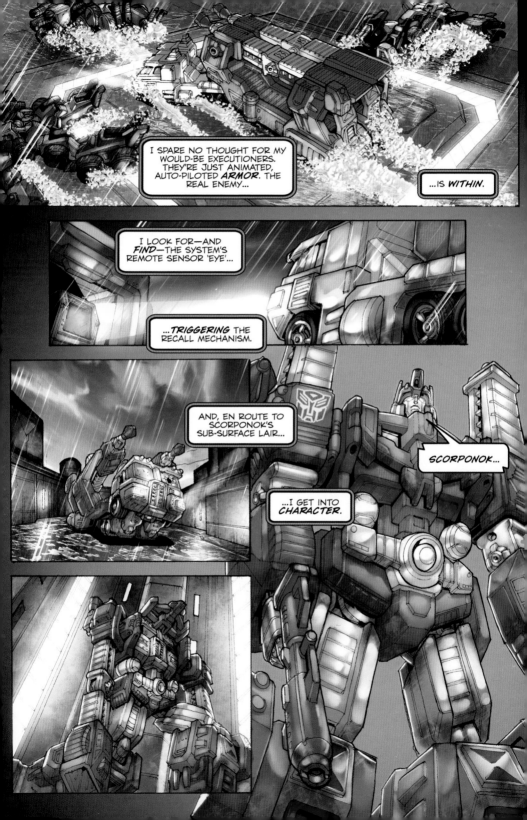

I SPARE NO THOUGHT FOR MY WOULD-BE EXECUTIONERS. THEY'RE JUST ANIMATED, AUTO-PILOTED *ARMOR*. THE REAL ENEMY...

...IS *WITHIN*.

I LOOK FOR—AND *FIND*—THE SYSTEM'S REMOTE SENSOR 'EYE'...

...*TRIGGERING* THE RECALL MECHANISM.

AND, EN ROUTE TO SCORPONOK'S SUB-SURFACE LAIR...

SCORPONOK...

...I GET INTO *CHARACTER*.

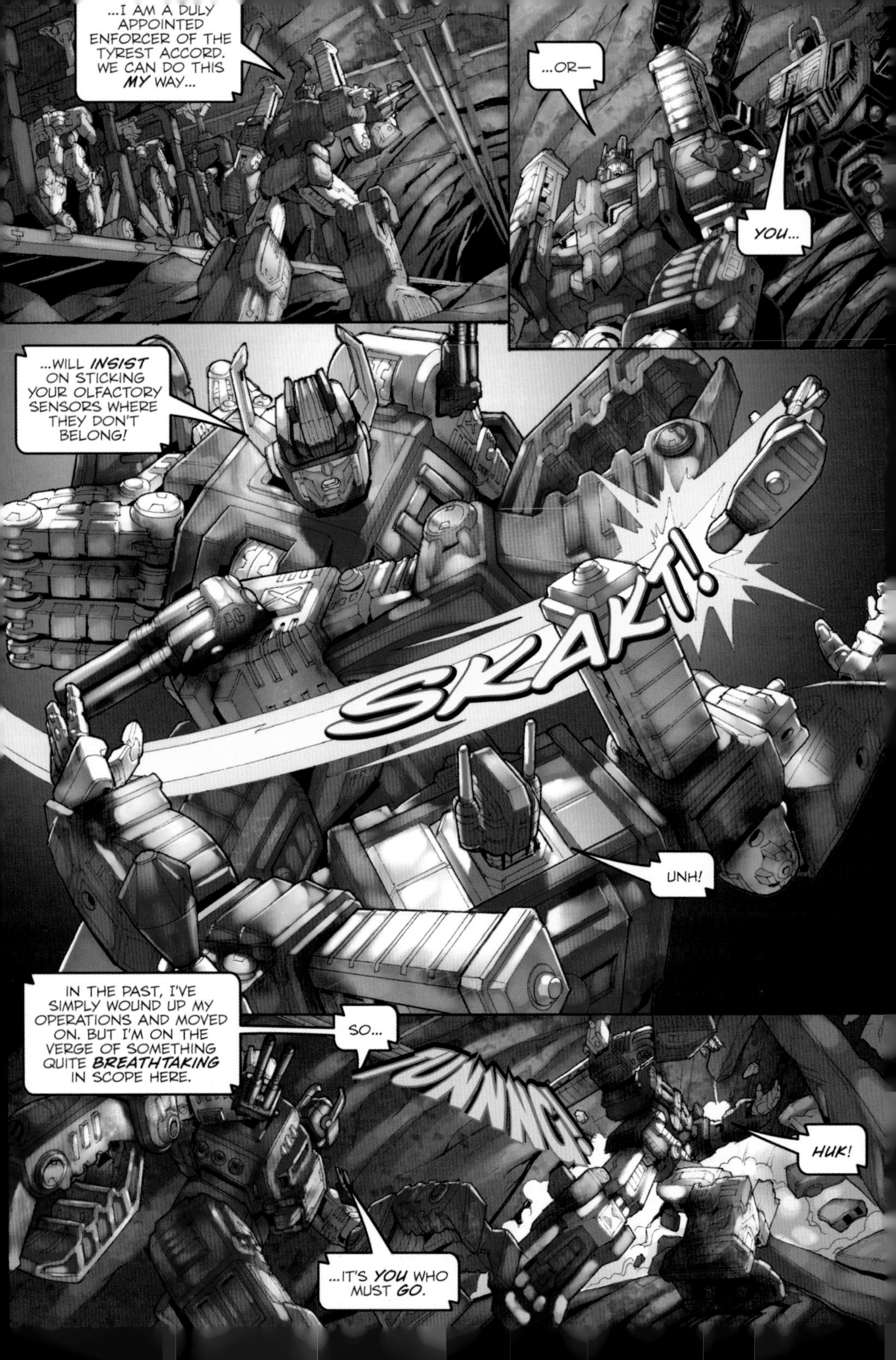
...I AM A DULY APPOINTED ENFORCER OF THE TYREST ACCORD. WE CAN DO THIS MY WAY...
...OR—
YOU...
...WILL INSIST ON STICKING YOUR OLFACTORY SENSORS WHERE THEY DON'T BELONG!
SKAKT!!
UNH!
IN THE PAST, I'VE SIMPLY WOUND UP MY OPERATIONS AND MOVED ON. BUT I'M ON THE VERGE OF SOMETHING QUITE BREATHTAKING IN SCOPE HERE.
SO...
HUK!
...IT'S YOU WHO MUST GO.

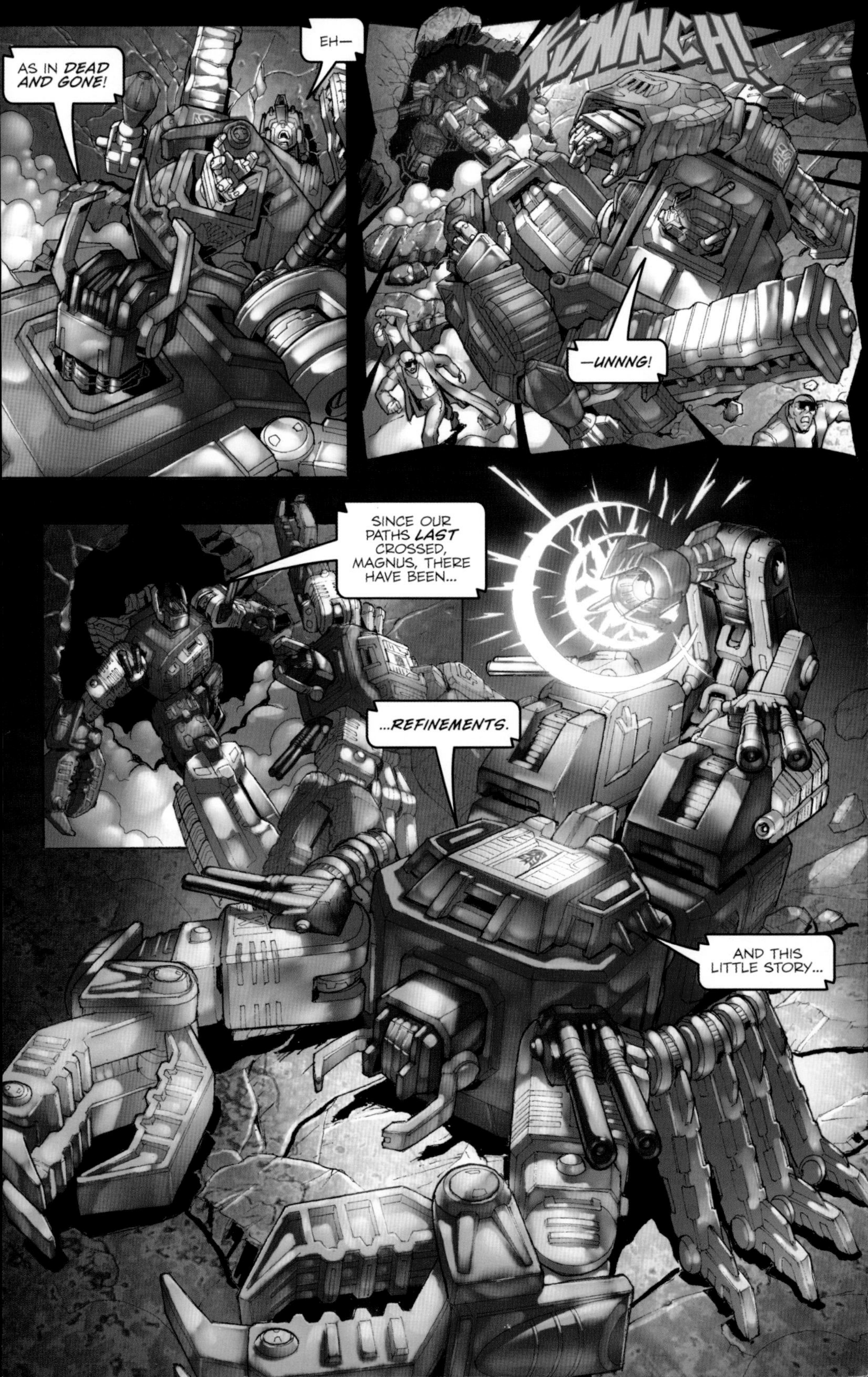
AS IN DEAD AND GONE!
EH—
KLUNNCH!
—UNNNG!
SINCE OUR PATHS LAST CROSSED, MAGNUS, THERE HAVE BEEN...
...REFINEMENTS.
AND THIS LITTLE STORY...

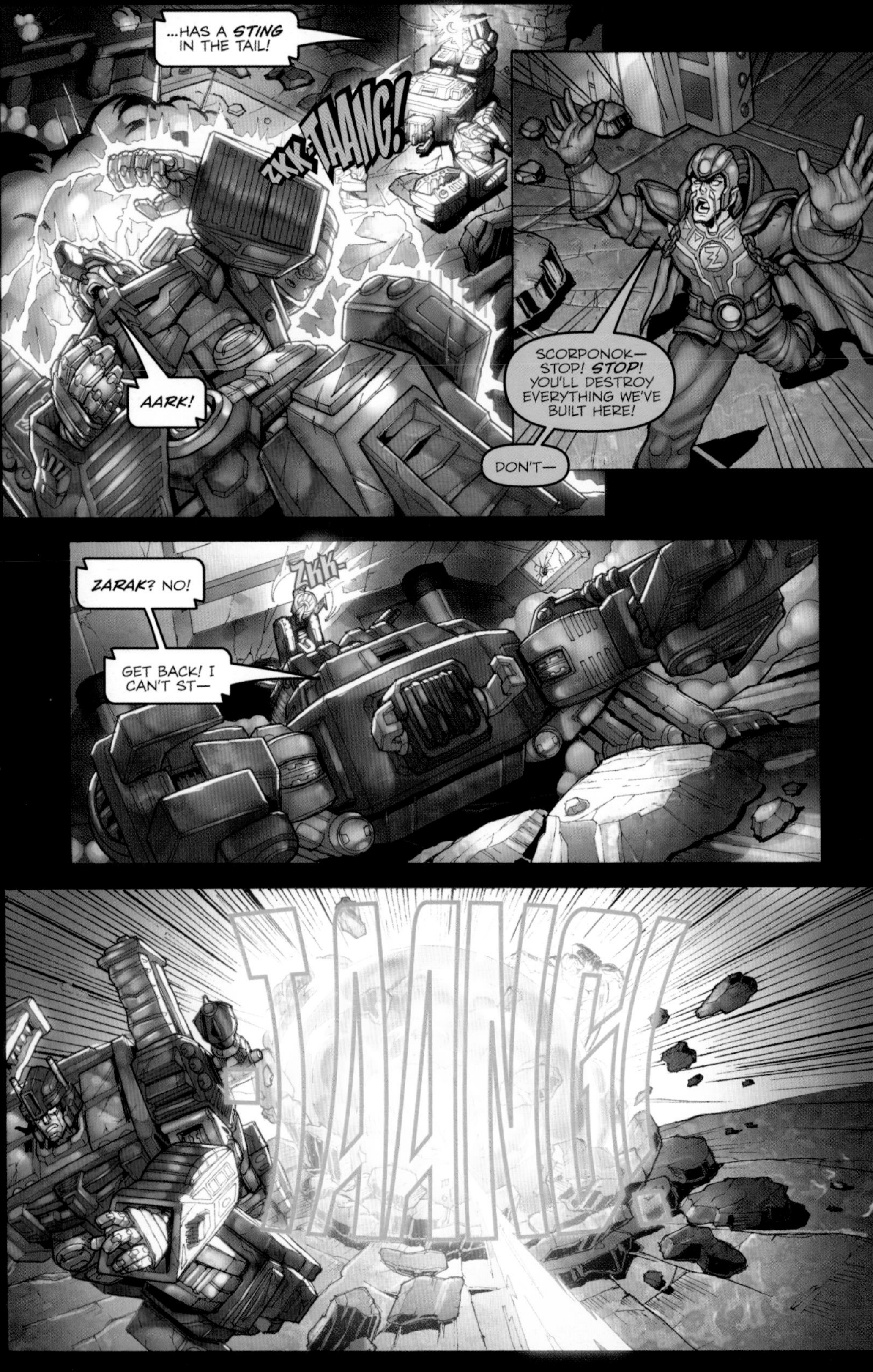
...HAS A STING IN THE TAIL!
ZKK-TAANG!
AARK!
SCORPONOK— STOP! STOP! YOU'LL DESTROY EVERYTHING WE'VE BUILT HERE!
DON'T—
ZAKK?! NO!
GET BACK! I CAN'T ST—
ZKK-
TAANG!

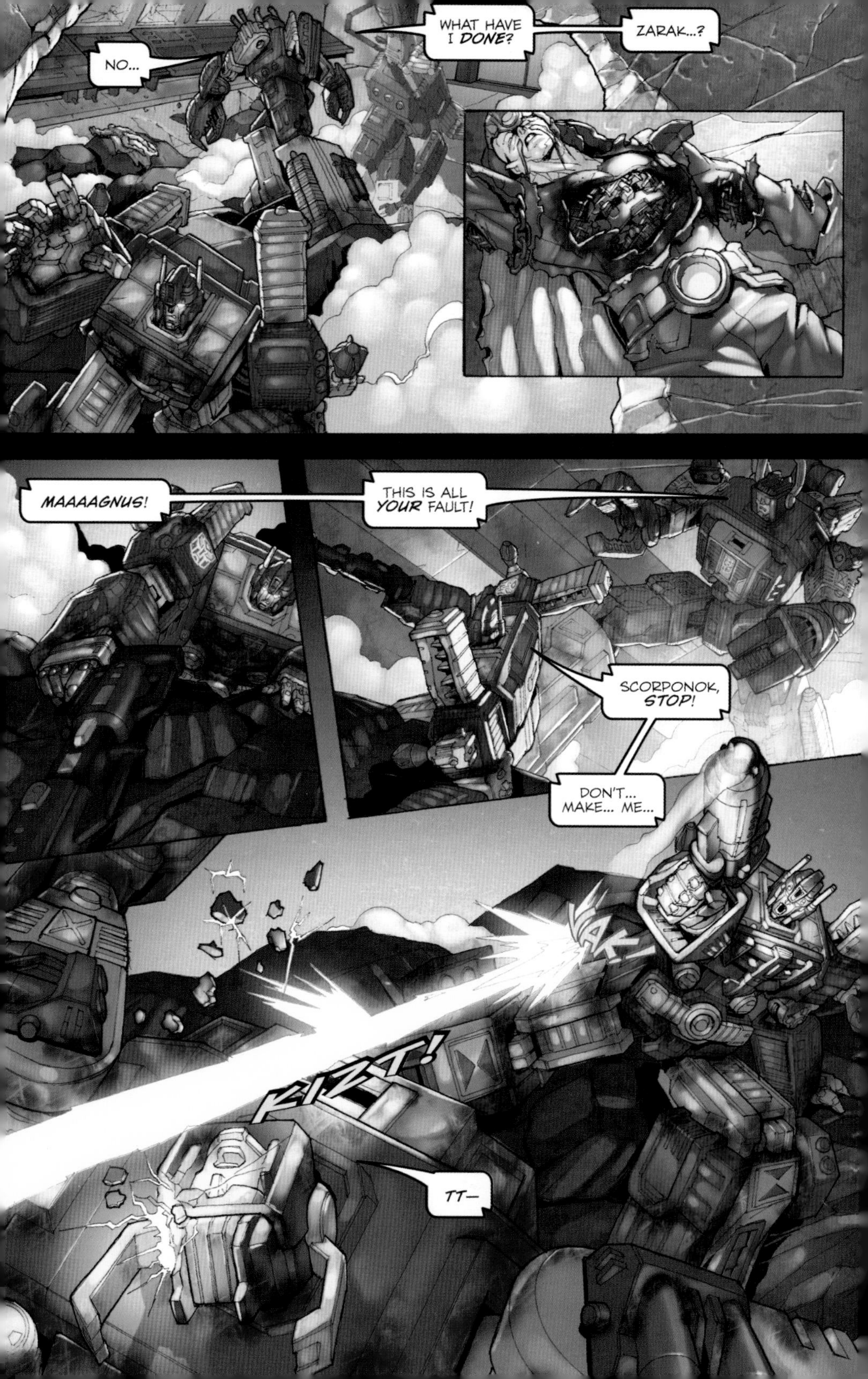
NO...
WHAT HAVE I *DONE*?
ZARAK...?
MAAAAGNUS!
THIS IS ALL *YOUR* FAULT!
SCORPONOK, *STOP!*
DON'T... MAKE... ME...
KRZZT!
TT—

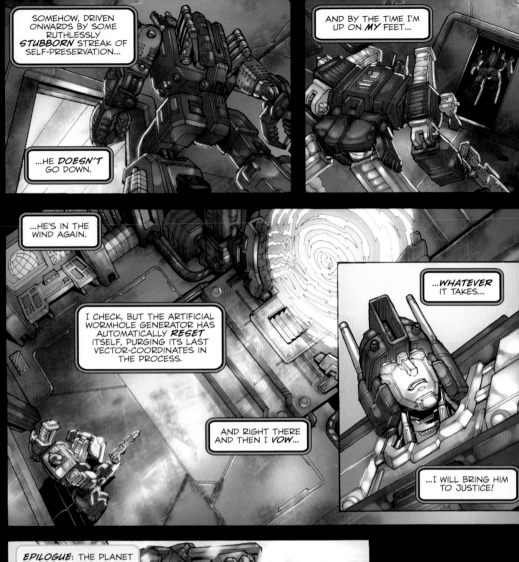

SOMEHOW, DRIVEN ONWARDS BY SOME RUTHLESSLY **STUBBORN** STREAK OF SELF-PRESERVATION...

...HE **DOESN'T** GO DOWN.

AND BY THE TIME I'M UP ON **MY** FEET...

...HE'S IN THE WIND AGAIN.

I CHECK, BUT THE ARTIFICIAL WORMHOLE GENERATOR HAS AUTOMATICALLY **RESET** ITSELF, PURGING ITS LAST VECTOR-COORDINATES IN THE PROCESS.

AND RIGHT THERE AND THEN I **VOW**...

...**WHATEVER** IT TAKES...

...I WILL BRING HIM TO JUSTICE!

EPILOGUE: THE PLANET **BURAS**, TWENTY-NINE STELLAR CYCLES LATER:

...UP TO HIS OLD TRICKS AGAIN. I'M BRINGING HIM IN. I'LL RENDEZVOUS WITH THE DECEPTICON **HIGH JUSTICE** ON KARASHI-DELTA.

I **NEVER** FORGET THAT VOW, BUT AS TIME PASSES I START TO WONDER... JUST HOW **FAR** WILL I GO TO GET THE JOB DONE!

SO... LET'S **DEAL!**

THE END?

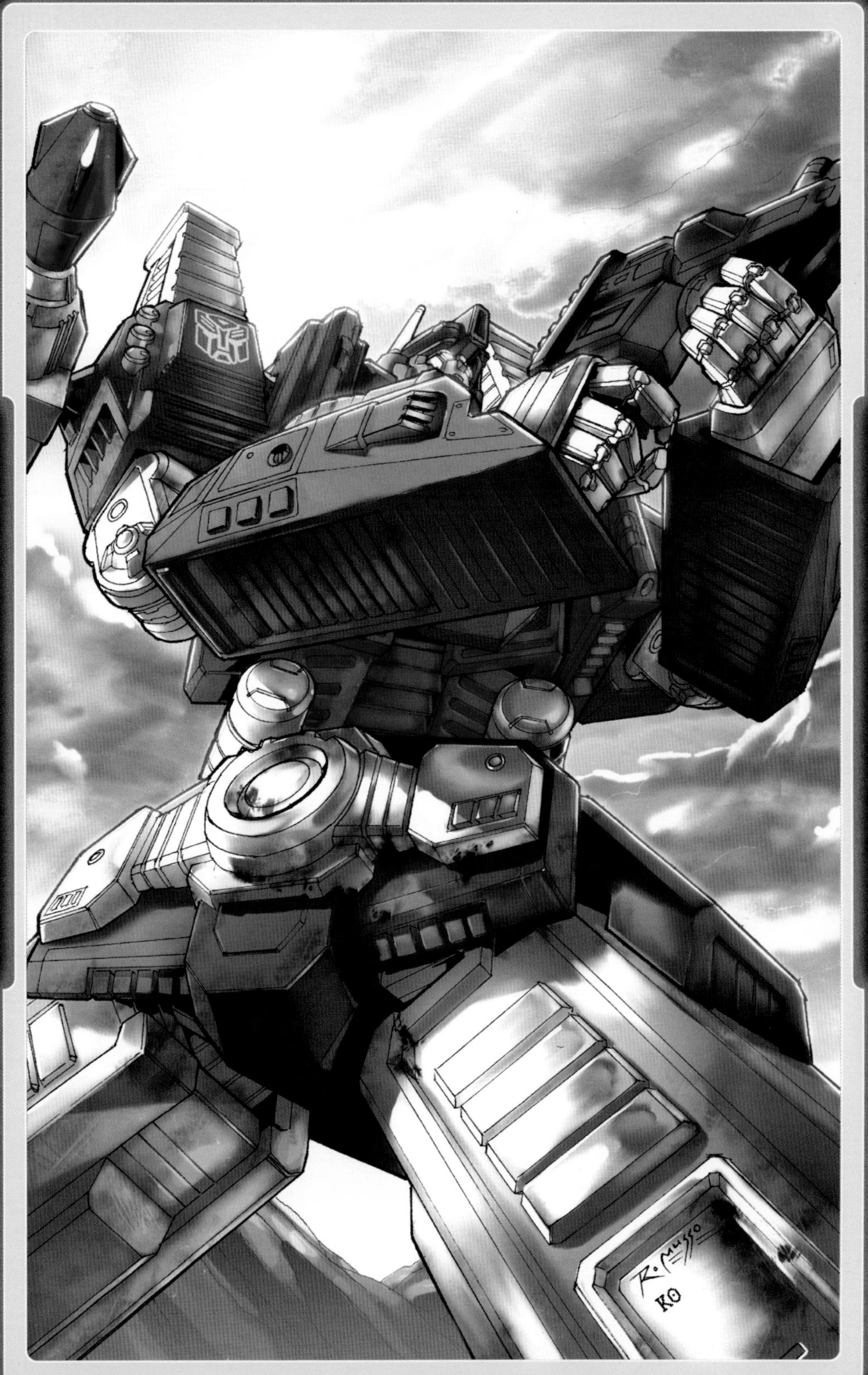
R. Musso
KO

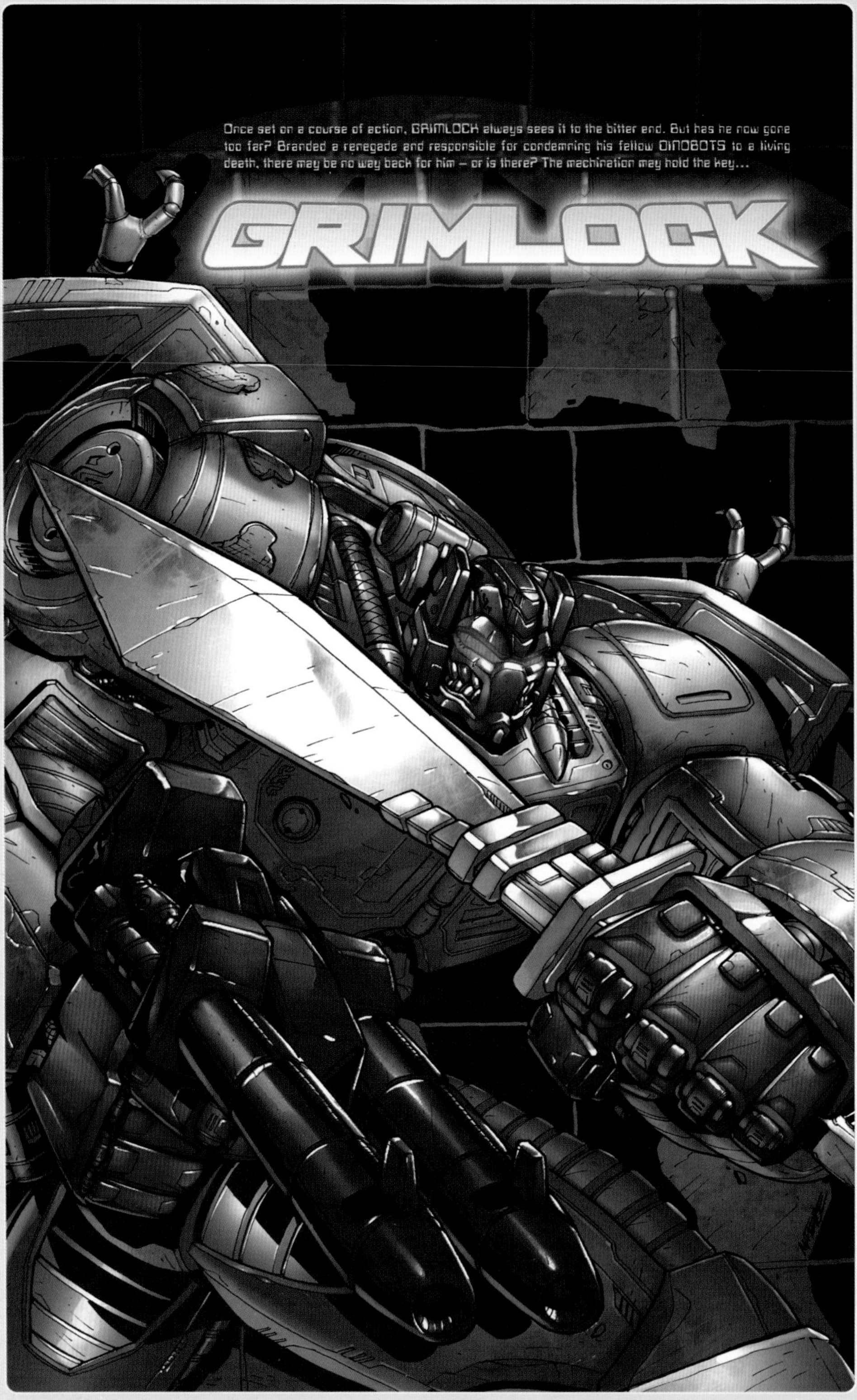
Once set on a course of action, GRIMLOCK always sees it to the bitter end. But has he now gone too far? Branded a renegade and responsible for condemning his fellow DINOBOTS to a living death, there may be no way back for him – or is there? The machination may hold the key...
GRIMLOCK

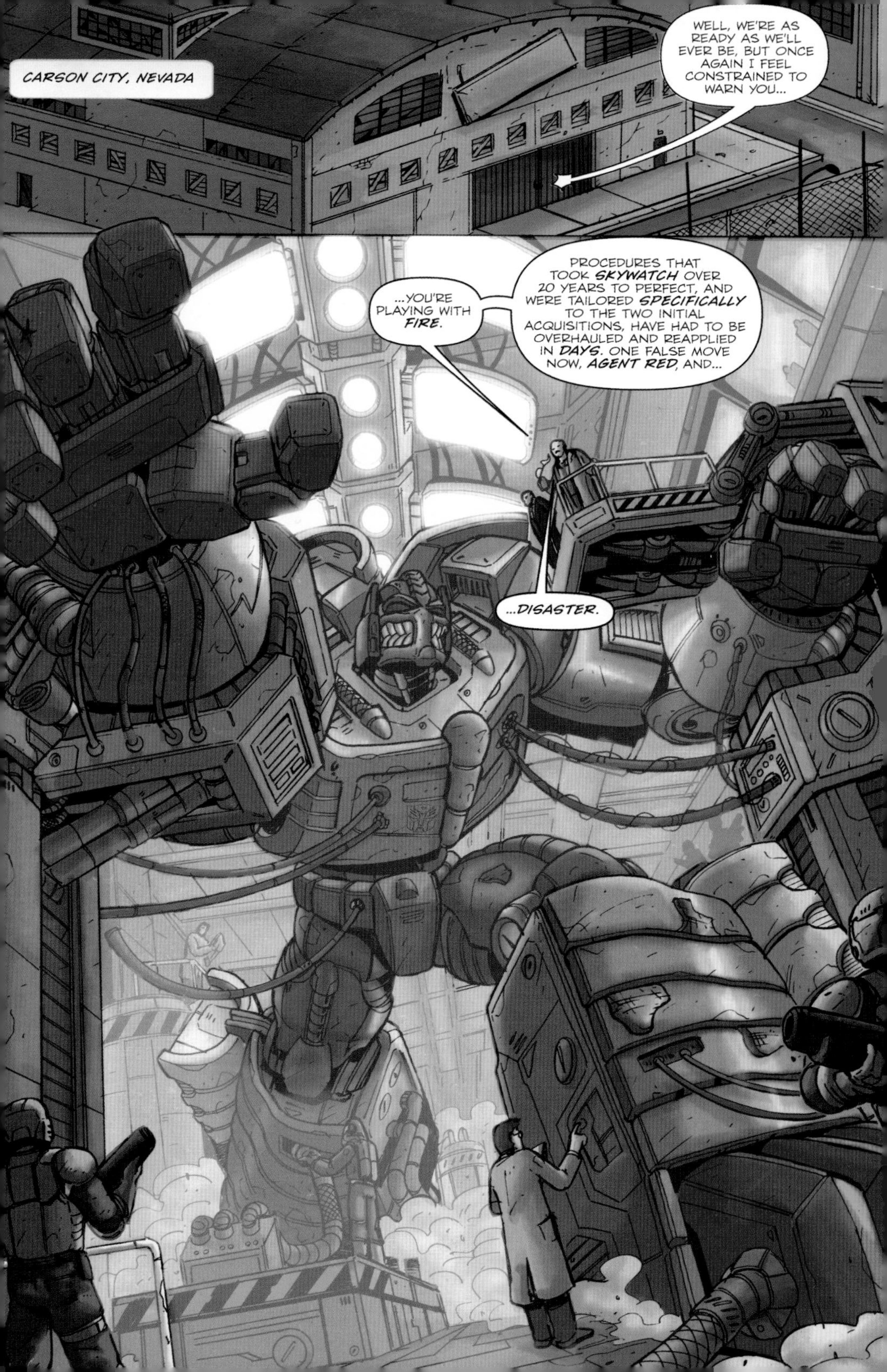
CARSON CITY, NEVADA
WELL, WE'RE AS READY AS WE'LL EVER BE, BUT ONCE AGAIN I FEEL CONSTRAINED TO WARN YOU...
...YOU'RE PLAYING WITH FIRE.
PROCEDURES THAT TOOK SKYWATCH OVER 20 YEARS TO PERFECT, AND WERE TAILORED SPECIFICALLY TO THE TWO INITIAL ACQUISITIONS, HAVE HAD TO BE OVERHAULED AND REAPPLIED IN DAYS. ONE FALSE MOVE NOW, AGENT RED, AND...
...DISASTER.

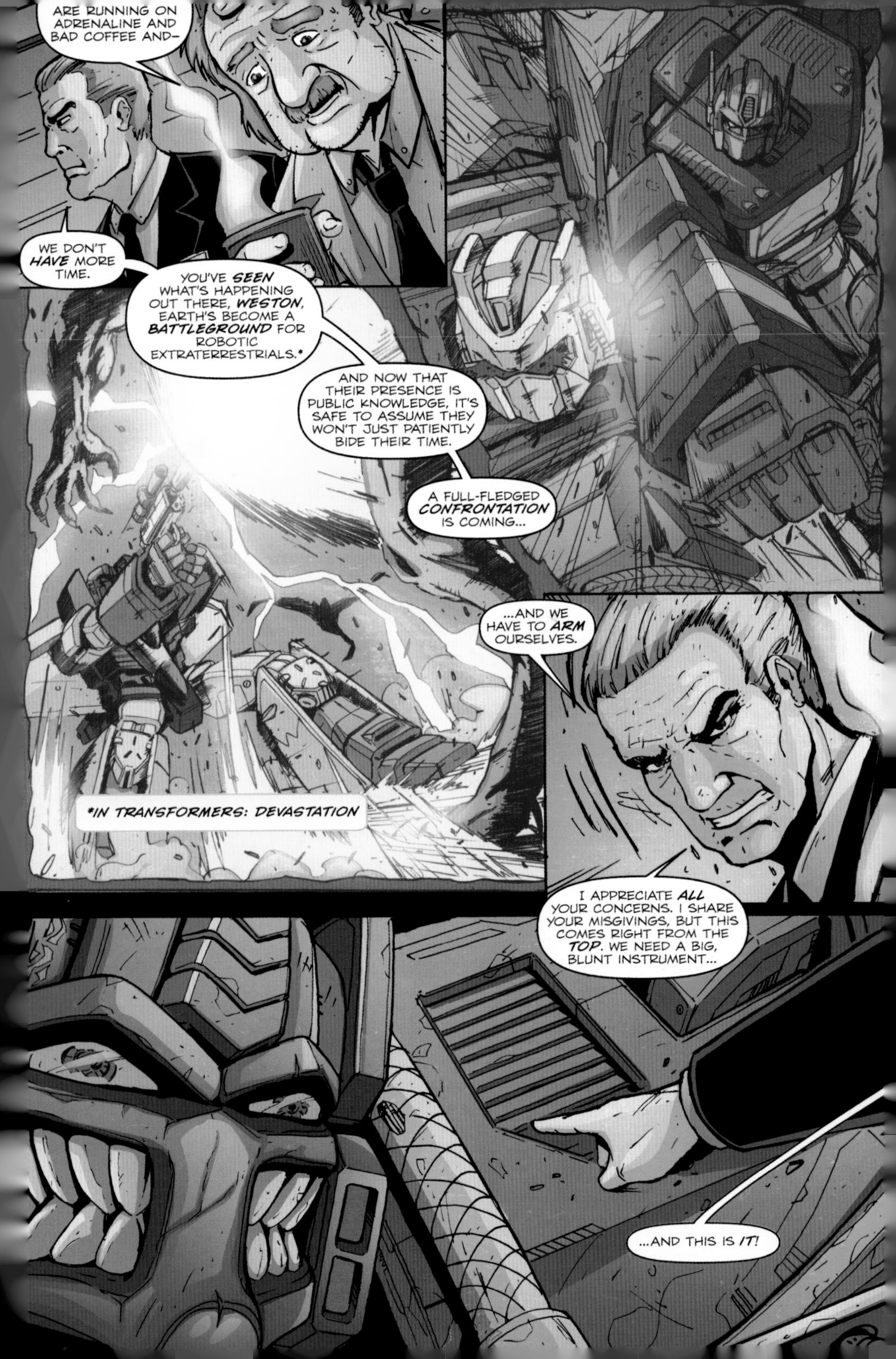
ARE RUNNING ON ADRENALINE AND BAD COFFEE AND–
WE DON'T *HAVE* MORE TIME.
YOU'VE *SEEN* WHAT'S HAPPENING OUT THERE, *WESTON*, EARTH'S BECOME A *BATTLEGROUND* FOR ROBOTIC EXTRATERRESTRIALS.*
AND NOW THAT THEIR PRESENCE IS PUBLIC KNOWLEDGE, IT'S SAFE TO ASSUME THEY WON'T JUST PATIENTLY BIDE THEIR TIME.
A FULL-FLEDGED *CONFRONTATION* IS COMING...
*IN TRANSFORMERS: DEVASTATION
...AND WE HAVE TO *ARM* OURSELVES.
I APPRECIATE *ALL* YOUR CONCERNS. I SHARE YOUR MISGIVINGS, BUT THIS COMES RIGHT FROM THE *TOP*. WE NEED A BIG, BLUNT INSTRUMENT...
...AND THIS IS *IT!*

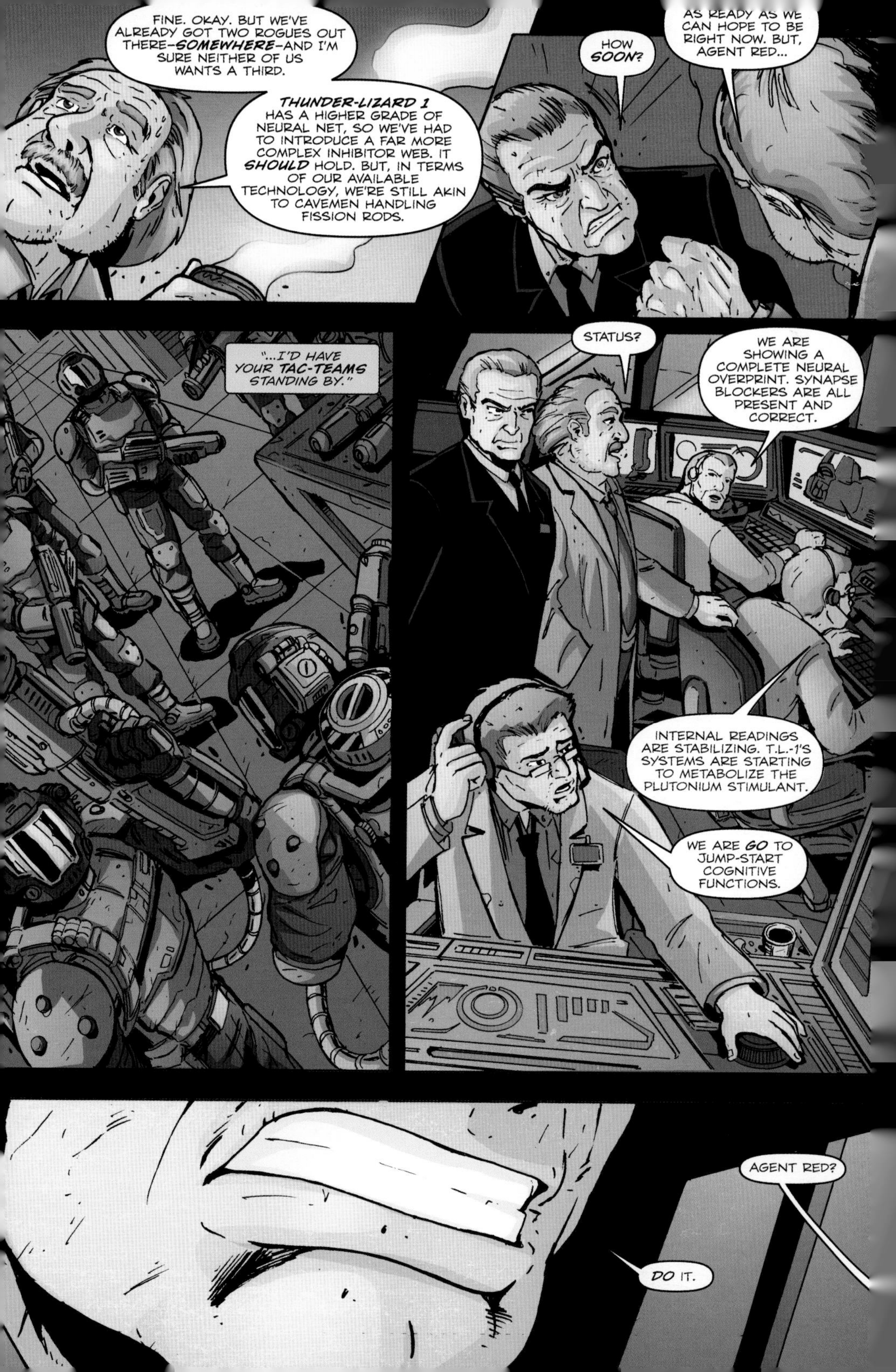

FINE. OKAY. BUT WE'VE ALREADY GOT TWO ROGUES OUT THERE–SOMEWHERE–AND I'M SURE NEITHER OF US WANTS A THIRD.
THUNDER-LIZARD 1 HAS A HIGHER GRADE OF NEURAL NET, SO WE'VE HAD TO INTRODUCE A FAR MORE COMPLEX INHIBITOR WEB. IT SHOULD HOLD. BUT, IN TERMS OF OUR AVAILABLE TECHNOLOGY, WE'RE STILL AKIN TO CAVEMEN HANDLING FISSION RODS.
HOW SOON?
AS READY AS WE CAN HOPE TO BE RIGHT NOW. BUT, AGENT RED...
"...I'D HAVE YOUR TAC-TEAMS STANDING BY."
STATUS?
WE ARE SHOWING A COMPLETE NEURAL OVERPRINT. SYNAPSE BLOCKERS ARE ALL PRESENT AND CORRECT.
INTERNAL READINGS ARE STABILIZING. T.L.-1'S SYSTEMS ARE STARTING TO METABOLIZE THE PLUTONIUM STIMULANT.
WE ARE GO TO JUMP-START COGNITIVE FUNCTIONS.
AGENT RED?
DO IT.

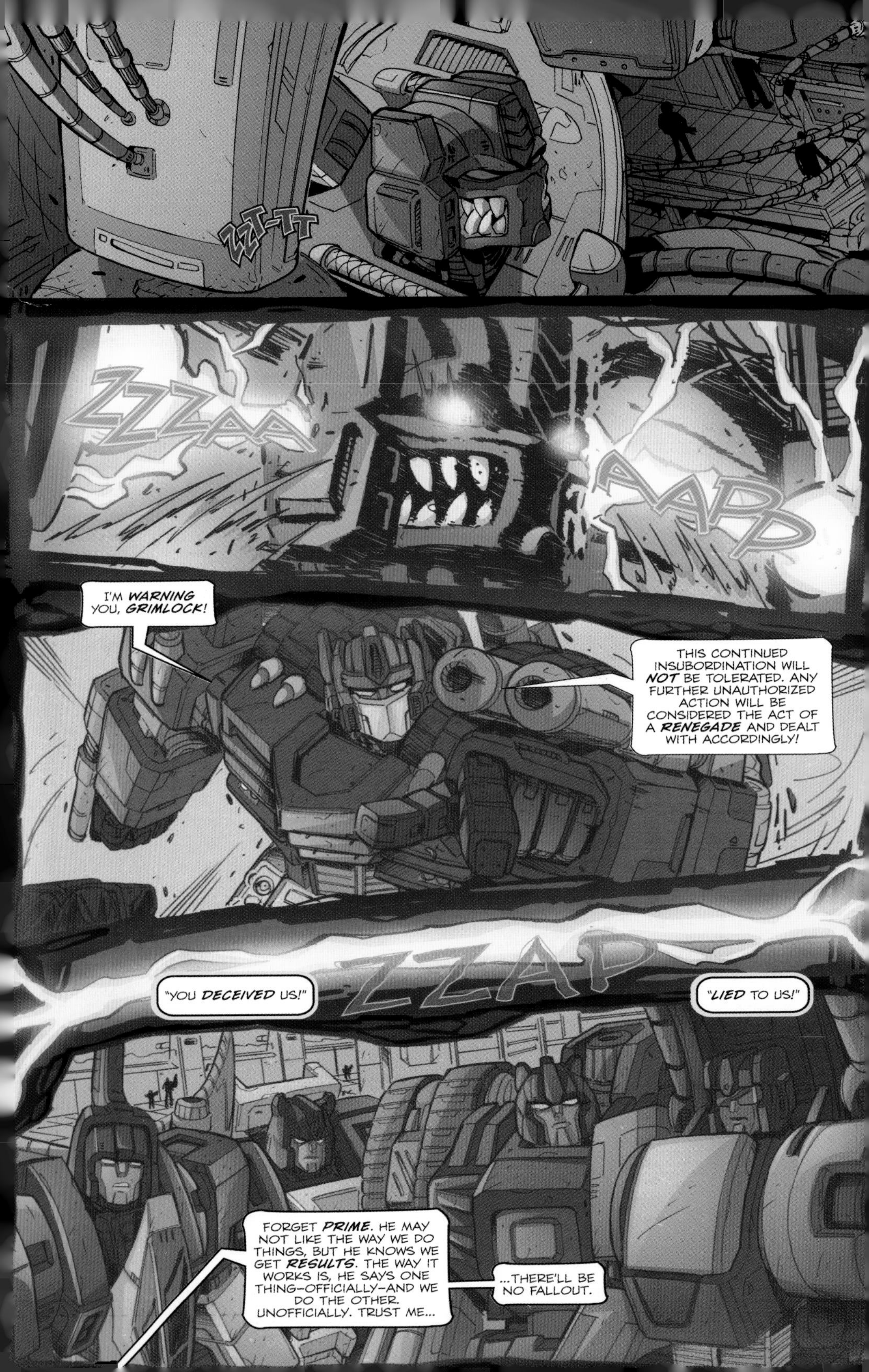
ZZT-TT
ZZZAA
AAPP
I'M WARNING YOU, GRIMLOCK!
THIS CONTINUED INSUBORDINATION WILL NOT BE TOLERATED. ANY FURTHER UNAUTHORIZED ACTION WILL BE CONSIDERED THE ACT OF A RENEGADE AND DEALT WITH ACCORDINGLY!
"YOU DECEIVED US!"
ZZAP
"LIED TO US!"
FORGET PRIME. HE MAY NOT LIKE THE WAY WE DO THINGS, BUT HE KNOWS WE GET RESULTS. THE WAY IT WORKS IS, HE SAYS ONE THING—OFFICIALLY—AND WE DO THE OTHER. UNOFFICIALLY. TRUST ME...
...THERE'LL BE NO FALLOUT.

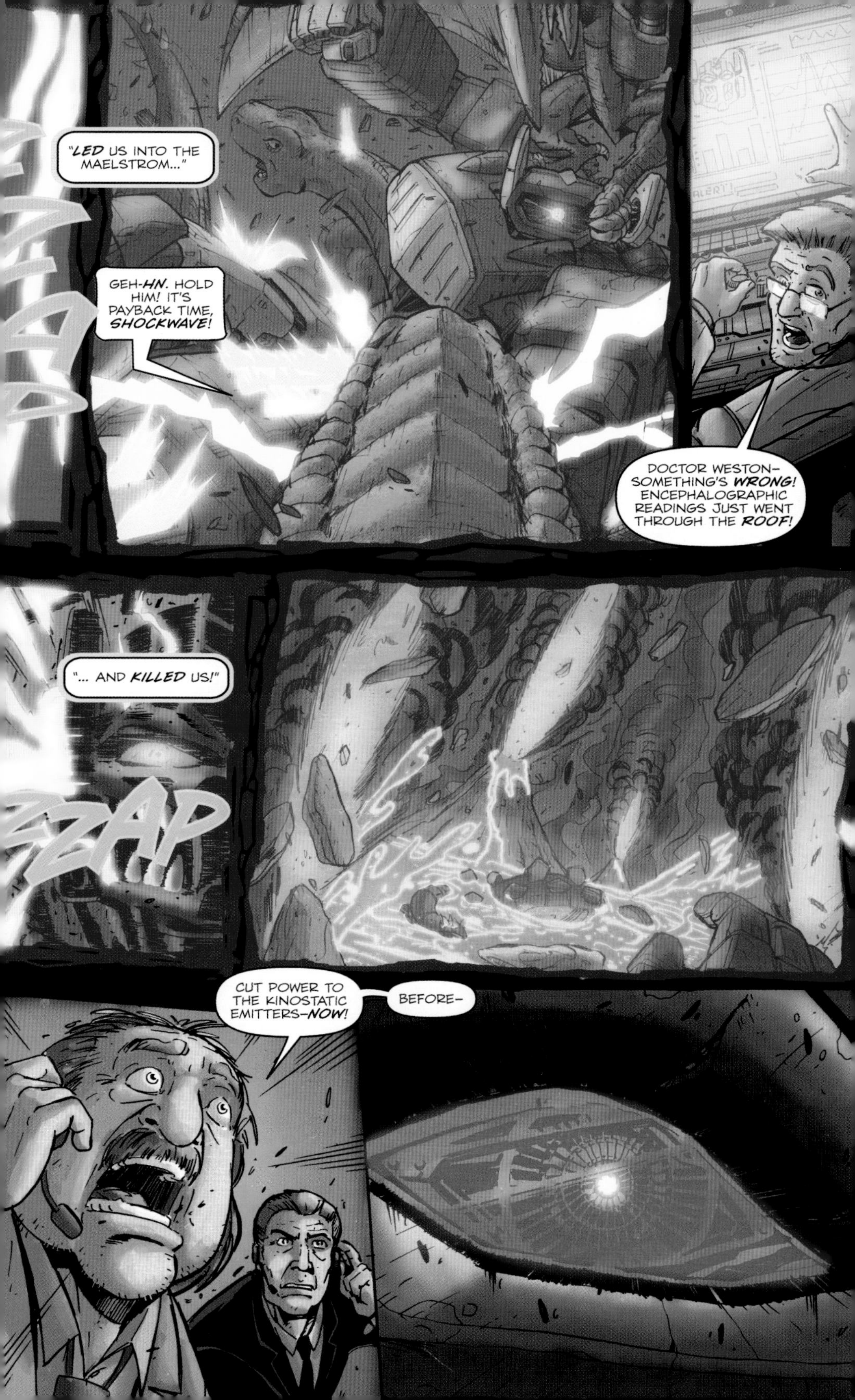
"LED US INTO THE MAELSTROM..."
GEH-HN. HOLD HIM! IT'S PAYBACK TIME, SHOCKWAVE!
DOCTOR WESTON-SOMETHING'S WRONG! ENCEPHALOGRAPHIC READINGS JUST WENT THROUGH THE ROOF!
"... AND KILLED US!"
CUT POWER TO THE KINOSTATIC EMITTERS-NOW!
BEFORE-

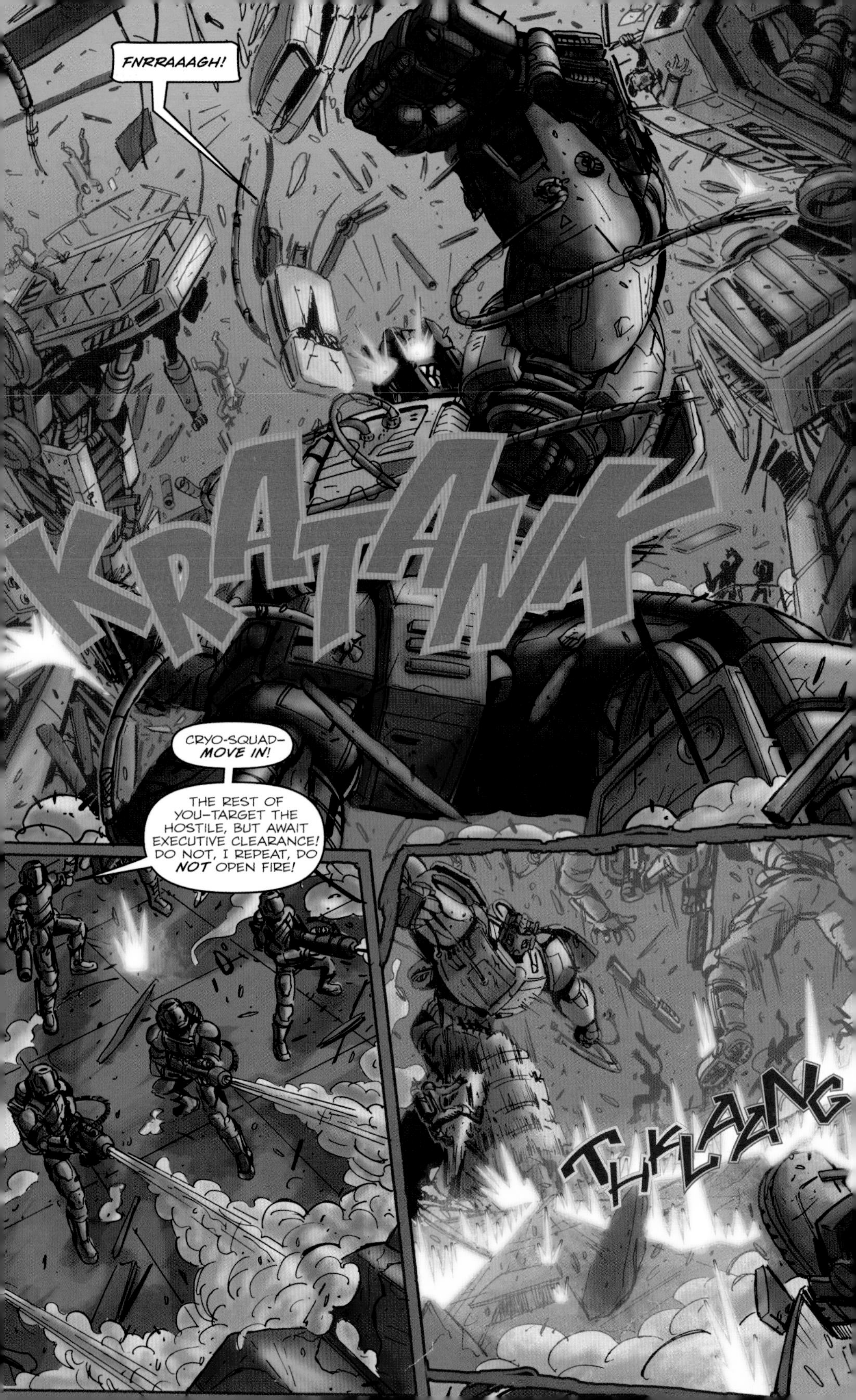
FNRRAAAGH!
KRATANK
CRYO-SQUAD- MOVE IN!
THE REST OF YOU--TARGET THE HOSTILE, BUT AWAIT EXECUTIVE CLEARANCE! DO NOT, I REPEAT, DO NOT OPEN FIRE!
THKLAZANG

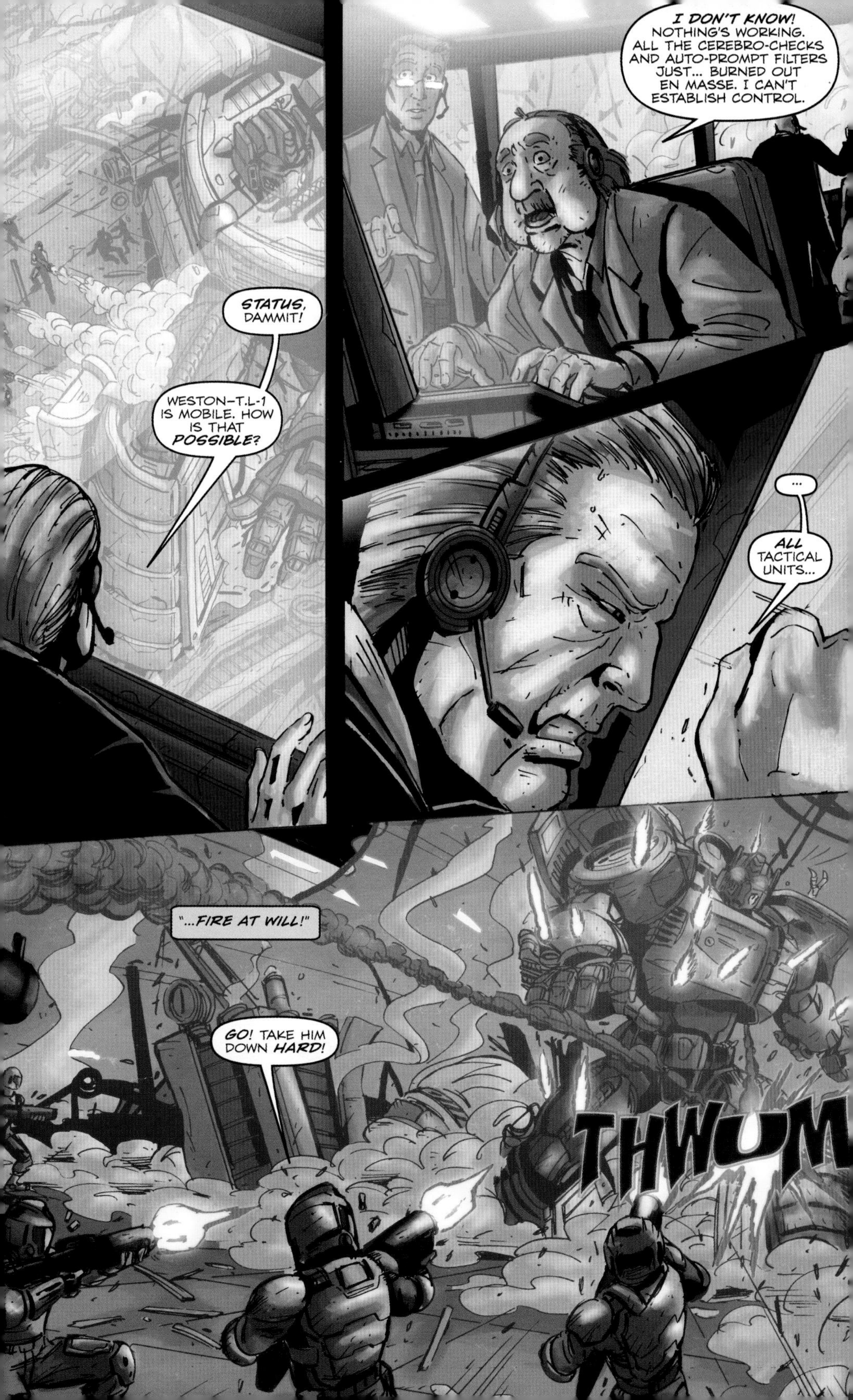

I DON'T KNOW! NOTHING'S WORKING. ALL THE CEREBRO-CHECKS AND AUTO-PROMPT FILTERS JUST... BURNED OUT EN MASSE. I CAN'T ESTABLISH CONTROL.
STATUS, DAMMIT!
WESTON-T.L-1 IS MOBILE. HOW IS THAT POSSIBLE?
...
ALL TACTICAL UNITS...
"...FIRE AT WILL!"
GO! TAKE HIM DOWN HARD!
THWUM

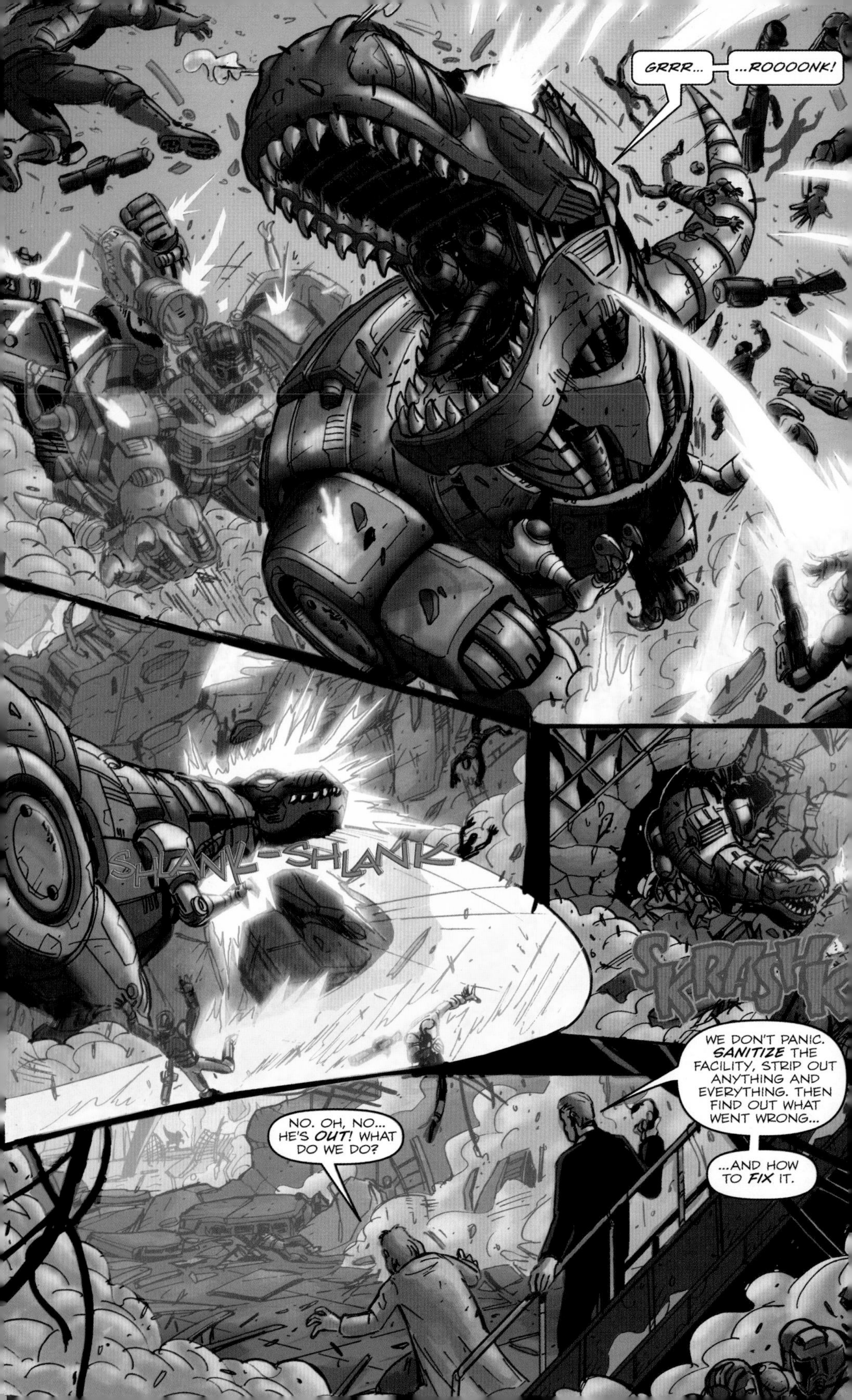
GRRR...
...ROOOONK!
SHLANK-SHLANK
SKRASHK
NO. OH, NO... HE'S *OUT*! WHAT DO WE DO?
WE DON'T PANIC. ***SANITIZE*** THE FACILITY, STRIP OUT ANYTHING AND EVERYTHING. THEN FIND OUT WHAT WENT WRONG...
...AND HOW TO *FIX* IT.

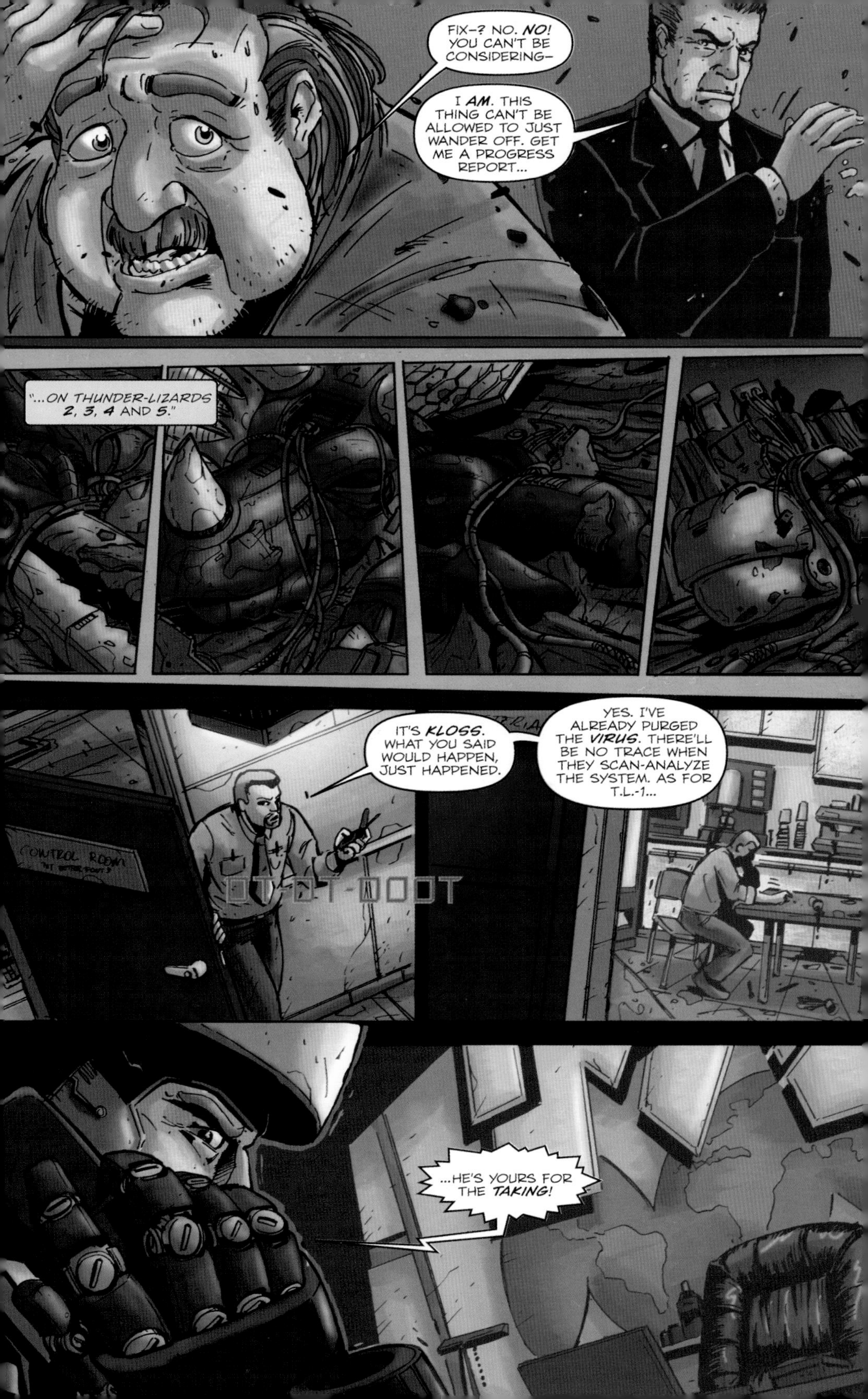
FIX–? NO. NO! YOU CAN'T BE CONSIDERING–
I AM. THIS THING CAN'T BE ALLOWED TO JUST WANDER OFF. GET ME A PROGRESS REPORT...
"...ON THUNDER-LIZARDS 2, 3, 4 AND 5."
IT'S KLOSS. WHAT YOU SAID WOULD HAPPEN, JUST HAPPENED.
YES. I'VE ALREADY PURGED THE VIRUS. THERE'LL BE NO TRACE WHEN THEY SCAN-ANALYZE THE SYSTEM. AS FOR T.L.-1...
...HE'S YOURS FOR THE TAKING!

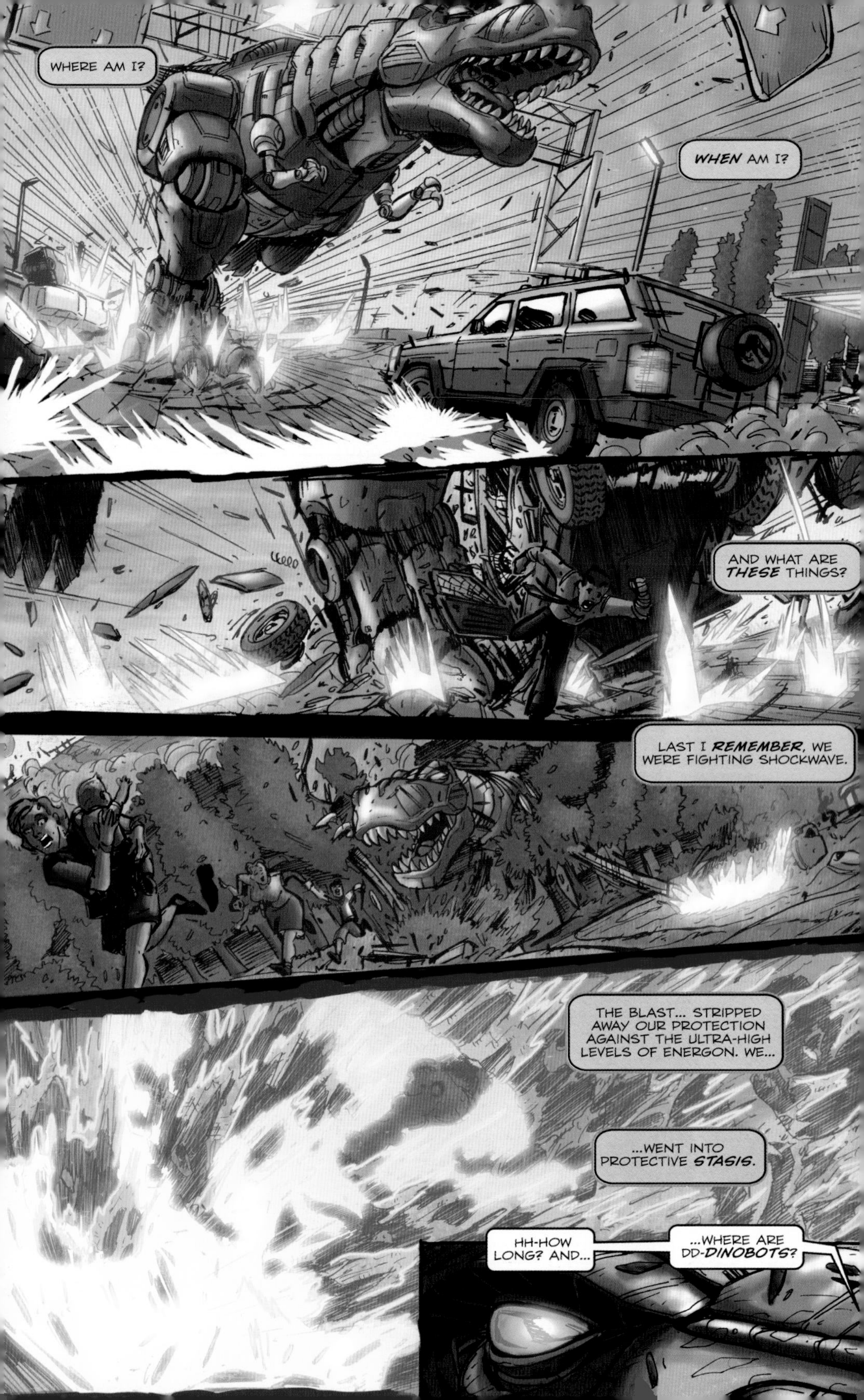

WHERE AM I?
WHEN AM I?
AND WHAT ARE *THESE* THINGS?
LAST I *REMEMBER*, WE WERE FIGHTING SHOCKWAVE.
THE BLAST... STRIPPED AWAY OUR PROTECTION AGAINST THE ULTRA-HIGH LEVELS OF ENERGON. WE...
...WENT INTO PROTECTIVE *STASIS*.
HH-HOW LONG? AND...
...WHERE ARE DD-*DINOBOTS*?

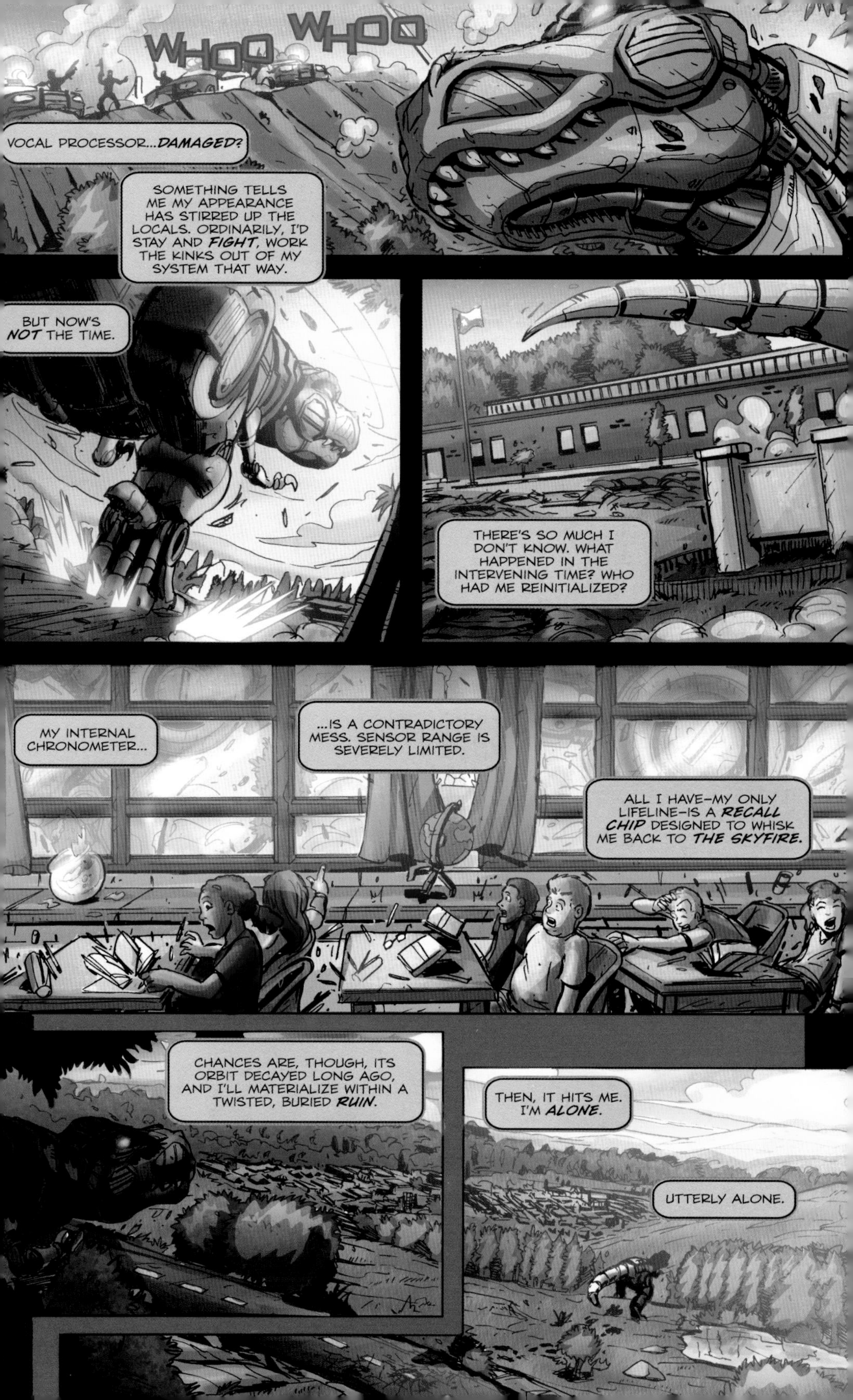
WHOO WHOO
VOCAL PROCESSOR...DAMAGED?
SOMETHING TELLS ME MY APPEARANCE HAS STIRRED UP THE LOCALS. ORDINARILY, I'D STAY AND FIGHT, WORK THE KINKS OUT OF MY SYSTEM THAT WAY.
BUT NOW'S NOT THE TIME.
THERE'S SO MUCH I DON'T KNOW. WHAT HAPPENED IN THE INTERVENING TIME? WHO HAD ME REINITIALIZED?
MY INTERNAL CHRONOMETER...
...IS A CONTRADICTORY MESS. SENSOR RANGE IS SEVERELY LIMITED.
ALL I HAVE—MY ONLY LIFELINE—IS A RECALL CHIP DESIGNED TO WHISK ME BACK TO THE SKYFIRE.
CHANCES ARE, THOUGH, ITS ORBIT DECAYED LONG AGO, AND I'LL MATERIALIZE WITHIN A TWISTED, BURIED RUIN.
THEN, IT HITS ME. I'M ALONE.
UTTERLY ALONE.

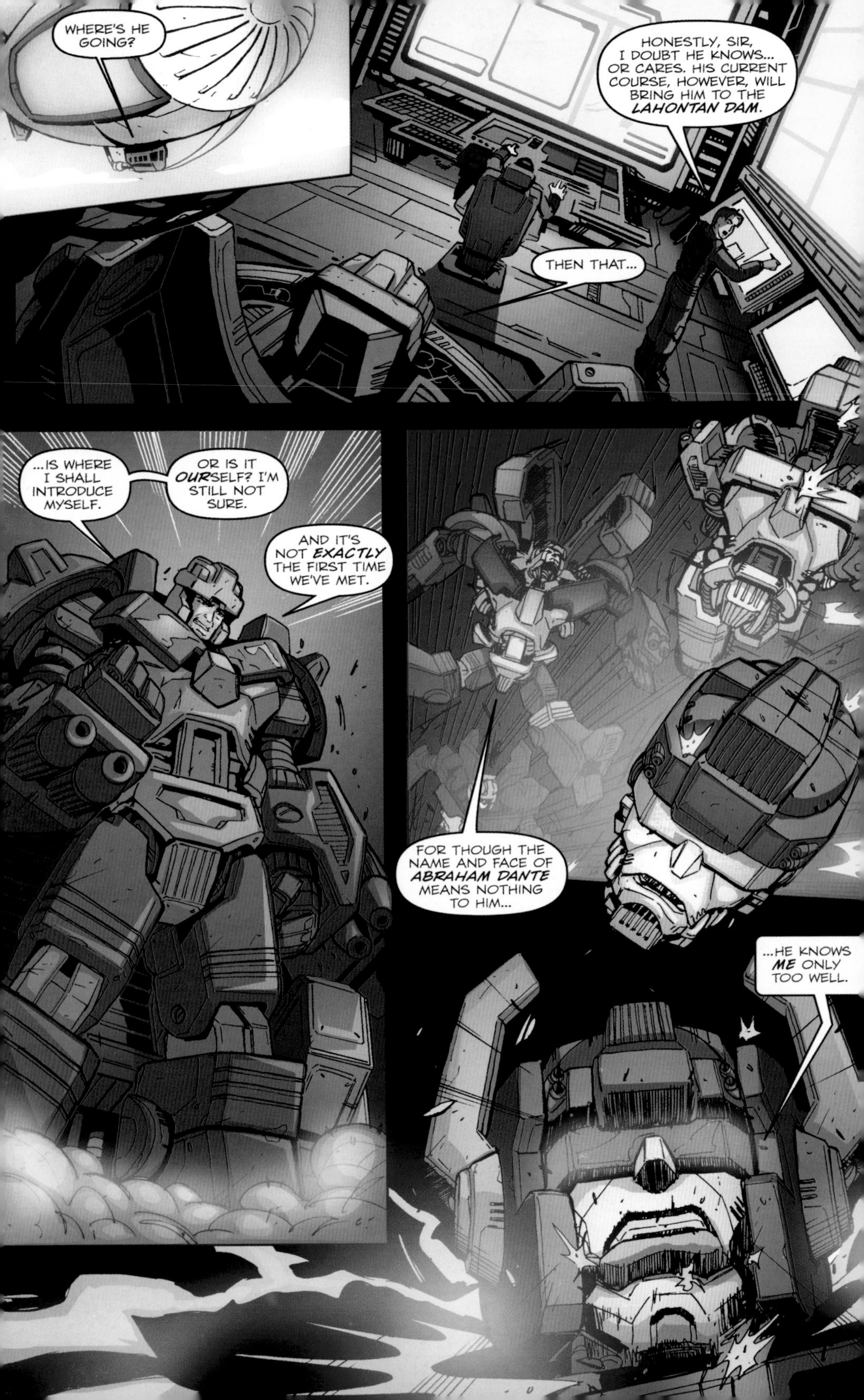
WHERE'S HE GOING?
HONESTLY, SIR, I DOUBT HE KNOWS... OR CARES. HIS CURRENT COURSE, HOWEVER, WILL BRING HIM TO THE LAHONTAN DAM.
THEN THAT...
...IS WHERE I SHALL INTRODUCE MYSELF.
OR IS IT OURSELF? I'M STILL NOT SURE.
AND IT'S NOT EXACTLY THE FIRST TIME WE'VE MET.
FOR THOUGH THE NAME AND FACE OF ABRAHAM DANTE MEANS NOTHING TO HIM...
...HE KNOWS ME ONLY TOO WELL.

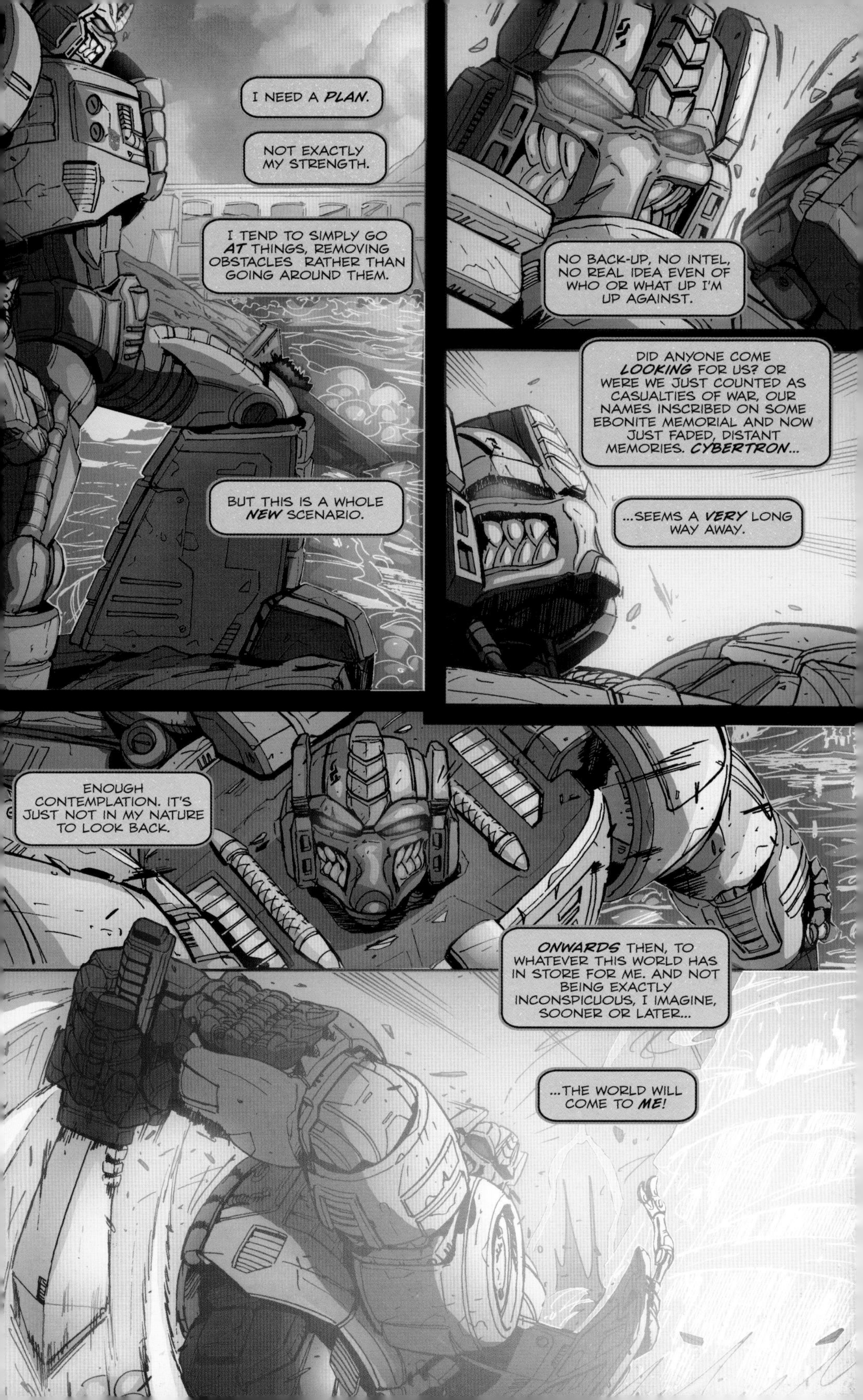
I NEED A *PLAN*.
NOT EXACTLY MY STRENGTH.
I TEND TO SIMPLY GO *AT* THINGS, REMOVING OBSTACLES RATHER THAN GOING AROUND THEM.
BUT THIS IS A WHOLE *NEW* SCENARIO.
NO BACK-UP, NO INTEL, NO REAL IDEA EVEN OF WHO OR WHAT UP I'M UP AGAINST.
DID ANYONE COME *LOOKING* FOR US? OR WERE WE JUST COUNTED AS CASUALTIES OF WAR, OUR NAMES INSCRIBED ON SOME EBONITE MEMORIAL AND NOW JUST FADED, DISTANT MEMORIES. *CYBERTRON*...
...SEEMS A *VERY* LONG WAY AWAY.
ENOUGH CONTEMPLATION. IT'S JUST NOT IN MY NATURE TO LOOK BACK.
ONWARDS THEN, TO WHATEVER THIS WORLD HAS IN STORE FOR ME. AND NOT BEING EXACTLY INCONSPICUOUS, I IMAGINE, SOONER OR LATER...
...THE WORLD WILL COME TO *ME!*

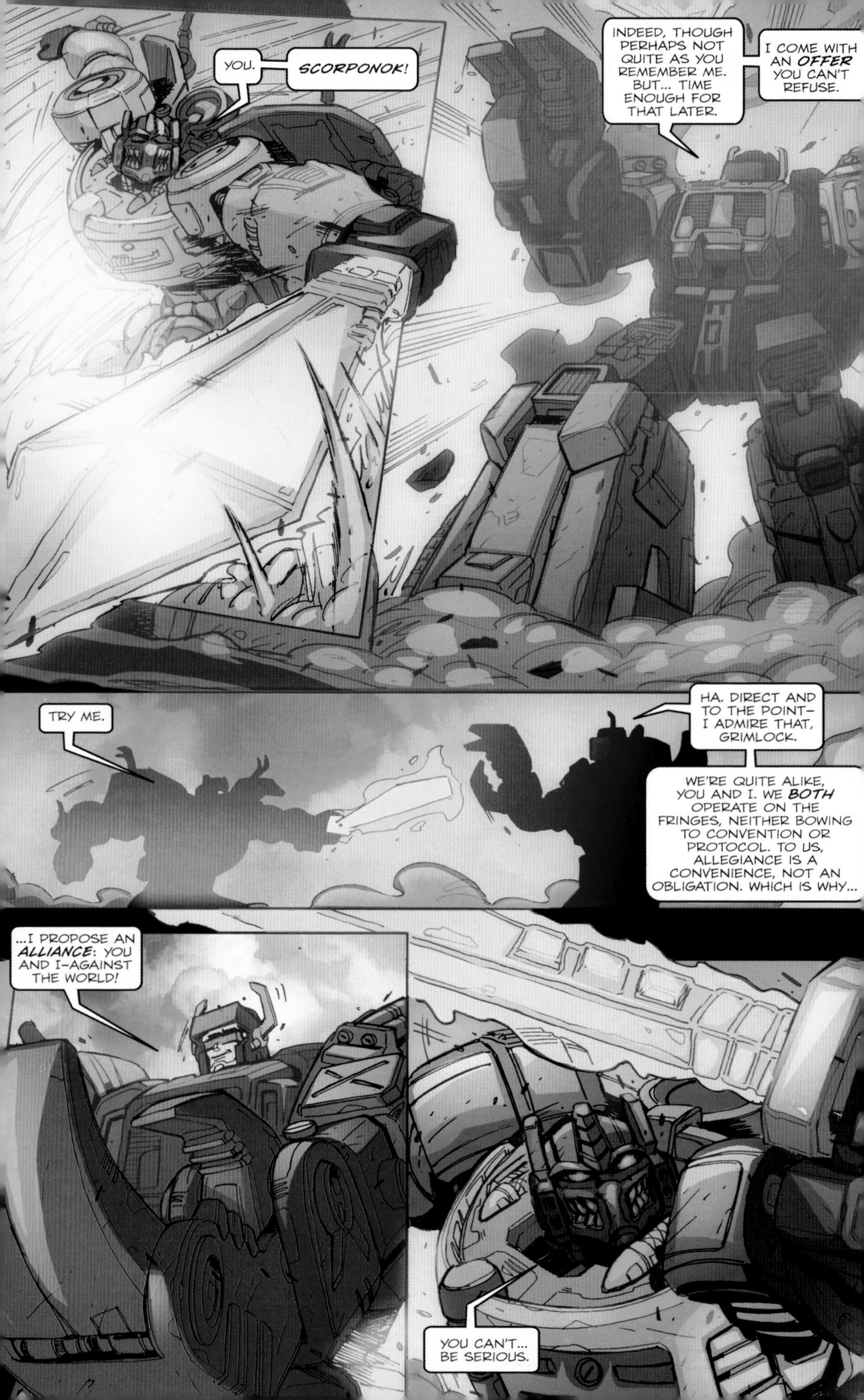
YOU.
SCORPONOK!
INDEED, THOUGH PERHAPS NOT QUITE AS YOU REMEMBER ME. BUT... TIME ENOUGH FOR THAT LATER.
I COME WITH AN OFFER YOU CAN'T REFUSE.
TRY ME.
HA. DIRECT AND TO THE POINT– I ADMIRE THAT, GRIMLOCK.
WE'RE QUITE ALIKE, YOU AND I. WE BOTH OPERATE ON THE FRINGES, NEITHER BOWING TO CONVENTION OR PROTOCOL. TO US, ALLEGIANCE IS A CONVENIENCE, NOT AN OBLIGATION. WHICH IS WHY...
...I PROPOSE AN ALLIANCE: YOU AND I–AGAINST THE WORLD!
YOU CAN'T... BE SERIOUS.

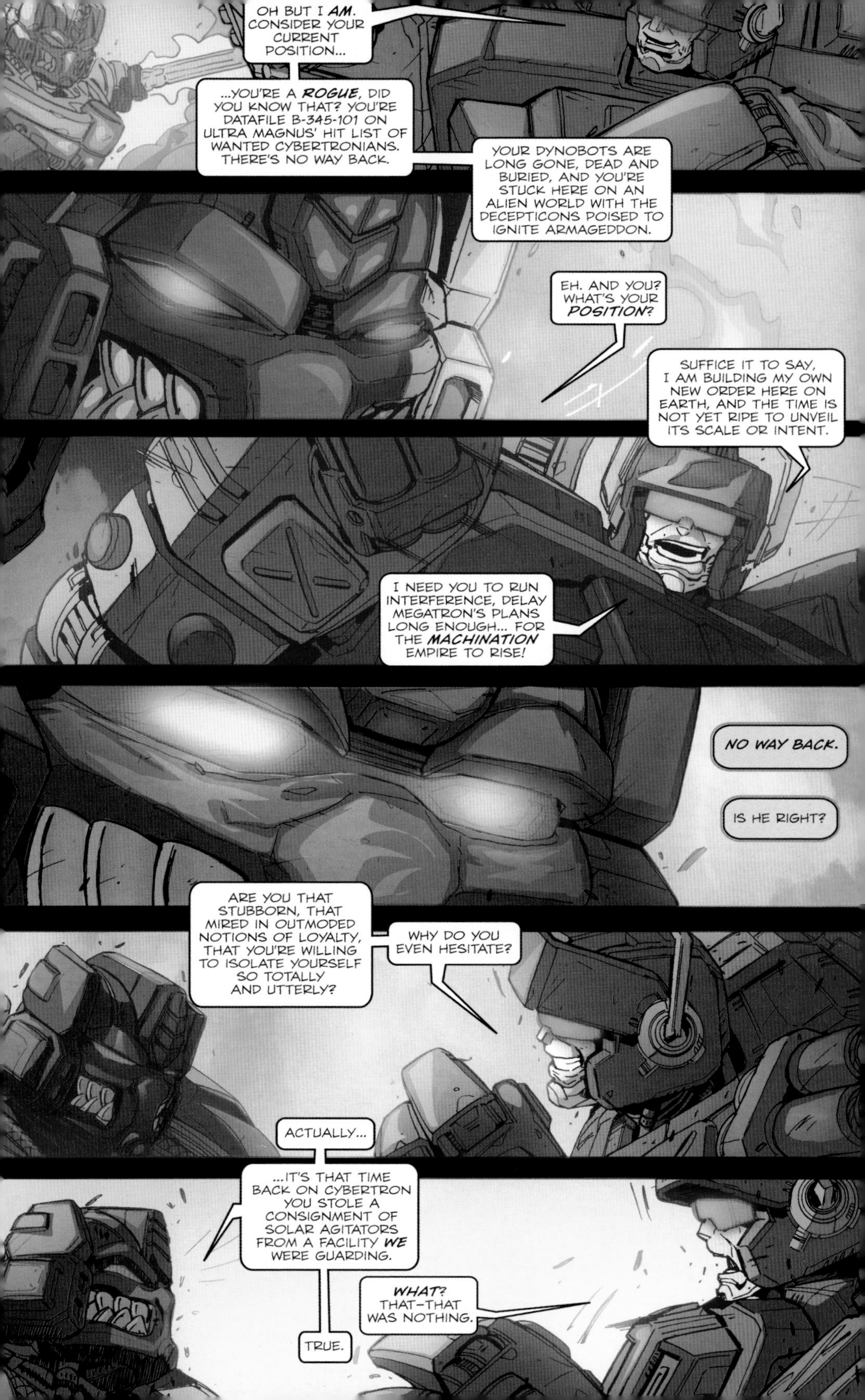
OH BUT I AM. CONSIDER YOUR CURRENT POSITION...
...YOU'RE A ROGUE, DID YOU KNOW THAT? YOU'RE DATAFILE B-345-101 ON ULTRA MAGNUS' HIT LIST OF WANTED CYBERTRONIANS. THERE'S NO WAY BACK.
YOUR DYNOBOTS ARE LONG GONE, DEAD AND BURIED, AND YOU'RE STUCK HERE ON AN ALIEN WORLD WITH THE DECEPTICONS POISED TO IGNITE ARMAGEDDON.
EH. AND YOU? WHAT'S YOUR POSITION?
SUFFICE IT TO SAY, I AM BUILDING MY OWN NEW ORDER HERE ON EARTH, AND THE TIME IS NOT YET RIPE TO UNVEIL ITS SCALE OR INTENT.
I NEED YOU TO RUN INTERFERENCE, DELAY MEGATRON'S PLANS LONG ENOUGH... FOR THE MACHINATION EMPIRE TO RISE!
NO WAY BACK.
IS HE RIGHT?
ARE YOU THAT STUBBORN, THAT MIRED IN OUTMODED NOTIONS OF LOYALTY, THAT YOU'RE WILLING TO ISOLATE YOURSELF SO TOTALLY AND UTTERLY?
WHY DO YOU EVEN HESITATE?
ACTUALLY...
...IT'S THAT TIME BACK ON CYBERTRON YOU STOLE A CONSIGNMENT OF SOLAR AGITATORS FROM A FACILITY WE WERE GUARDING.
WHAT? THAT–THAT WAS NOTHING.
TRUE.

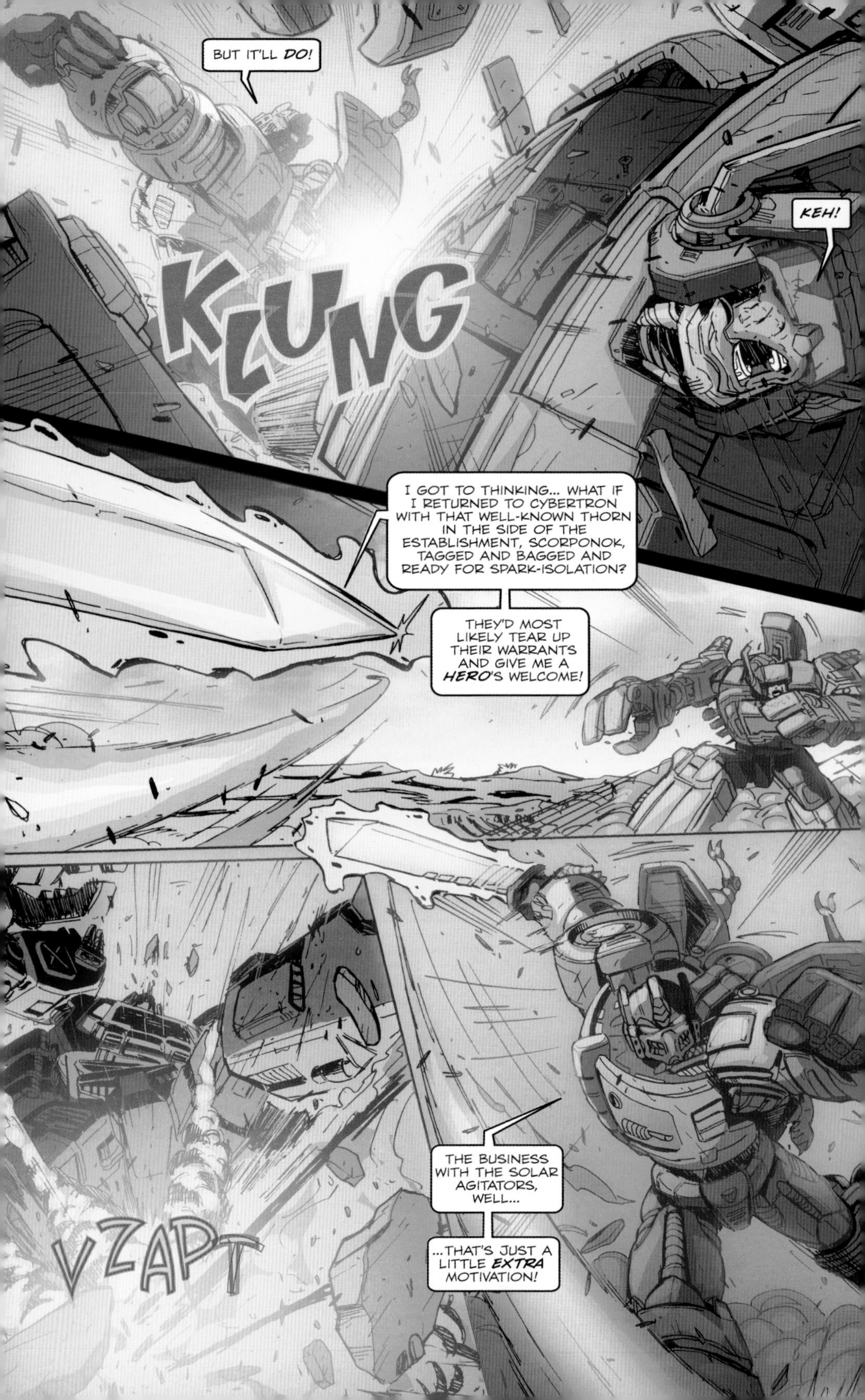
BUT IT'LL DO!
KLUNG
KEH!
I GOT TO THINKING... WHAT IF I RETURNED TO CYBERTRON WITH THAT WELL-KNOWN THORN IN THE SIDE OF THE ESTABLISHMENT, SCORPONOK, TAGGED AND BAGGED AND READY FOR SPARK-ISOLATION?
THEY'D MOST LIKELY TEAR UP THEIR WARRANTS AND GIVE ME A HERO'S WELCOME!
THE BUSINESS WITH THE SOLAR AGITATORS, WELL...
...THAT'S JUST A LITTLE EXTRA MOTIVATION!
VZAPT

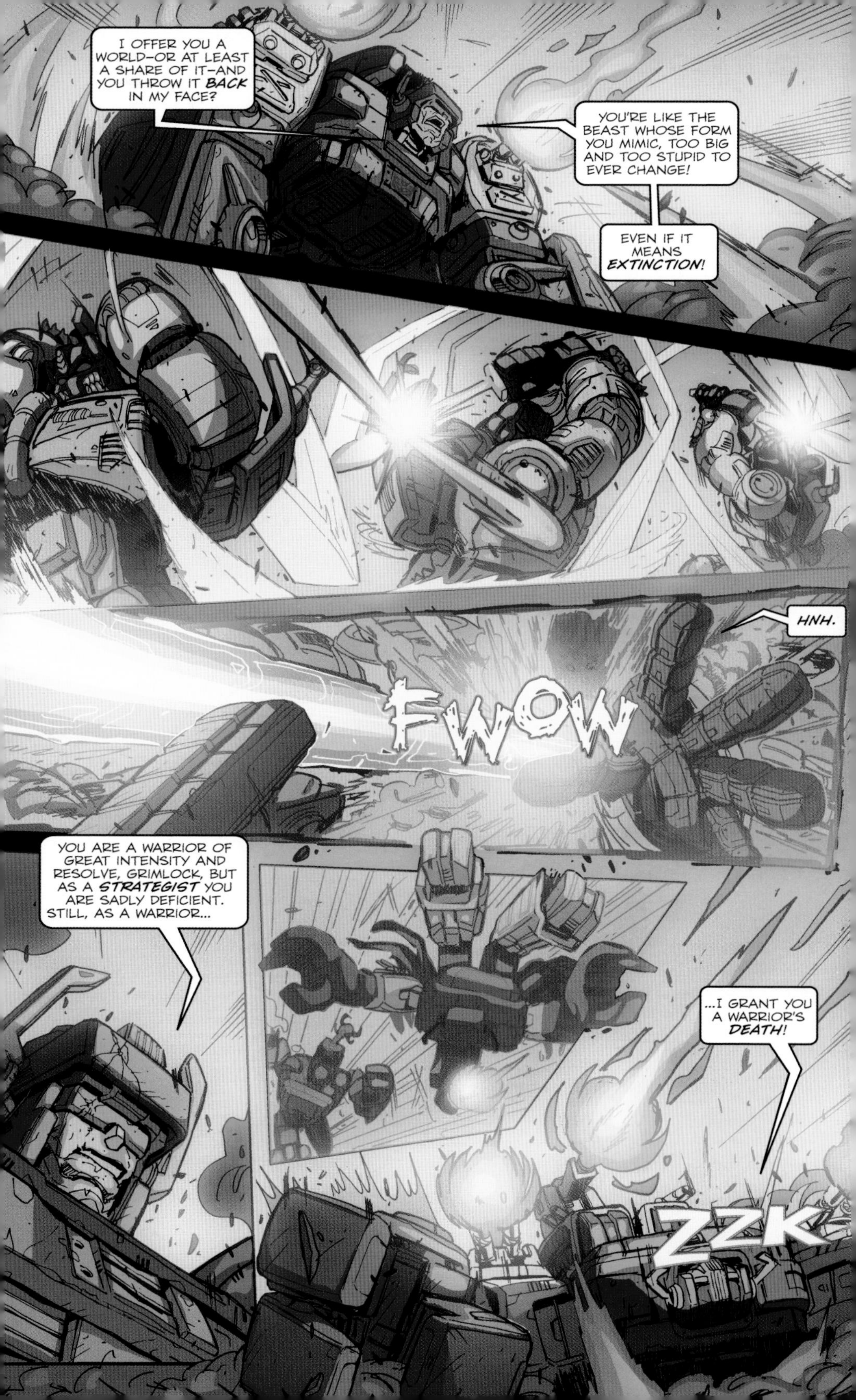
I OFFER YOU A WORLD—OR AT LEAST A SHARE OF IT—AND YOU THROW IT *BACK* IN MY FACE?
YOU'RE LIKE THE BEAST WHOSE FORM YOU MIMIC, TOO BIG AND TOO STUPID TO EVER CHANGE!
EVEN IF IT MEANS *EXTINCTION*!
HNH.
FWOW
YOU ARE A WARRIOR OF GREAT INTENSITY AND RESOLVE, GRIMLOCK, BUT AS A *STRATEGIST* YOU ARE SADLY DEFICIENT. STILL, AS A WARRIOR...
...I GRANT YOU A WARRIOR'S *DEATH*!
ZZK

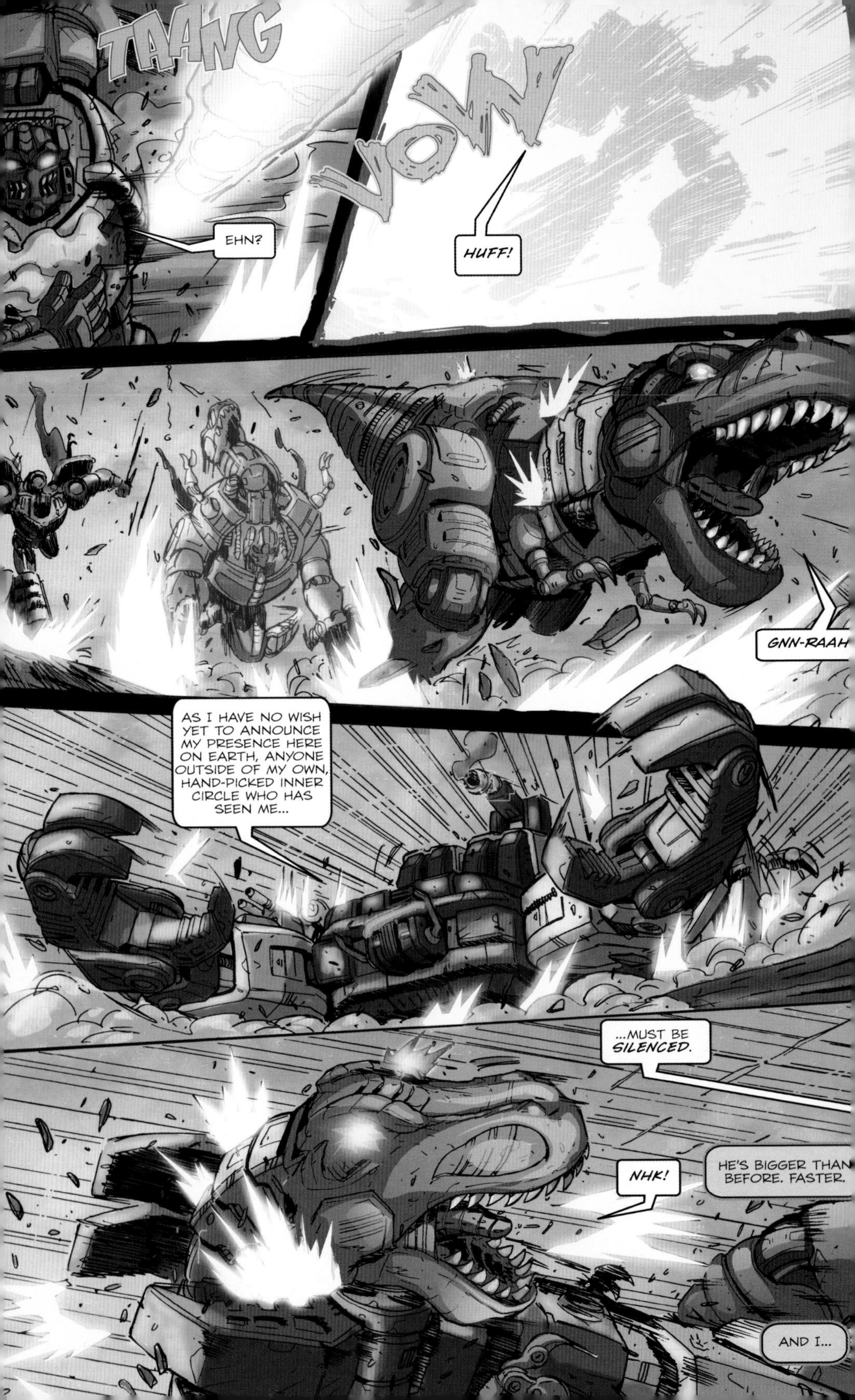
TAANG
VOOM
EHN?
HUFF!
GNN-RAAH
AS I HAVE NO WISH YET TO ANNOUNCE MY PRESENCE HERE ON EARTH, ANYONE OUTSIDE OF MY OWN, HAND-PICKED INNER CIRCLE WHO HAS SEEN ME...
...MUST BE SILENCED.
HE'S BIGGER THAN BEFORE. FASTER.
NHK!
AND I...

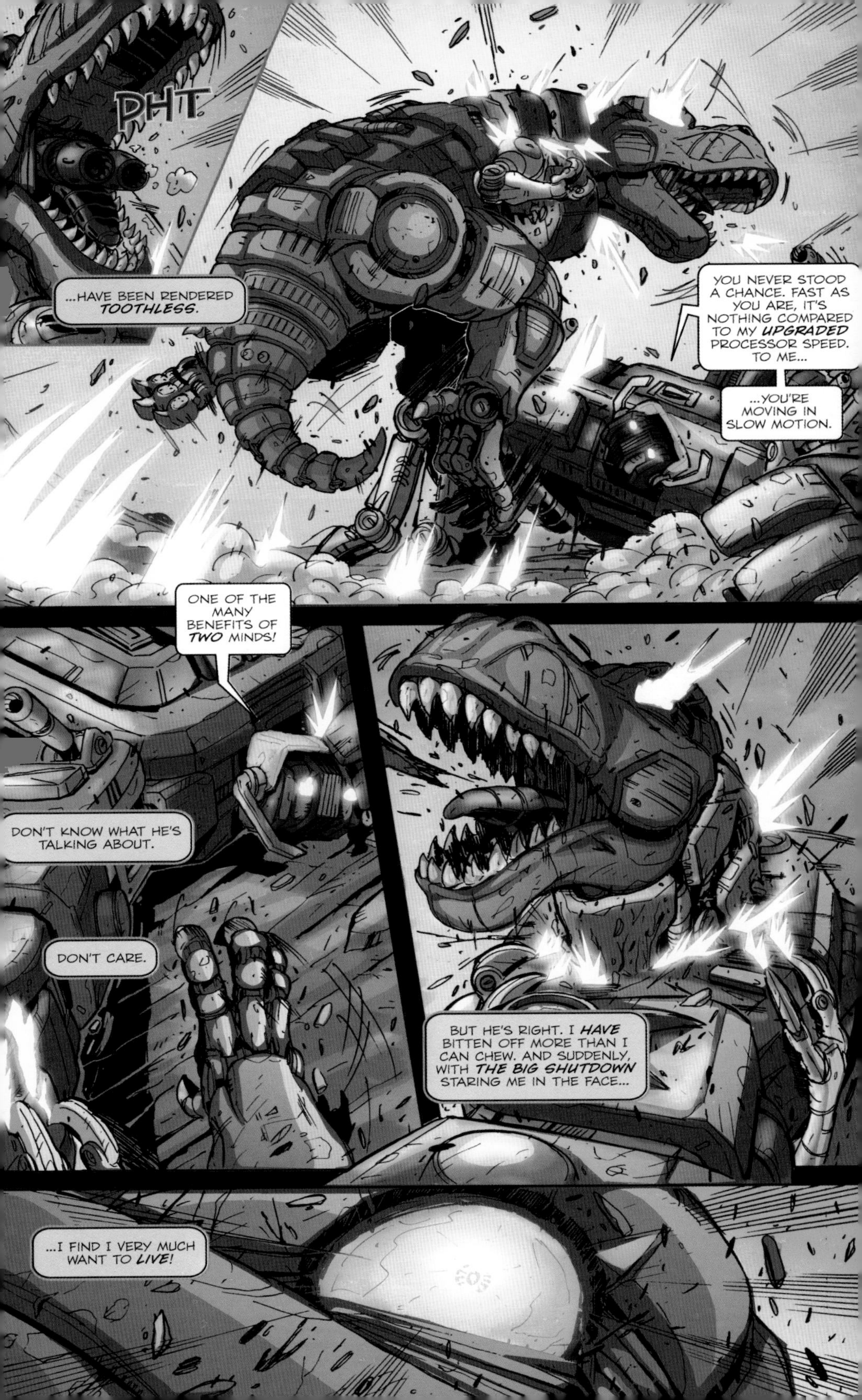
PHT
...HAVE BEEN RENDERED TOOTHLESS.
YOU NEVER STOOD A CHANCE. FAST AS YOU ARE, IT'S NOTHING COMPARED TO MY UPGRADED PROCESSOR SPEED. TO ME...
...YOU'RE MOVING IN SLOW MOTION.
ONE OF THE MANY BENEFITS OF TWO MINDS!
DON'T KNOW WHAT HE'S TALKING ABOUT.
DON'T CARE.
BUT HE'S RIGHT. I HAVE BITTEN OFF MORE THAN I CAN CHEW. AND SUDDENLY, WITH THE BIG SHUTDOWN STARING ME IN THE FACE...
...I FIND I VERY MUCH WANT TO LIVE!

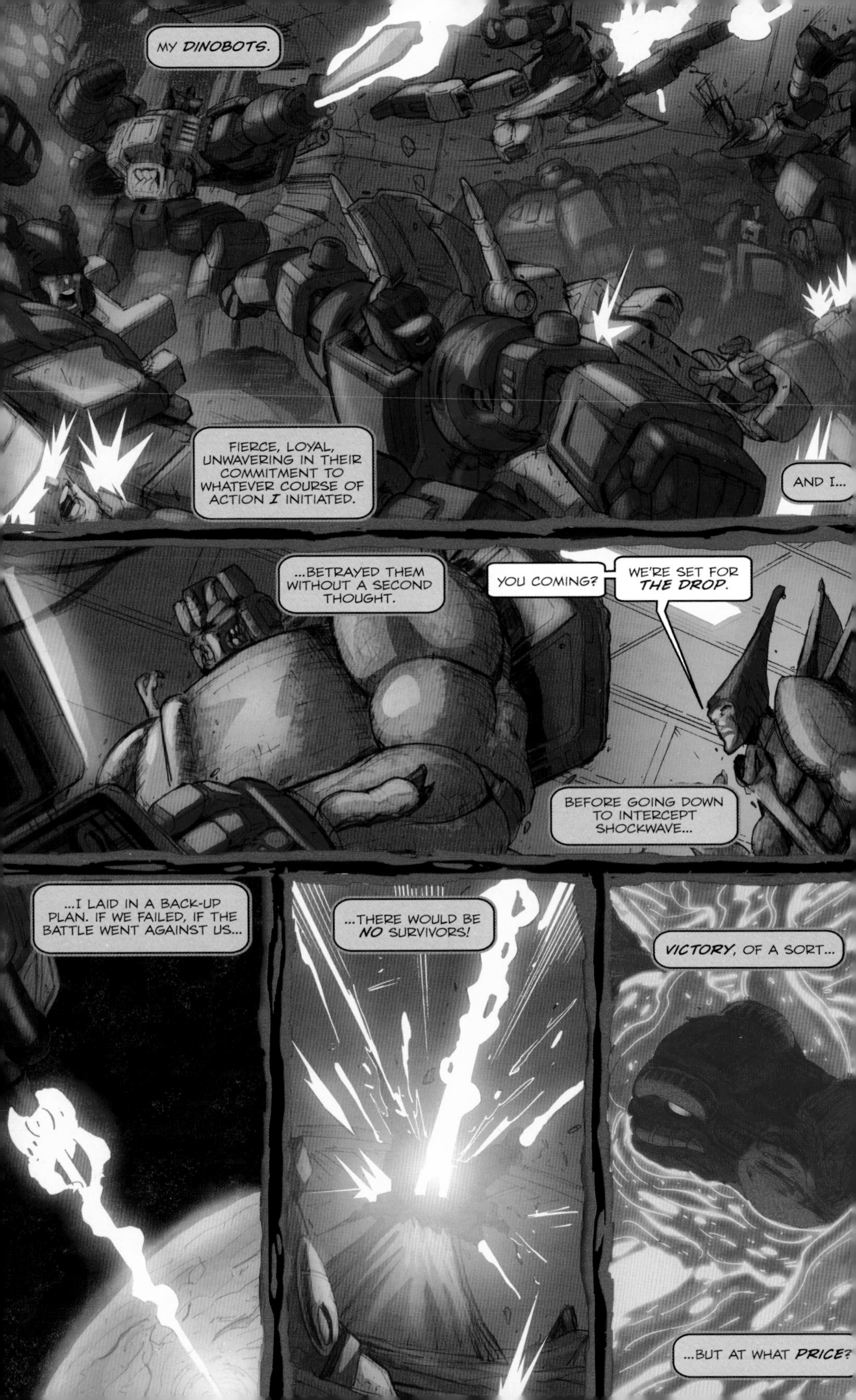
MY DINOBOTS.
FIERCE, LOYAL, UNWAVERING IN THEIR COMMITMENT TO WHATEVER COURSE OF ACTION I INITIATED.
AND I...
...BETRAYED THEM WITHOUT A SECOND THOUGHT.
YOU COMING?
WE'RE SET FOR THE DROP.
BEFORE GOING DOWN TO INTERCEPT SHOCKWAVE...
...I LAID IN A BACK-UP PLAN. IF WE FAILED, IF THE BATTLE WENT AGAINST US...
...THERE WOULD BE NO SURVIVORS!
VICTORY, OF A SORT...
...BUT AT WHAT PRICE?

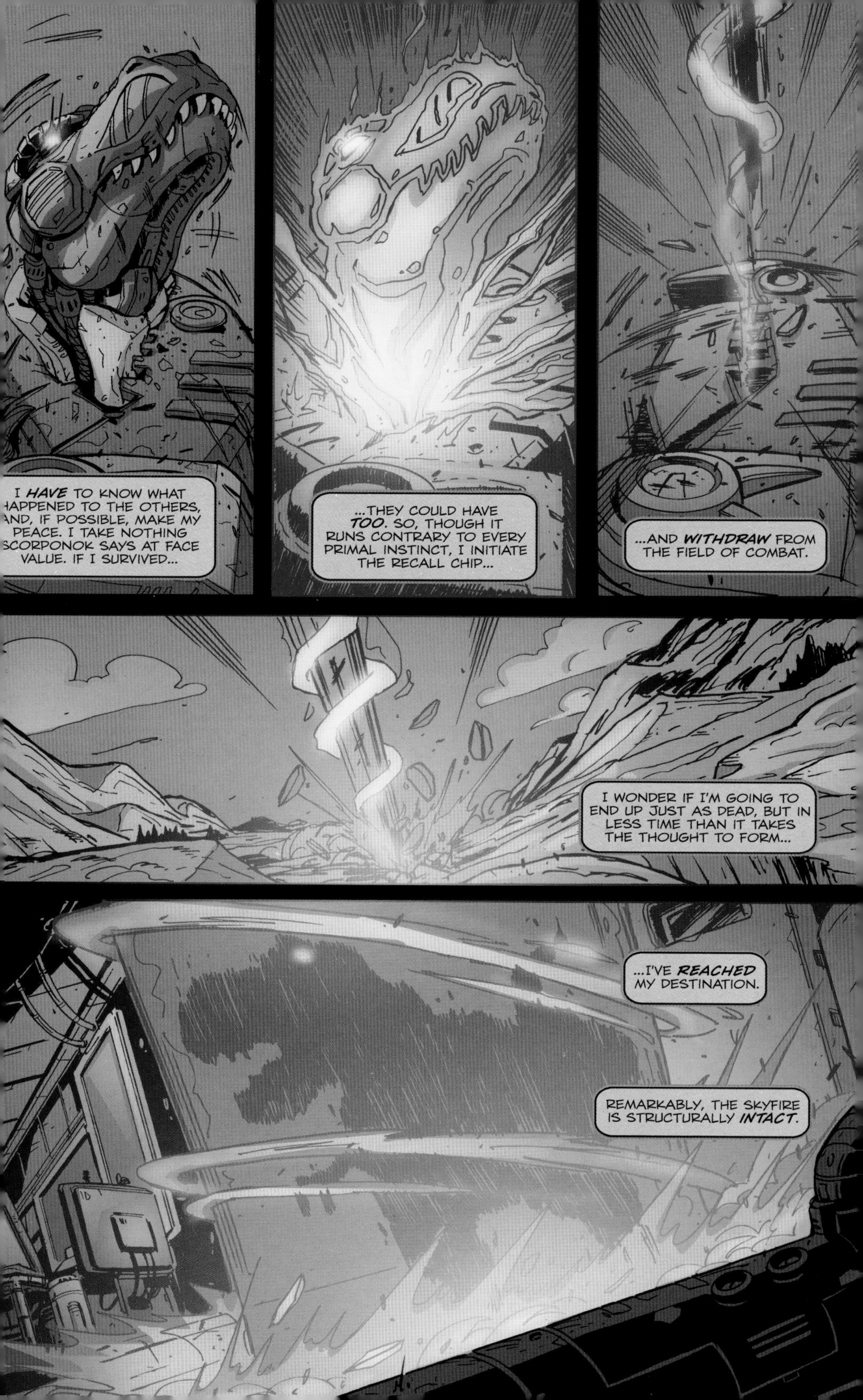
I HAVE TO KNOW WHAT HAPPENED TO THE OTHERS, AND, IF POSSIBLE, MAKE MY PEACE. I TAKE NOTHING SCORPONOK SAYS AT FACE VALUE. IF I SURVIVED...
...THEY COULD HAVE TOO. SO, THOUGH IT RUNS CONTRARY TO EVERY PRIMAL INSTINCT, I INITIATE THE RECALL CHIP...
...AND WITHDRAW FROM THE FIELD OF COMBAT.
I WONDER IF I'M GOING TO END UP JUST AS DEAD, BUT IN LESS TIME THAN IT TAKES THE THOUGHT TO FORM...
...I'VE REACHED MY DESTINATION.
REMARKABLY, THE SKYFIRE IS STRUCTURALLY INTACT.

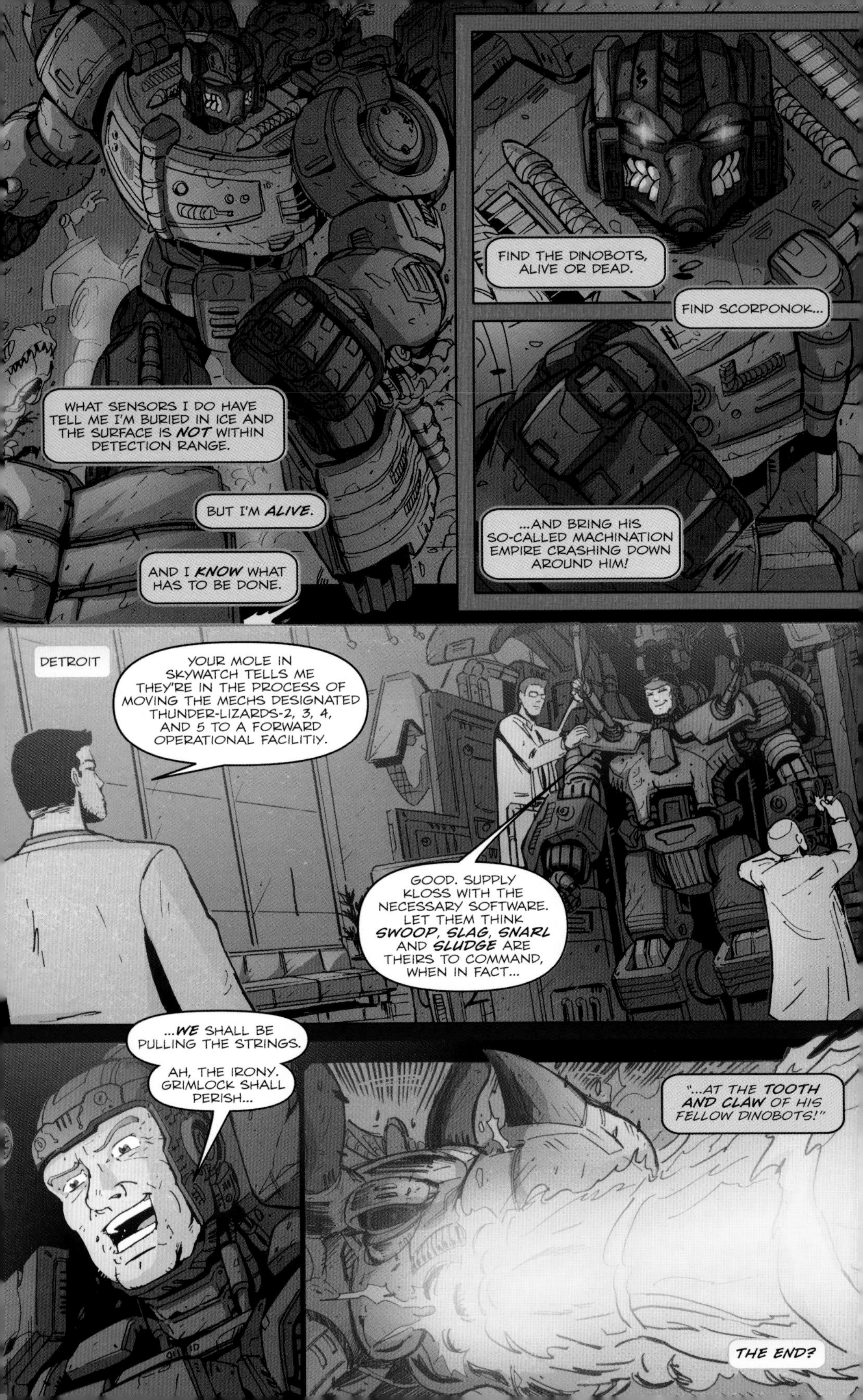
WHAT SENSORS I DO HAVE TELL ME I'M BURIED IN ICE AND THE SURFACE IS *NOT* WITHIN DETECTION RANGE.
BUT I'M *ALIVE*.
AND I *KNOW* WHAT HAS TO BE DONE.
FIND THE DINOBOTS, ALIVE OR DEAD.
FIND SCORPONOK...
...AND BRING HIS SO-CALLED MACHINATION EMPIRE CRASHING DOWN AROUND HIM!
DETROIT
YOUR MOLE IN SKYWATCH TELLS ME THEY'RE IN THE PROCESS OF MOVING THE MECHS DESIGNATED THUNDER-LIZARDS-2, 3, 4, AND 5 TO A FORWARD OPERATIONAL FACILITIY.
GOOD. SUPPLY KLOSS WITH THE NECESSARY SOFTWARE. LET THEM THINK *SWOOP, SLAG, SNARL* AND *SLUDGE* ARE THEIRS TO COMMAND, WHEN IN FACT...
...*WE* SHALL BE PULLING THE STRINGS.
AH, THE IRONY. GRIMLOCK SHALL PERISH...
"...AT THE *TOOTH AND CLAW* OF HIS FELLOW DINOBOTS!"
THE END?

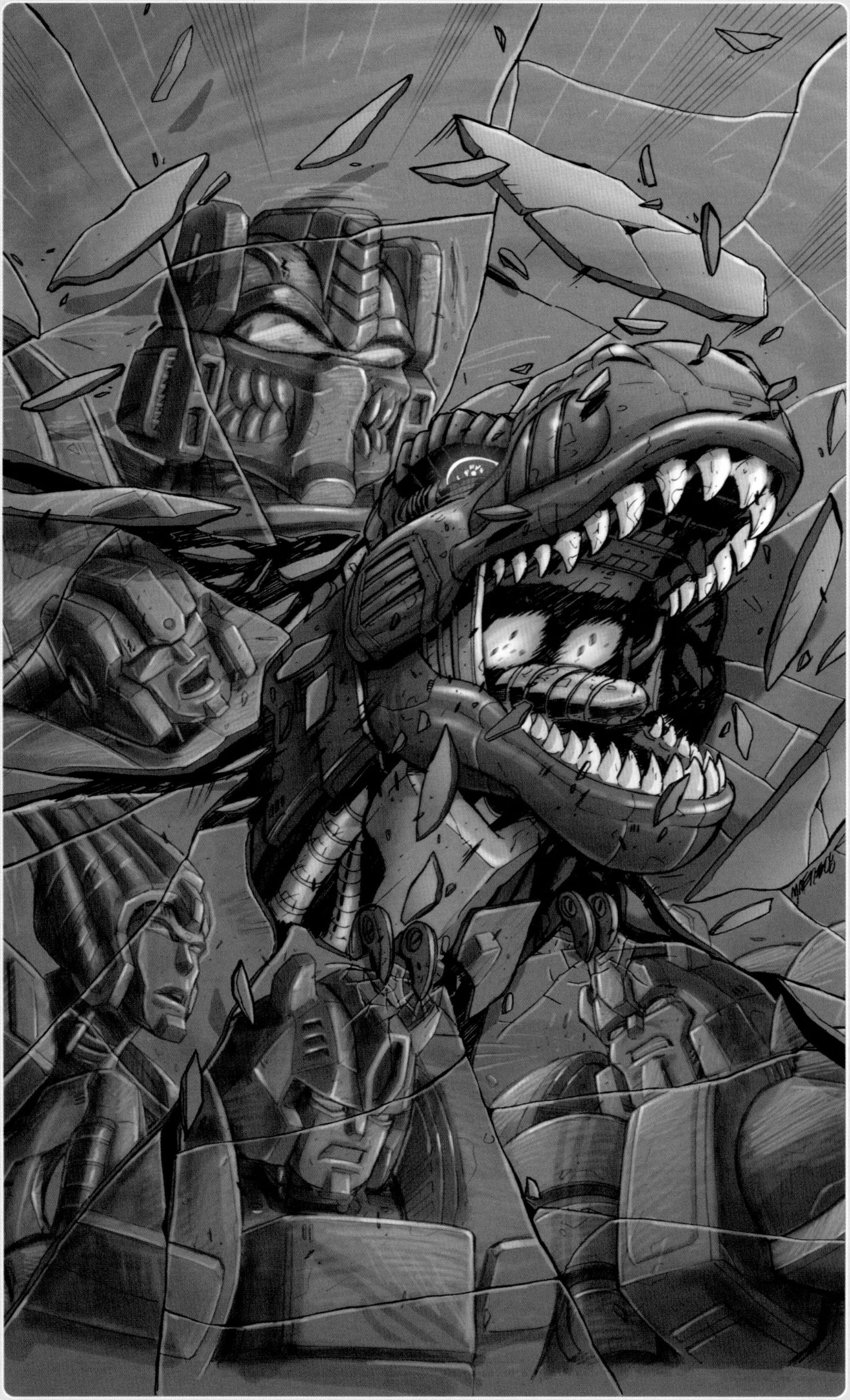

He is one of the most feared and powerful DECEPTICONS, but where others are ruled by greed, ambition or an unchecked lust for power, his only master is cold, clear, dispassionate logic. Spur plus reaction equals outcome. This equation shapes and defines his thoughts and deeds. Infinitely patient, he sees the shape of things to come and so acts accordingly...

SHOCKWAVE

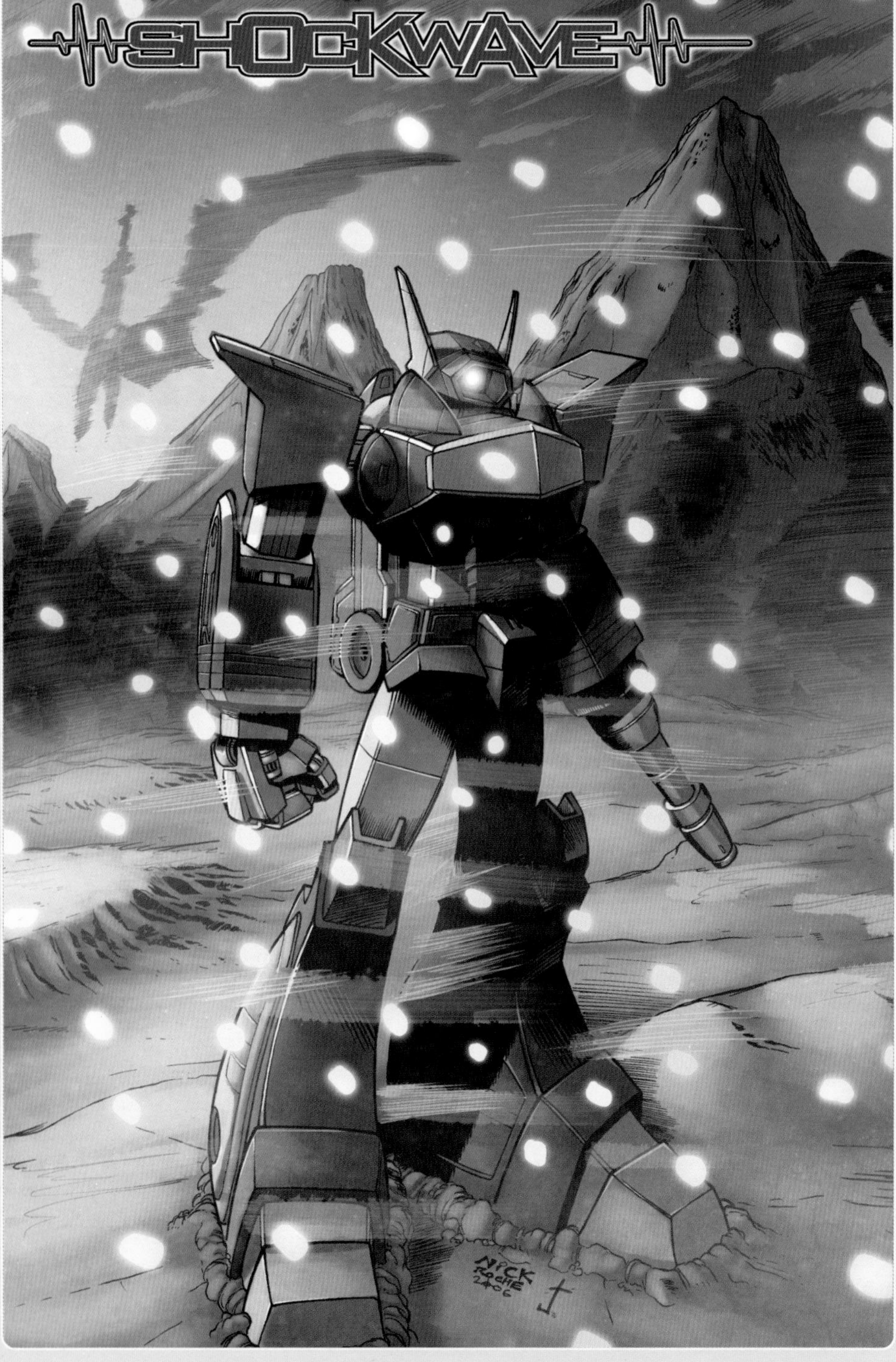

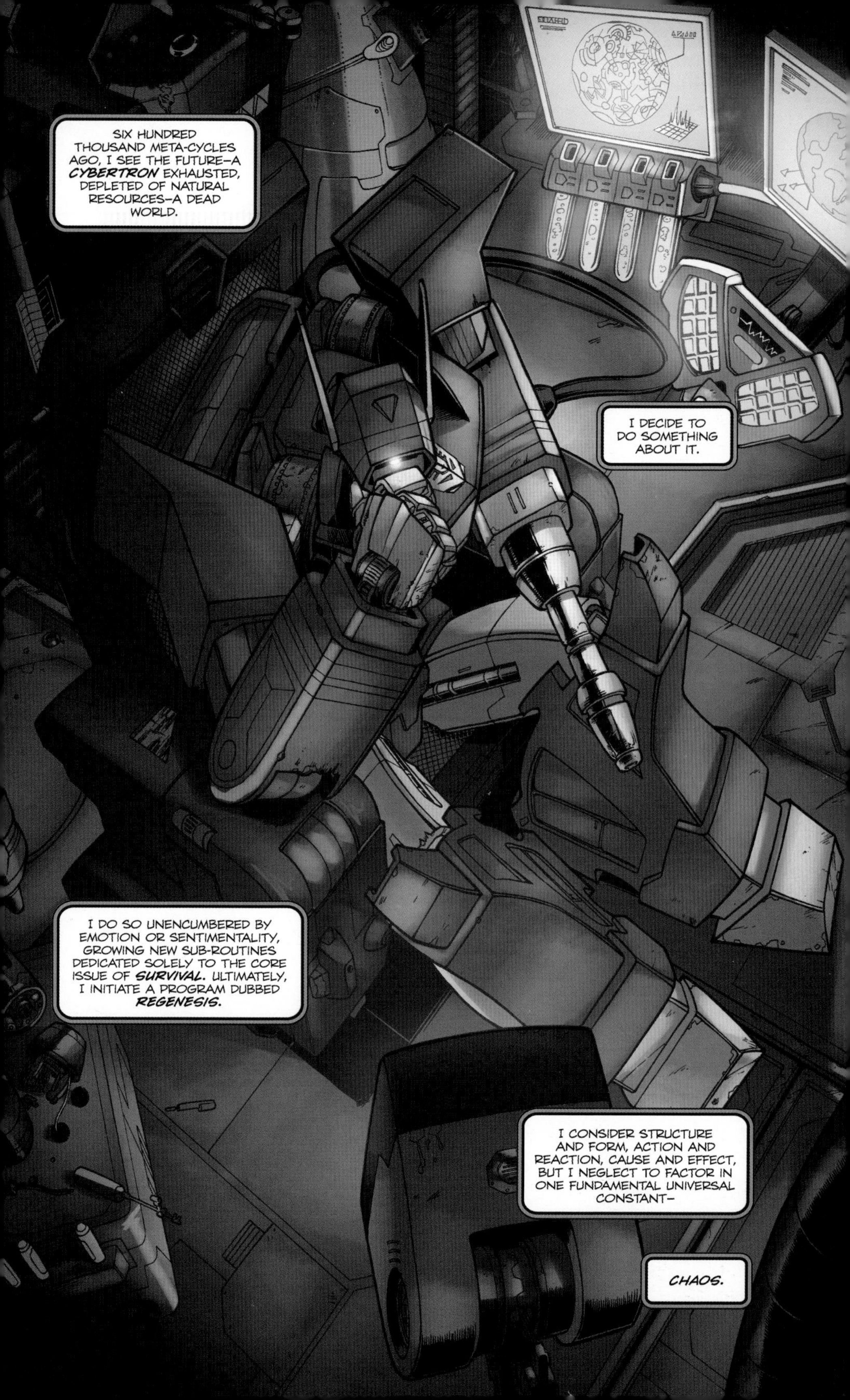
SIX HUNDRED THOUSAND META-CYCLES AGO, I SEE THE FUTURE–A *CYBERTRON* EXHAUSTED, DEPLETED OF NATURAL RESOURCES–A DEAD WORLD.
I DECIDE TO DO SOMETHING ABOUT IT.
I DO SO UNENCUMBERED BY EMOTION OR SENTIMENTALITY, GROWING NEW SUB-ROUTINES DEDICATED SOLELY TO THE CORE ISSUE OF *SURVIVAL*. ULTIMATELY, I INITIATE A PROGRAM DUBBED *REGENESIS*.
I CONSIDER STRUCTURE AND FORM, ACTION AND REACTION, CAUSE AND EFFECT, BUT I NEGLECT TO FACTOR IN ONE FUNDAMENTAL UNIVERSAL CONSTANT–
CHAOS.

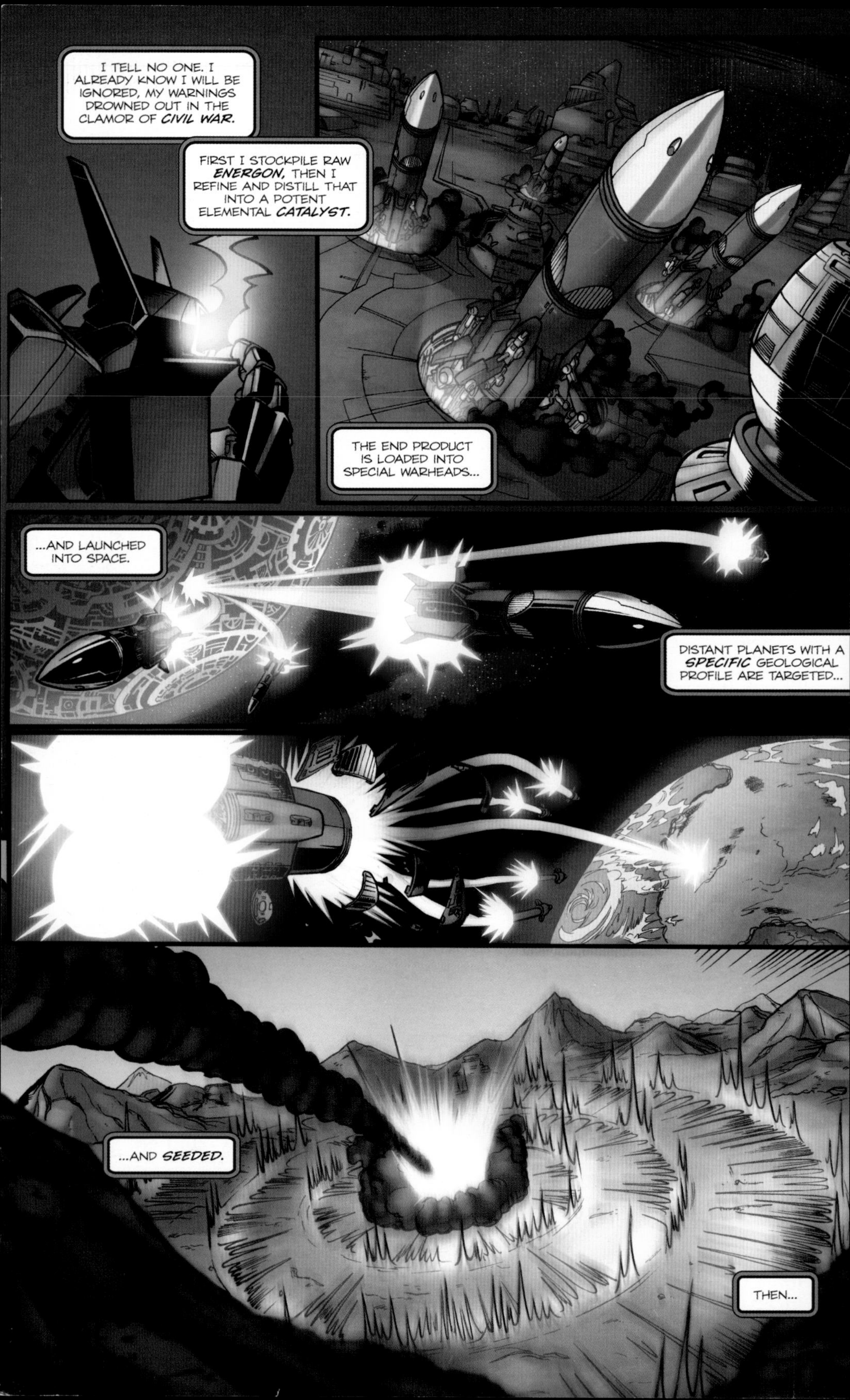
I TELL NO ONE. I ALREADY KNOW I WILL BE IGNORED, MY WARNINGS DROWNED OUT IN THE CLAMOR OF CIVIL WAR.
FIRST I STOCKPILE RAW ENERGON, THEN I REFINE AND DISTILL THAT INTO A POTENT ELEMENTAL CATALYST.
THE END PRODUCT IS LOADED INTO SPECIAL WARHEADS...
...AND LAUNCHED INTO SPACE.
DISTANT PLANETS WITH A SPECIFIC GEOLOGICAL PROFILE ARE TARGETED...
...AND SEEDED.
THEN...

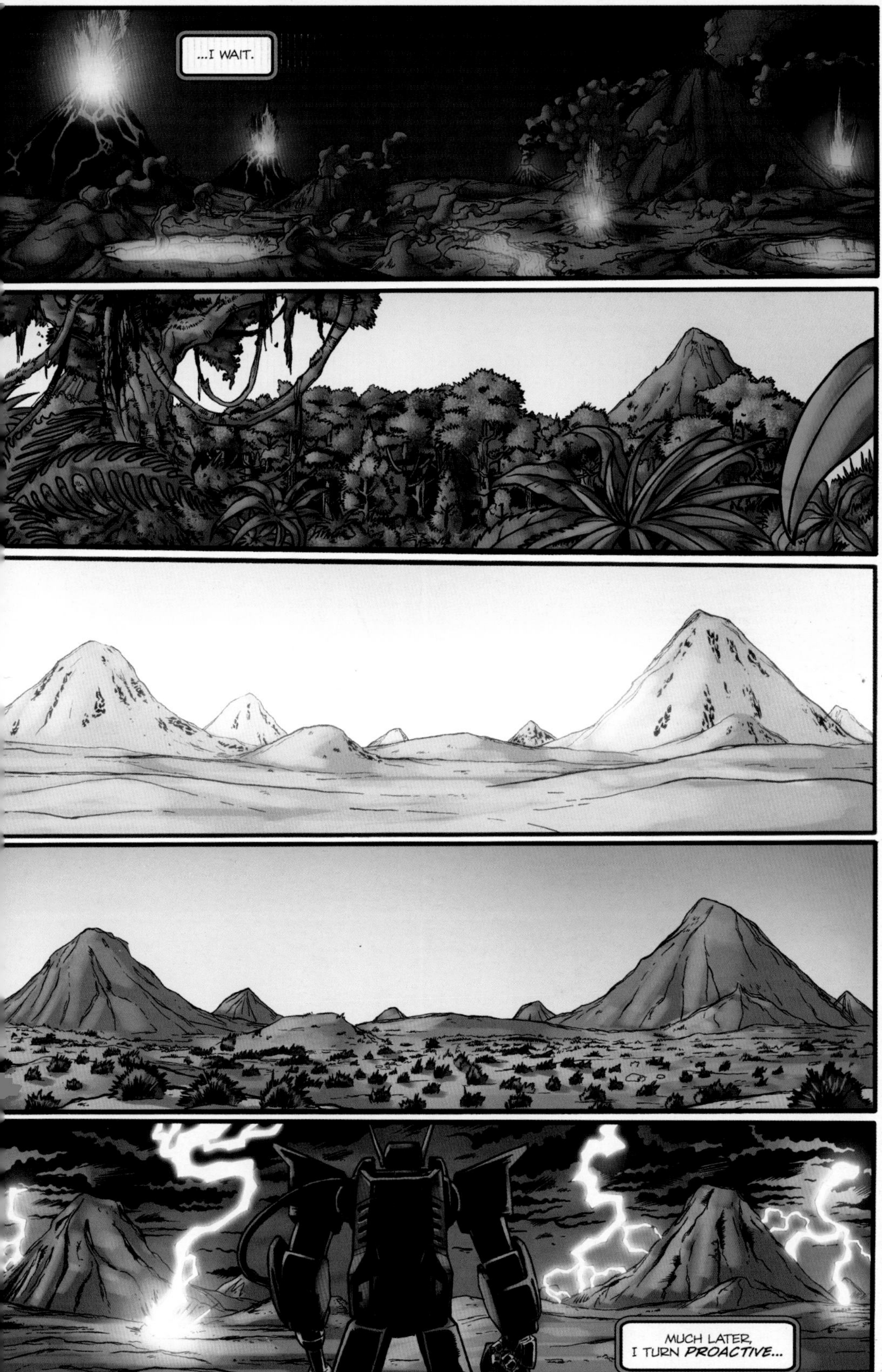
...I WAIT.
MUCH LATER, I TURN PROACTIVE...

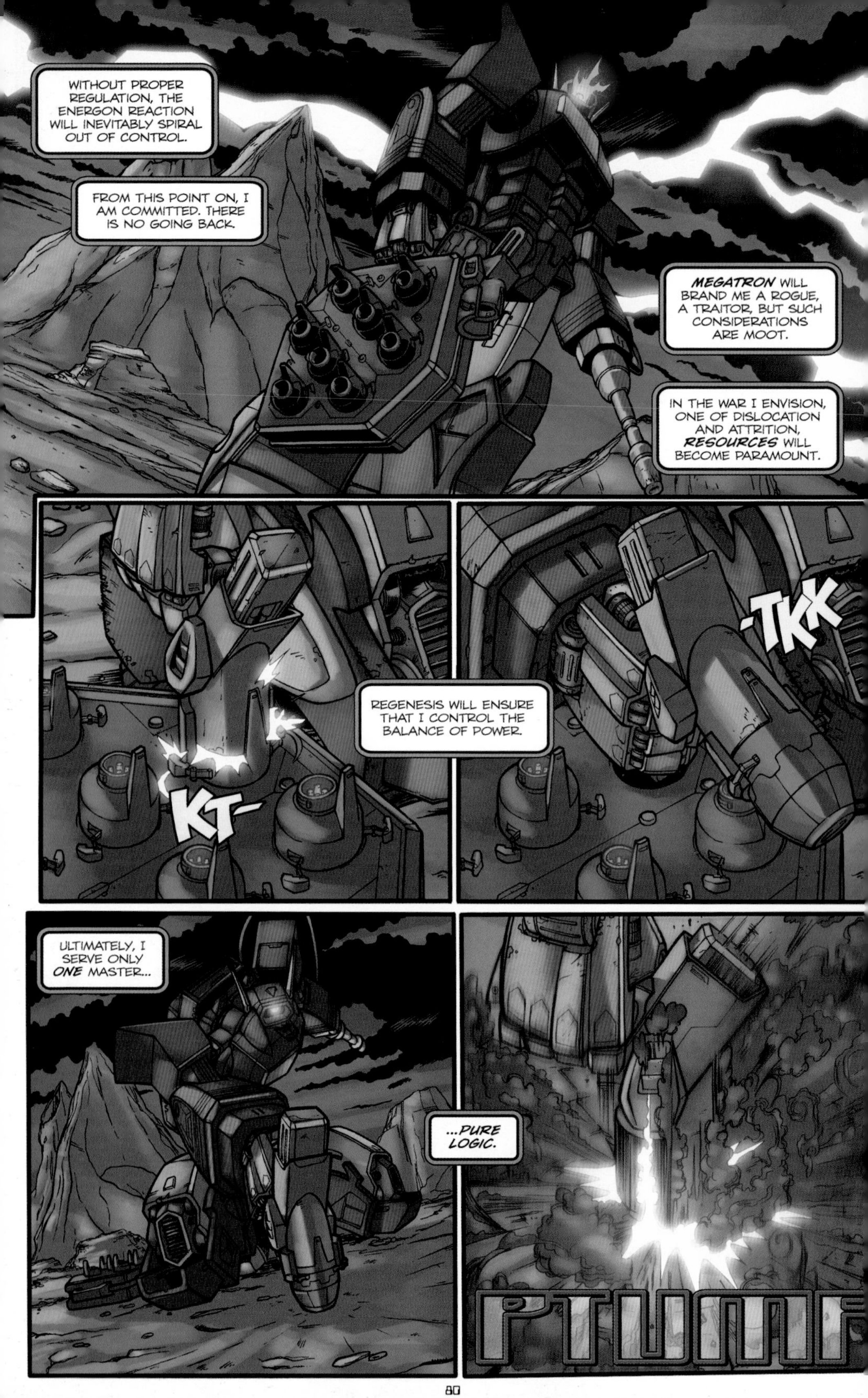
WITHOUT PROPER REGULATION, THE ENERGON REACTION WILL INEVITABLY SPIRAL OUT OF CONTROL.
FROM THIS POINT ON, I AM COMMITTED. THERE IS NO GOING BACK.
MEGATRON WILL BRAND ME A ROGUE, A TRAITOR, BUT SUCH CONSIDERATIONS ARE MOOT.
IN THE WAR I ENVISION, ONE OF DISLOCATION AND ATTRITION, RESOURCES WILL BECOME PARAMOUNT.
KT-
REGENESIS WILL ENSURE THAT I CONTROL THE BALANCE OF POWER.
-TKK
ULTIMATELY, I SERVE ONLY ONE MASTER...
...PURE LOGIC.
P'TUNNF

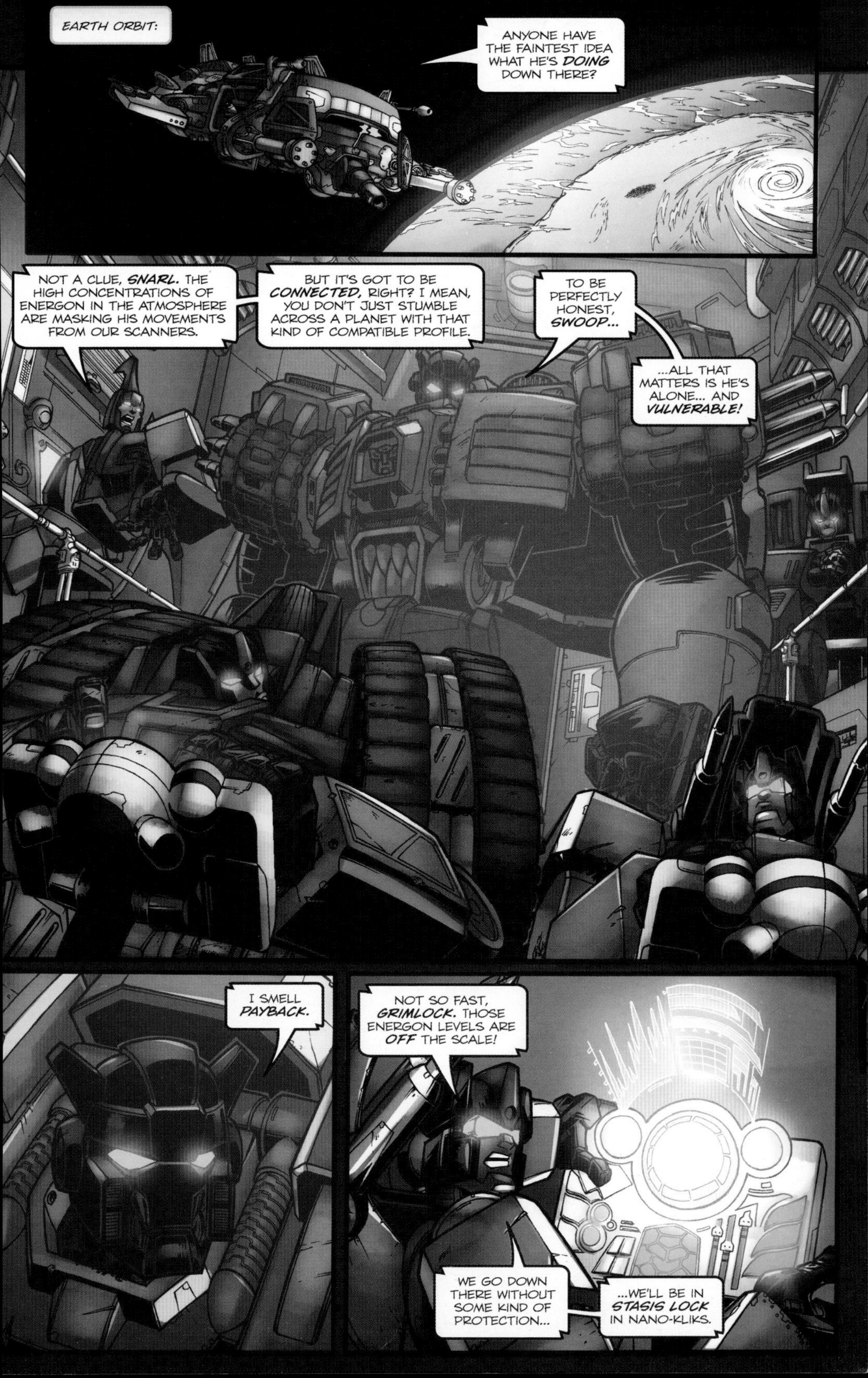

EARTH ORBIT:
ANYONE HAVE THE FAINTEST IDEA WHAT HE'S DOING DOWN THERE?
NOT A CLUE, SNARL. THE HIGH CONCENTRATIONS OF ENERGON IN THE ATMOSPHERE ARE MASKING HIS MOVEMENTS FROM OUR SCANNERS.
BUT IT'S GOT TO BE CONNECTED, RIGHT? I MEAN, YOU DON'T JUST STUMBLE ACROSS A PLANET WITH THAT KIND OF COMPATIBLE PROFILE.
TO BE PERFECTLY HONEST, SWOOP...
...ALL THAT MATTERS IS HE'S ALONE... AND VULNERABLE!
I SMELL PAYBACK.
NOT SO FAST, GRIMLOCK. THOSE ENERGON LEVELS ARE OFF THE SCALE!
WE GO DOWN THERE WITHOUT SOME KIND OF PROTECTION...
...WE'LL BE IN STASIS LOCK IN NANO-KLIKS.

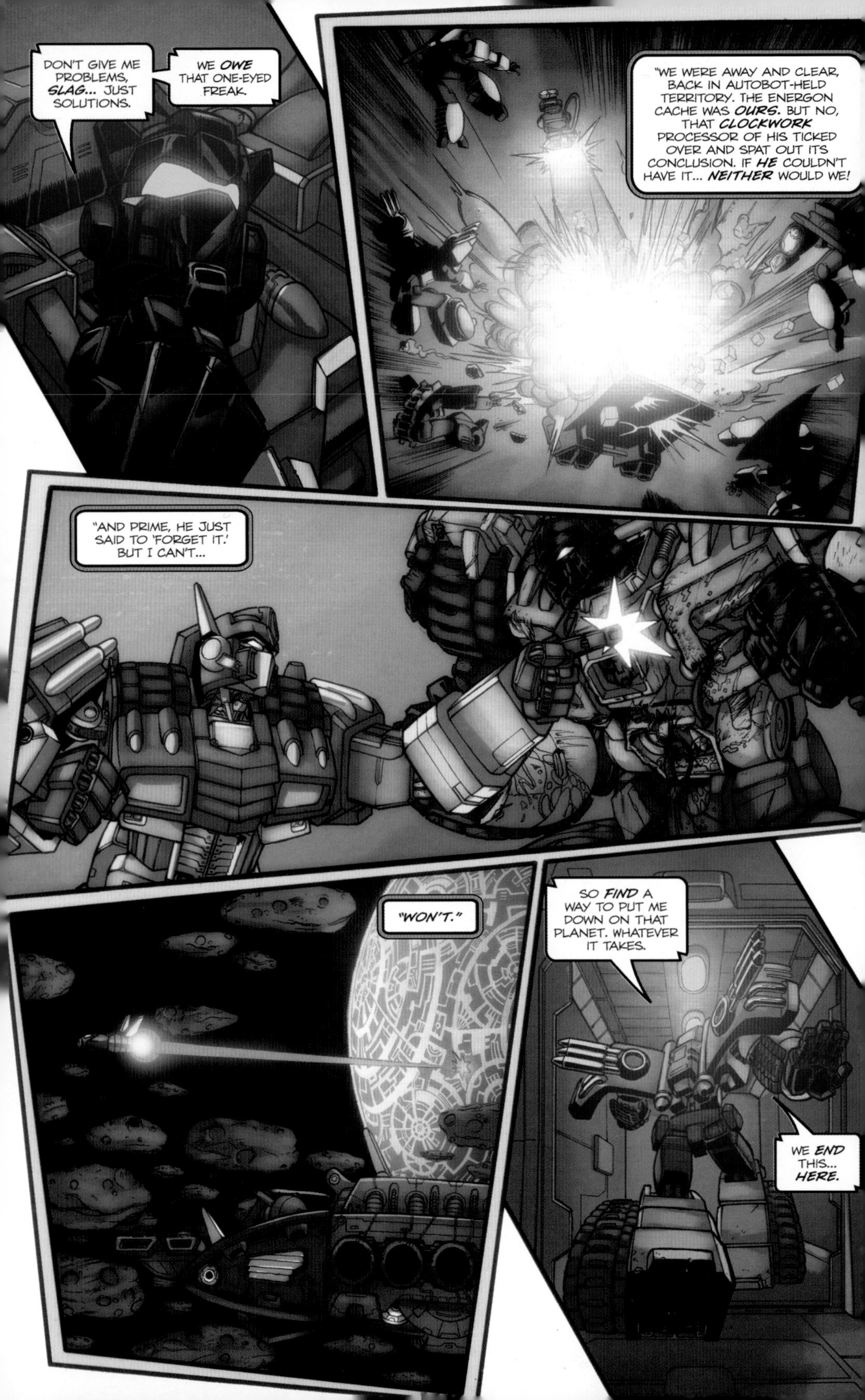
DON'T GIVE ME PROBLEMS, SLAG... JUST SOLUTIONS.
WE OWE THAT ONE-EYED FREAK.
"WE WERE AWAY AND CLEAR, BACK IN AUTOBOT-HELD TERRITORY. THE ENERGON CACHE WAS OURS. BUT NO, THAT CLOCKWORK PROCESSOR OF HIS TICKED OVER AND SPAT OUT ITS CONCLUSION. IF HE COULDN'T HAVE IT... NEITHER WOULD WE!
"AND PRIME, HE JUST SAID TO 'FORGET IT.' BUT I CAN'T...
"WON'T."
SO FIND A WAY TO PUT ME DOWN ON THAT PLANET. WHATEVER IT TAKES.
WE END THIS... HERE.

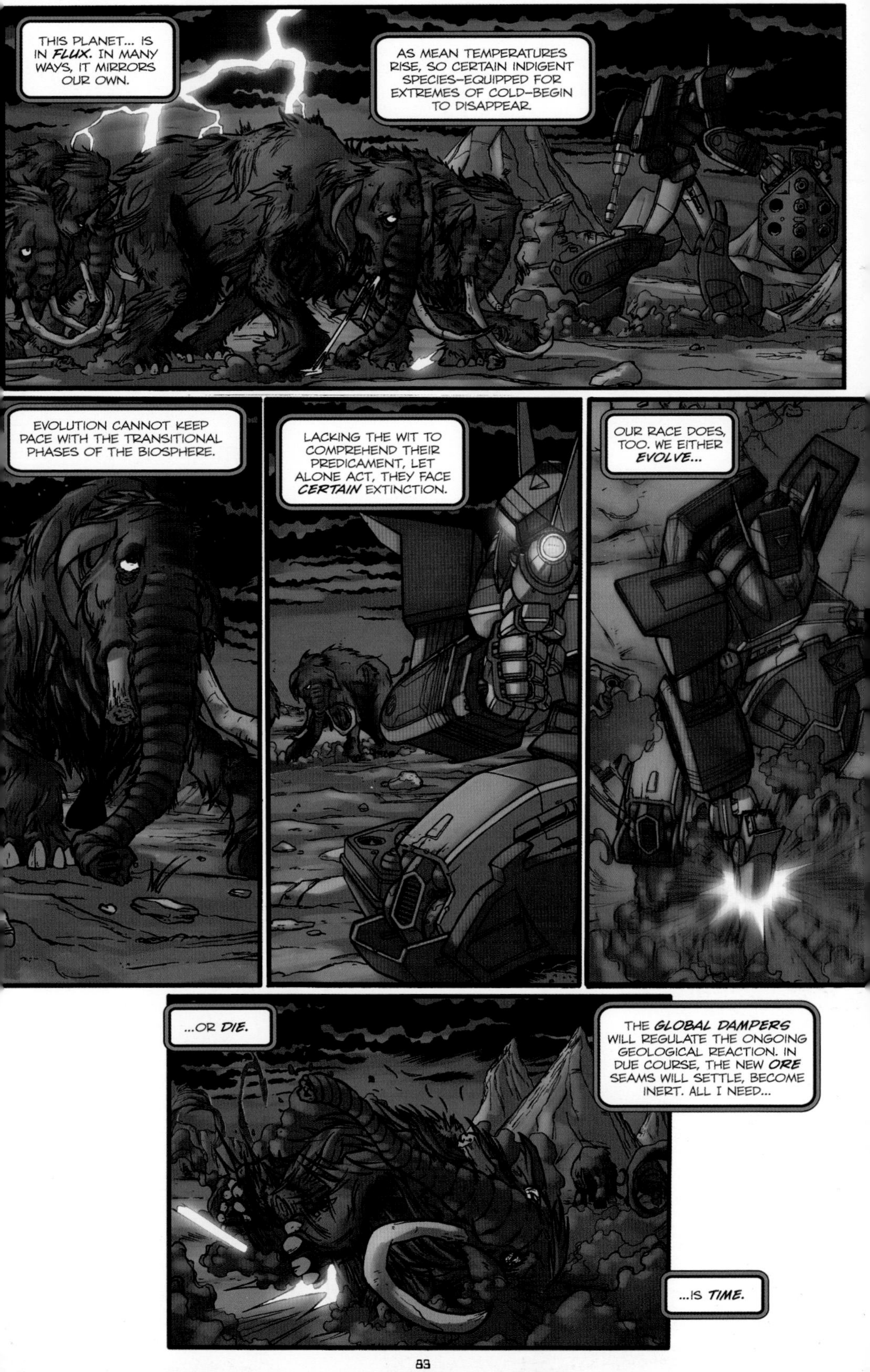
THIS PLANET... IS IN FLUX. IN MANY WAYS, IT MIRRORS OUR OWN.
AS MEAN TEMPERATURES RISE, SO CERTAIN INDIGENT SPECIES—EQUIPPED FOR EXTREMES OF COLD—BEGIN TO DISAPPEAR.
EVOLUTION CANNOT KEEP PACE WITH THE TRANSITIONAL PHASES OF THE BIOSPHERE.
LACKING THE WIT TO COMPREHEND THEIR PREDICAMENT, LET ALONE ACT, THEY FACE CERTAIN EXTINCTION.
OUR RACE DOES, TOO. WE EITHER EVOLVE...
...OR DIE.
THE GLOBAL DAMPERS WILL REGULATE THE ONGOING GEOLOGICAL REACTION. IN DUE COURSE, THE NEW ORE SEAMS WILL SETTLE, BECOME INERT. ALL I NEED...
...IS TIME.

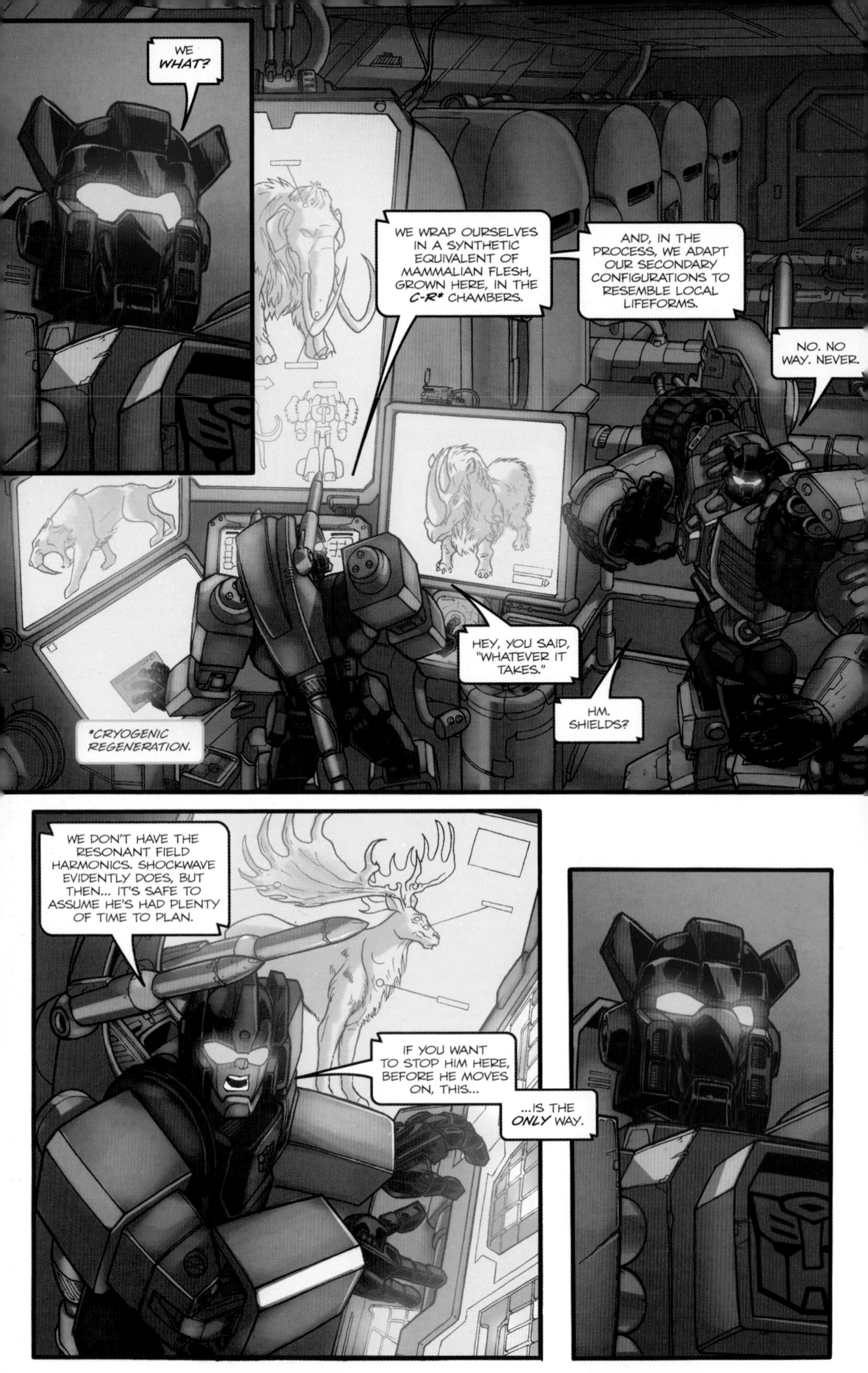
WE *WHAT?*
WE WRAP OURSELVES IN A SYNTHETIC EQUIVALENT OF MAMMALIAN FLESH, GROWN HERE, IN THE *C-R** CHAMBERS.
AND, IN THE PROCESS, WE ADAPT OUR SECONDARY CONFIGURATIONS TO RESEMBLE LOCAL LIFEFORMS.
NO. NO WAY. NEVER.
HEY, YOU SAID, "WHATEVER IT TAKES."
HM. SHIELDS?
*CRYOGENIC REGENERATION.
WE DON'T HAVE THE RESONANT FIELD HARMONICS. SHOCKWAVE EVIDENTLY DOES, BUT THEN... IT'S SAFE TO ASSUME HE'S HAD PLENTY OF TIME TO PLAN.
IF YOU WANT TO STOP HIM HERE, BEFORE HE MOVES ON, THIS...
...IS THE *ONLY* WAY.

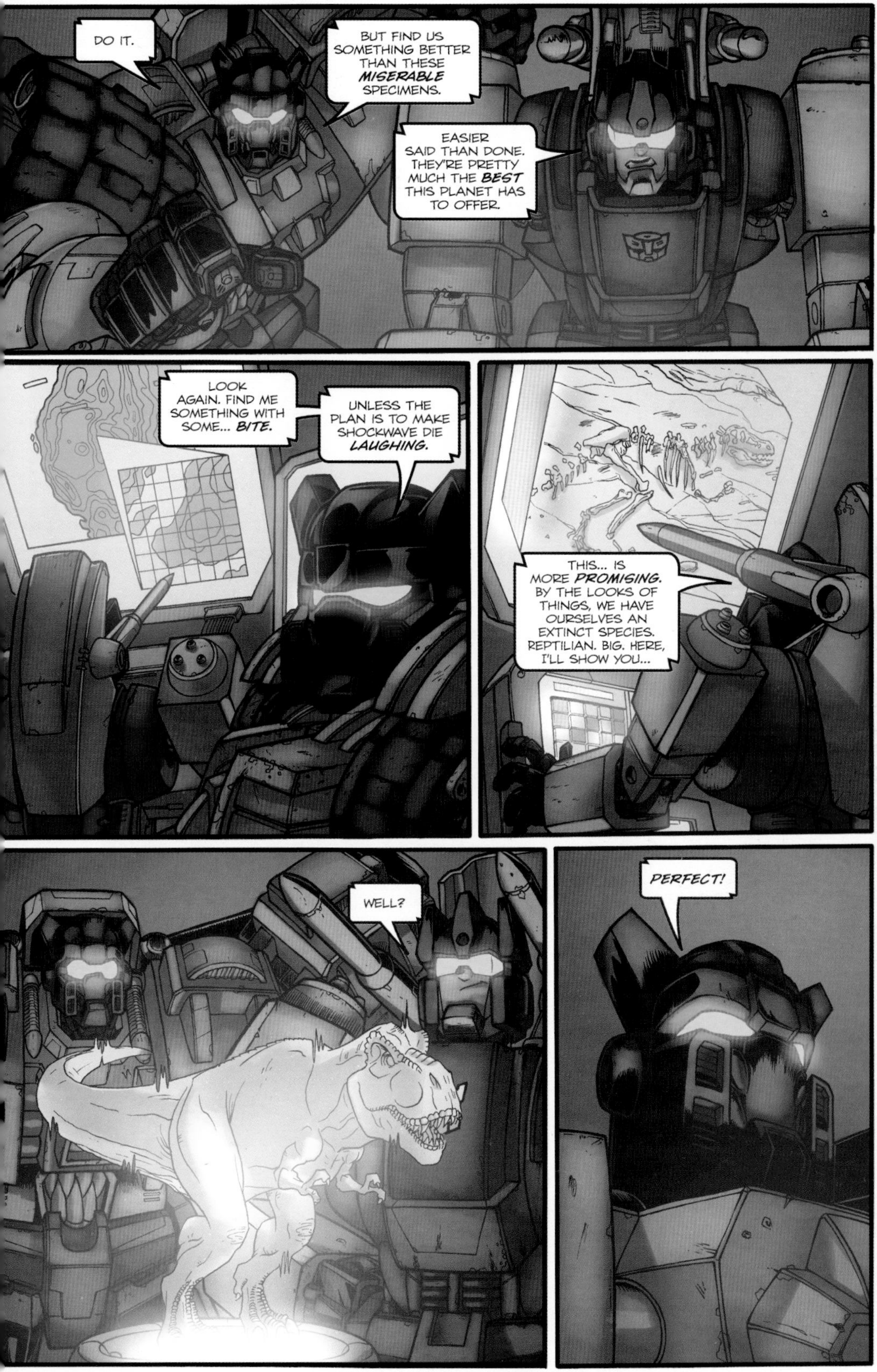
DO IT.
BUT FIND US SOMETHING BETTER THAN THESE MISERABLE SPECIMENS.
EASIER SAID THAN DONE. THEY'RE PRETTY MUCH THE BEST THIS PLANET HAS TO OFFER.
LOOK AGAIN. FIND ME SOMETHING WITH SOME... BITE.
UNLESS THE PLAN IS TO MAKE SHOCKWAVE DIE LAUGHING.
THIS... IS MORE PROMISING. BY THE LOOKS OF THINGS, WE HAVE OURSELVES AN EXTINCT SPECIES. REPTILIAN. BIG. HERE, I'LL SHOW YOU...
WELL?
PERFECT!

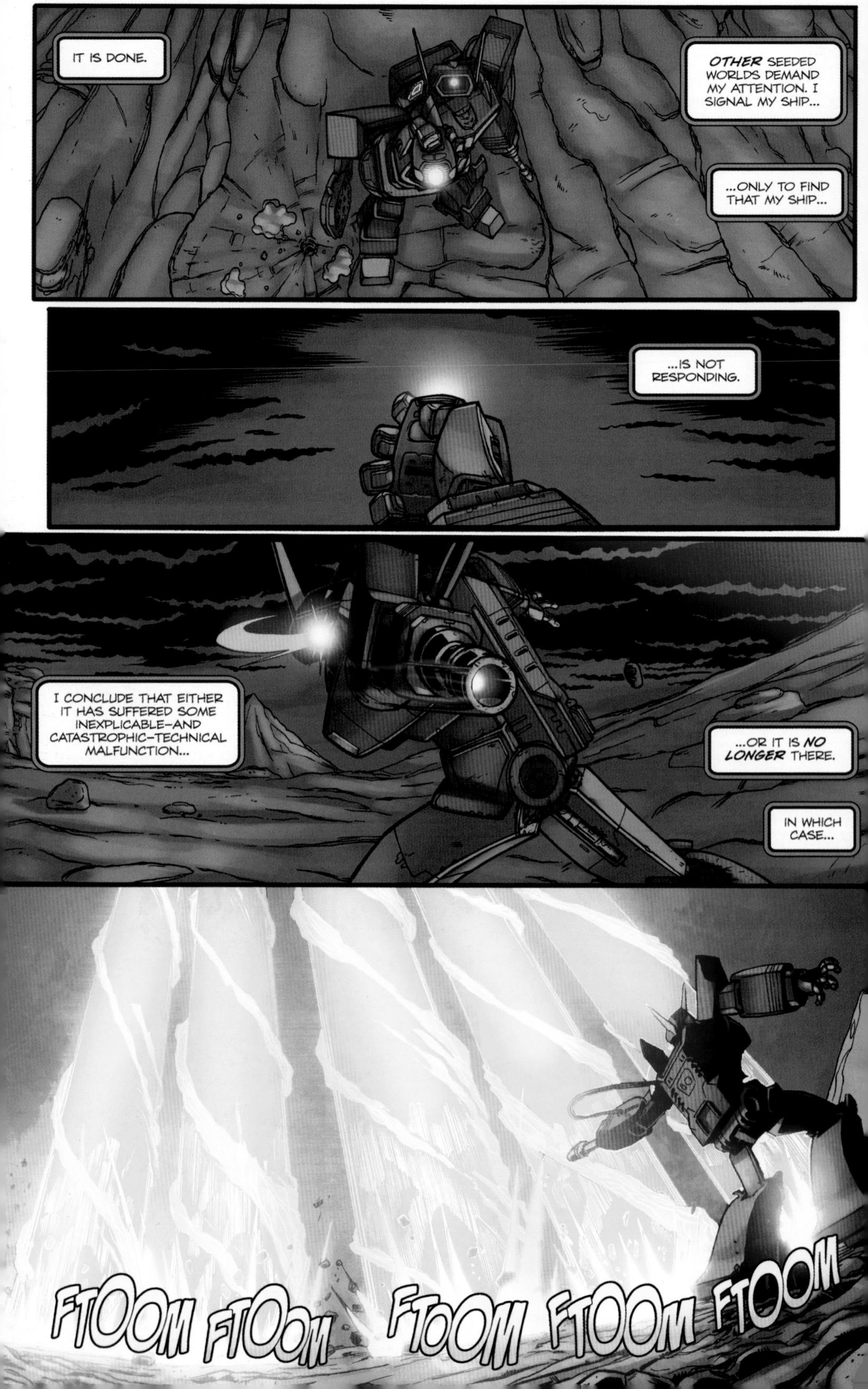
IT IS DONE.
OTHER SEEDED WORLDS DEMAND MY ATTENTION. I SIGNAL MY SHIP...
...ONLY TO FIND THAT MY SHIP...
...IS NOT RESPONDING.
I CONCLUDE THAT EITHER IT HAS SUFFERED SOME INEXPLICABLE–AND CATASTROPHIC–TECHNICAL MALFUNCTION...
...OR IT IS NO LONGER THERE.
IN WHICH CASE...
FTOOM FTOOM FTOOM FTOOM FTOOM

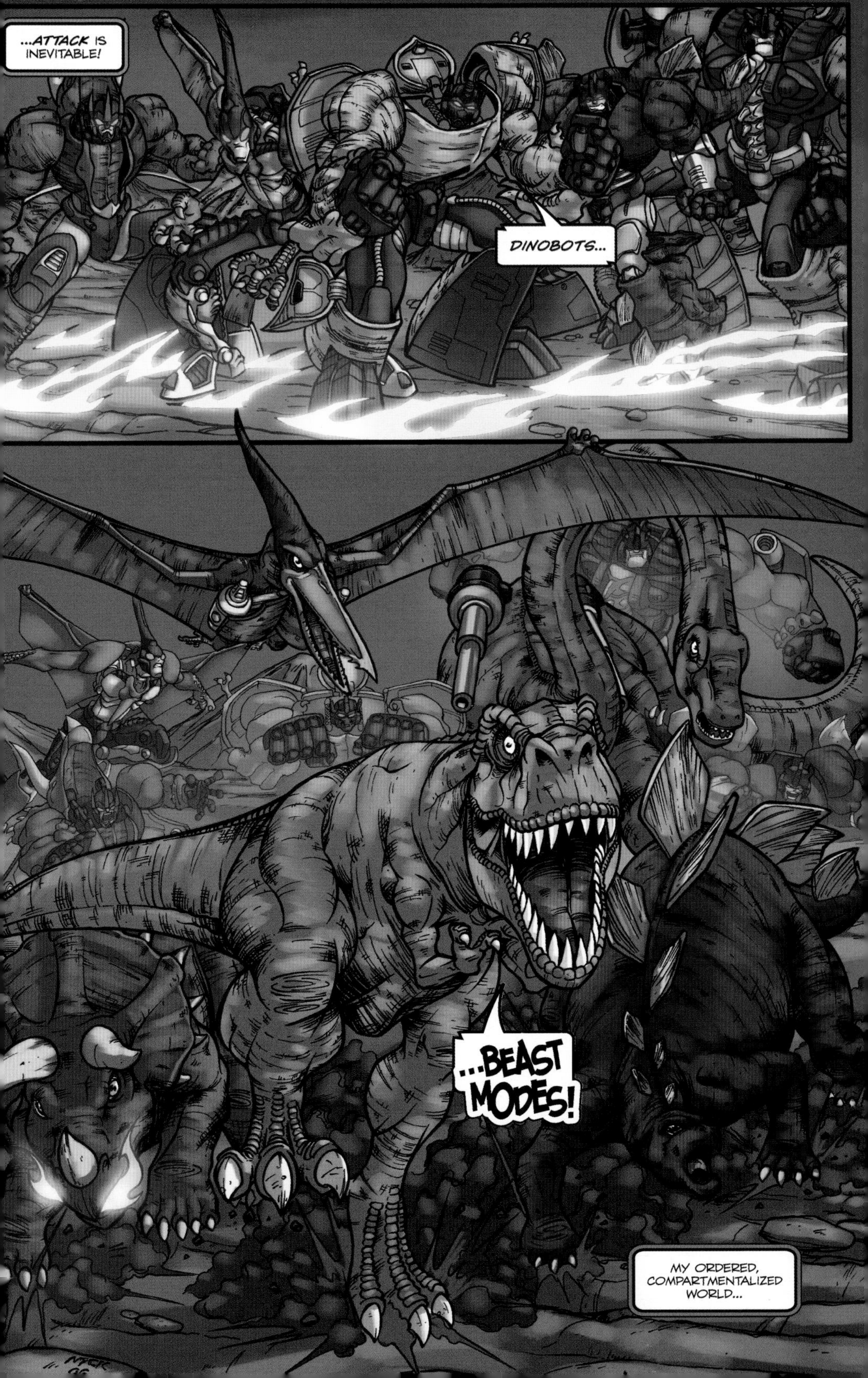
...ATTACK IS INEVITABLE!
DINOBOTS...
...BEAST MODES!
MY ORDERED, COMPARTMENTALIZED WORLD...

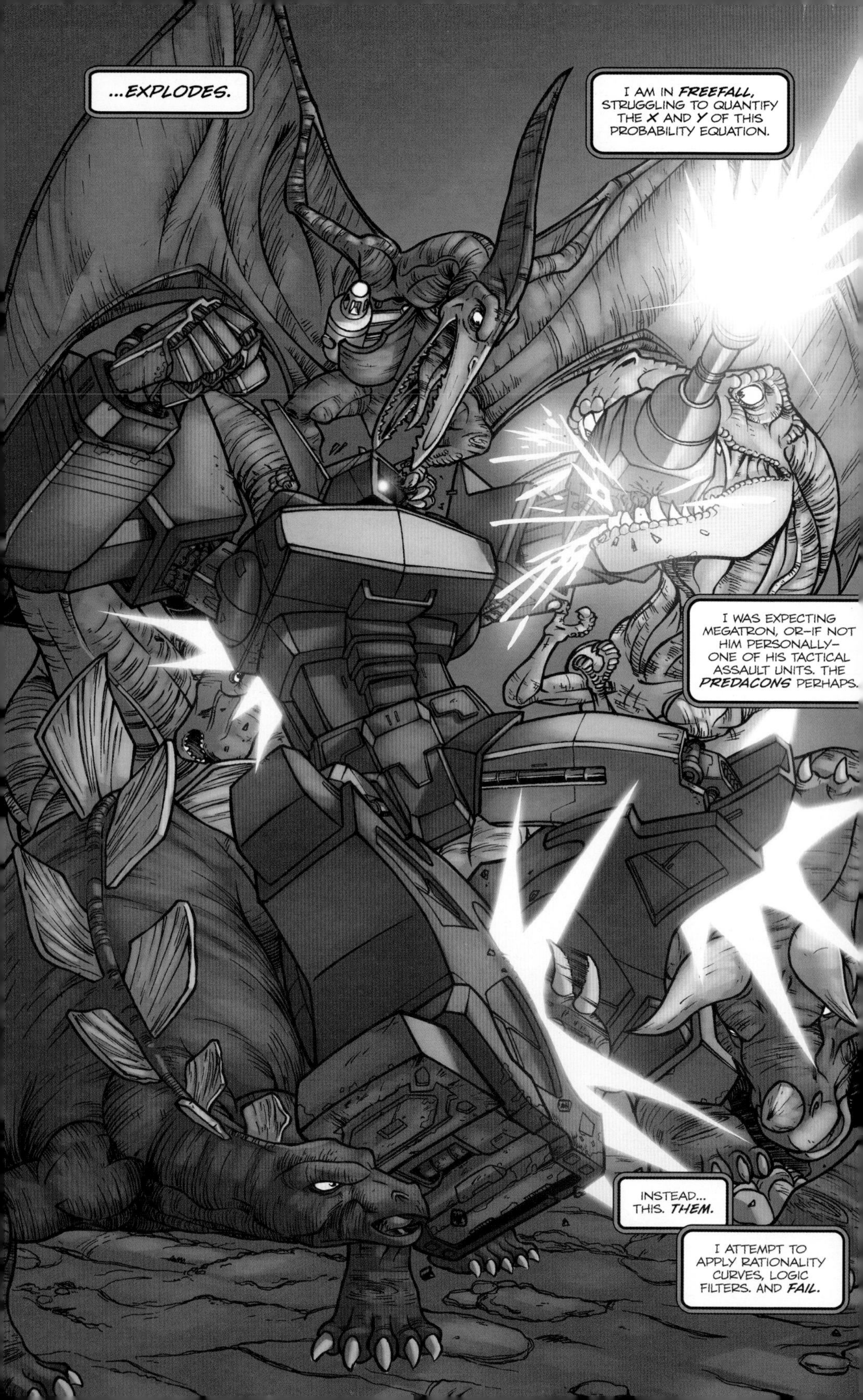
...EXPLODES.
I AM IN FREEFALL, STRUGGLING TO QUANTIFY THE X AND Y OF THIS PROBABILITY EQUATION.
I WAS EXPECTING MEGATRON, OR--IF NOT HIM PERSONALLY-- ONE OF HIS TACTICAL ASSAULT UNITS. THE PREDACONS PERHAPS.
INSTEAD... THIS. THEM.
I ATTEMPT TO APPLY RATIONALITY CURVES, LOGIC FILTERS. AND FAIL.

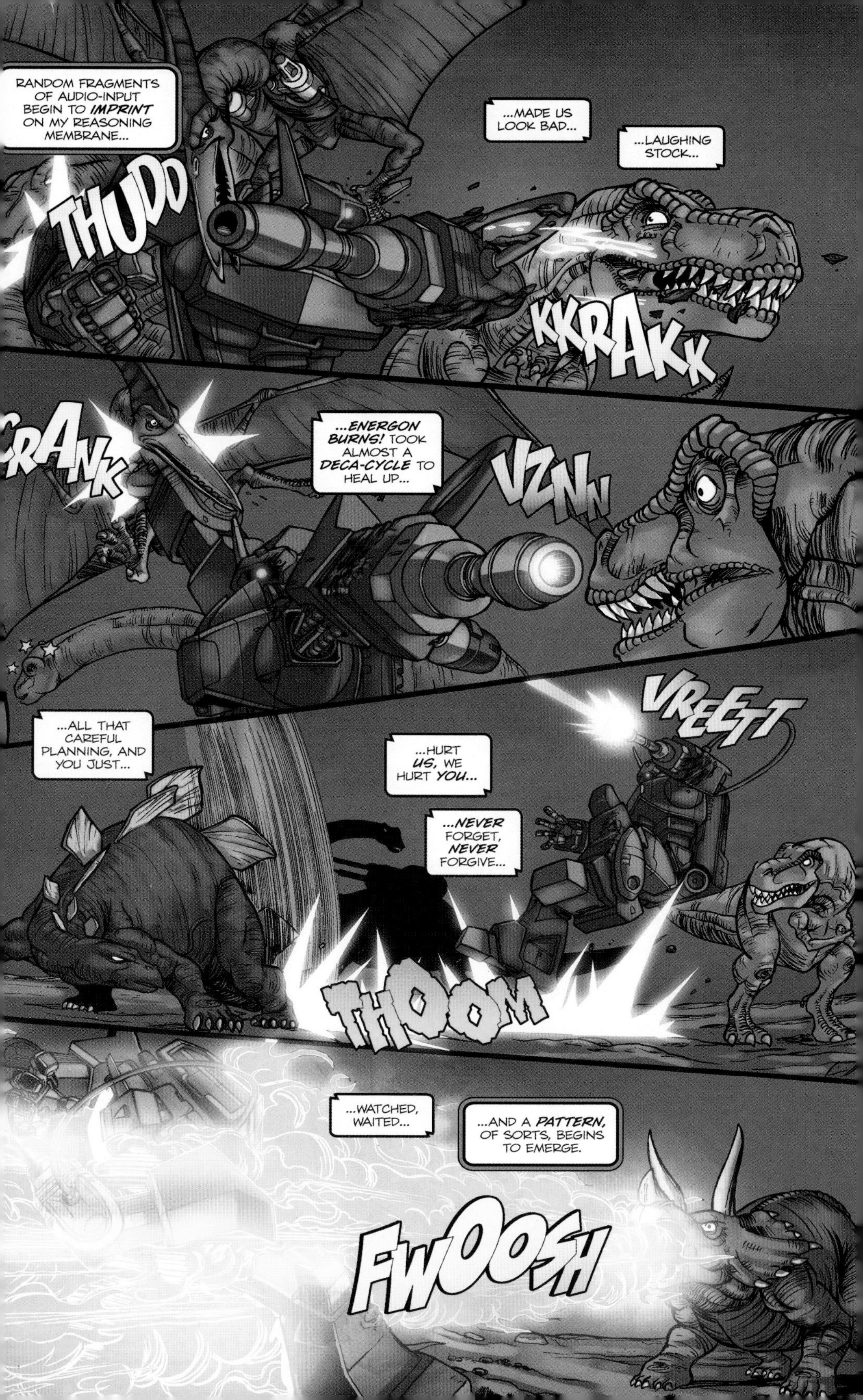
RANDOM FRAGMENTS OF AUDIO-INPUT BEGIN TO *IMPRINT* ON MY REASONING MEMBRANE...
...MADE US LOOK BAD...
...LAUGHING STOCK...
THUDD
KKRAKK
CRANK
...*ENERGON BURNS!* TOOK ALMOST A *DECA-CYCLE* TO HEAL UP...
VZNNN
VREETT
...ALL THAT CAREFUL PLANNING, AND YOU JUST...
...HURT *US,* WE HURT *YOU...*
...*NEVER* FORGET, *NEVER* FORGIVE...
THOOM
...WATCHED, WAITED...
...AND A *PATTERN,* OF SORTS, BEGINS TO EMERGE.
FWOOSH

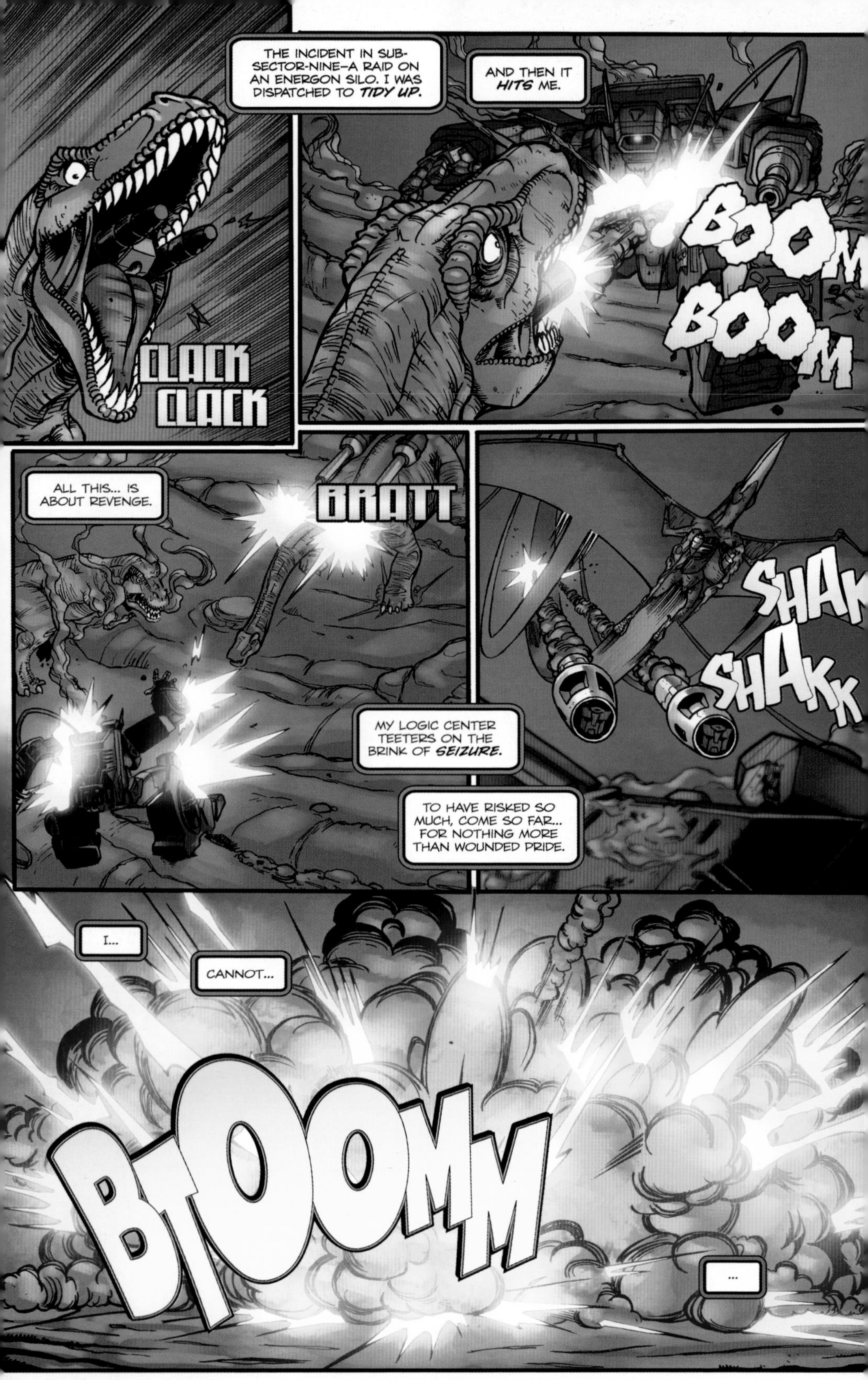

CLACK
CLACK
THE INCIDENT IN SUB-SECTOR-NINE—A RAID ON AN ENERGON SILO. I WAS DISPATCHED TO *TIDY UP.*
AND THEN IT *HITS* ME.
BOOM
BOOM
ALL THIS... IS ABOUT REVENGE.
BRATT
SHAK
SHAKK
MY LOGIC CENTER TEETERS ON THE BRINK OF *SEIZURE.*
TO HAVE RISKED SO MUCH, COME SO FAR... FOR NOTHING MORE THAN WOUNDED PRIDE.
I...
CANNOT...
BTOOMM
...

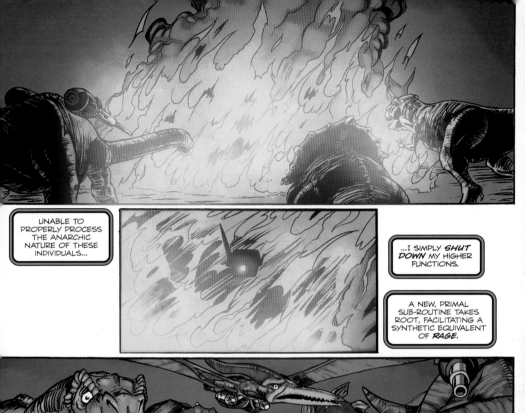

UNABLE TO PROPERLY PROCESS THE ANARCHIC NATURE OF THESE INDIVIDUALS...

...I SIMPLY *SHUT DOWN* MY HIGHER FUNCTIONS.

A NEW, PRIMAL SUB-ROUTINE TAKES ROOT, FACILITATING A SYNTHETIC EQUIVALENT OF *RAGE*.

I...

...EVOLVE.

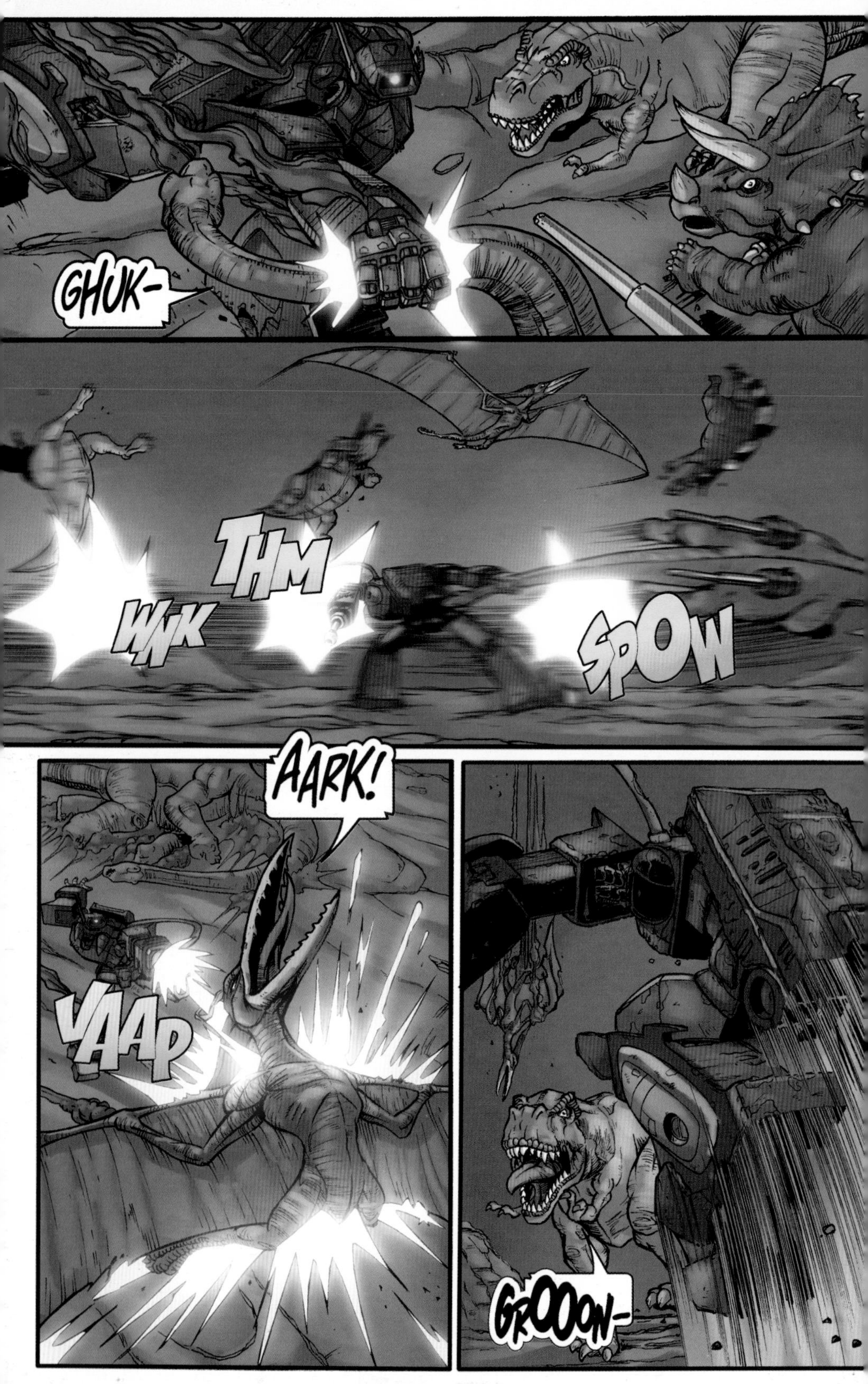
GHUK-
THM
WNK
SPOW
AARK!
VAAP
GROOOON-

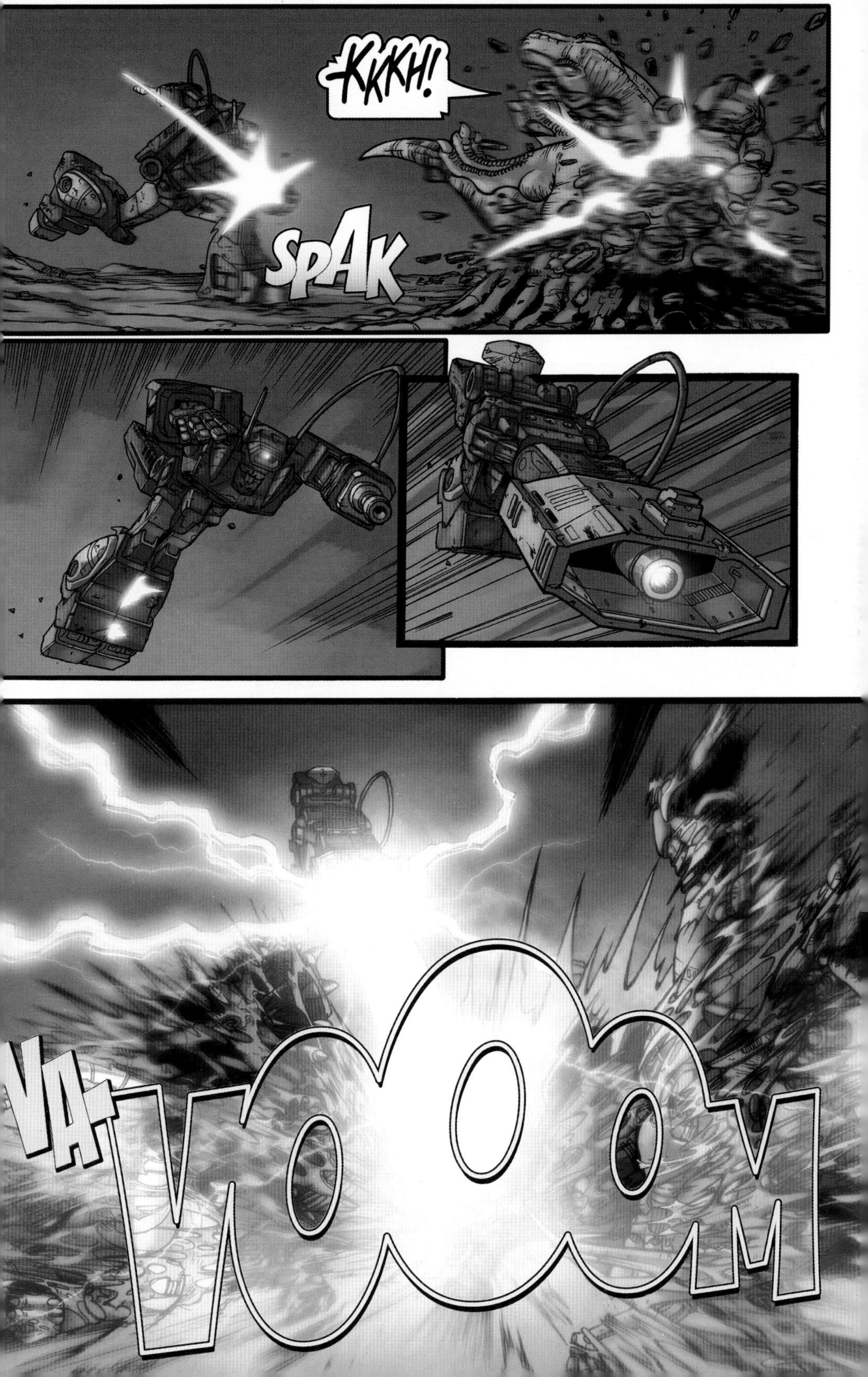

KKKH!
SPAK
VA-VOOOOM

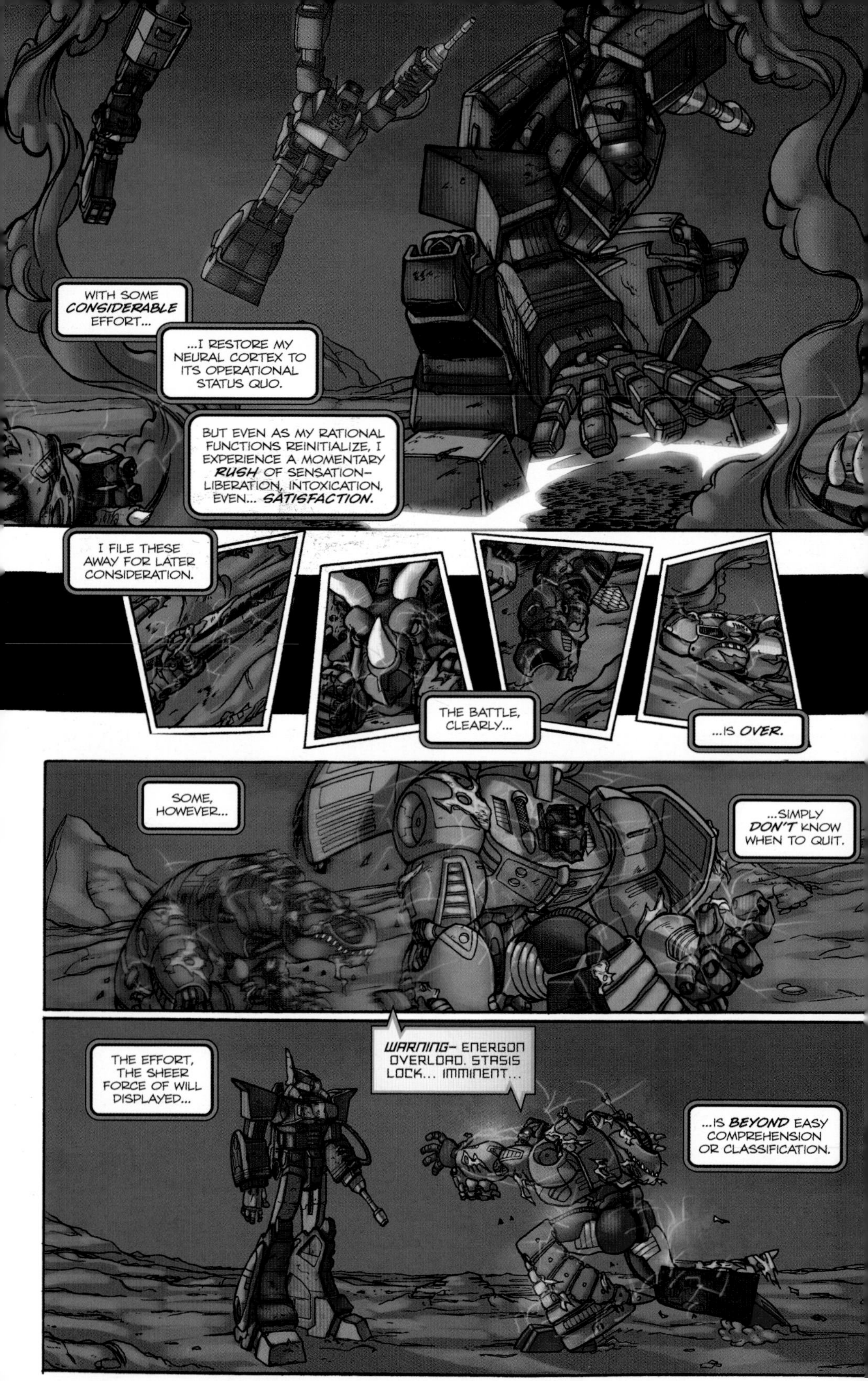
WITH SOME CONSIDERABLE EFFORT...
...I RESTORE MY NEURAL CORTEX TO ITS OPERATIONAL STATUS QUO.
BUT EVEN AS MY RATIONAL FUNCTIONS REINITIALIZE, I EXPERIENCE A MOMENTARY RUSH OF SENSATION– LIBERATION, INTOXICATION, EVEN... SATISFACTION.
I FILE THESE AWAY FOR LATER CONSIDERATION.
THE BATTLE, CLEARLY...
...IS OVER.
SOME, HOWEVER...
...SIMPLY DON'T KNOW WHEN TO QUIT.
THE EFFORT, THE SHEER FORCE OF WILL DISPLAYED...
WARNING– ENERGON OVERLOAD. STASIS LOCK... IMMINENT...
...IS BEYOND EASY COMPREHENSION OR CLASSIFICATION.

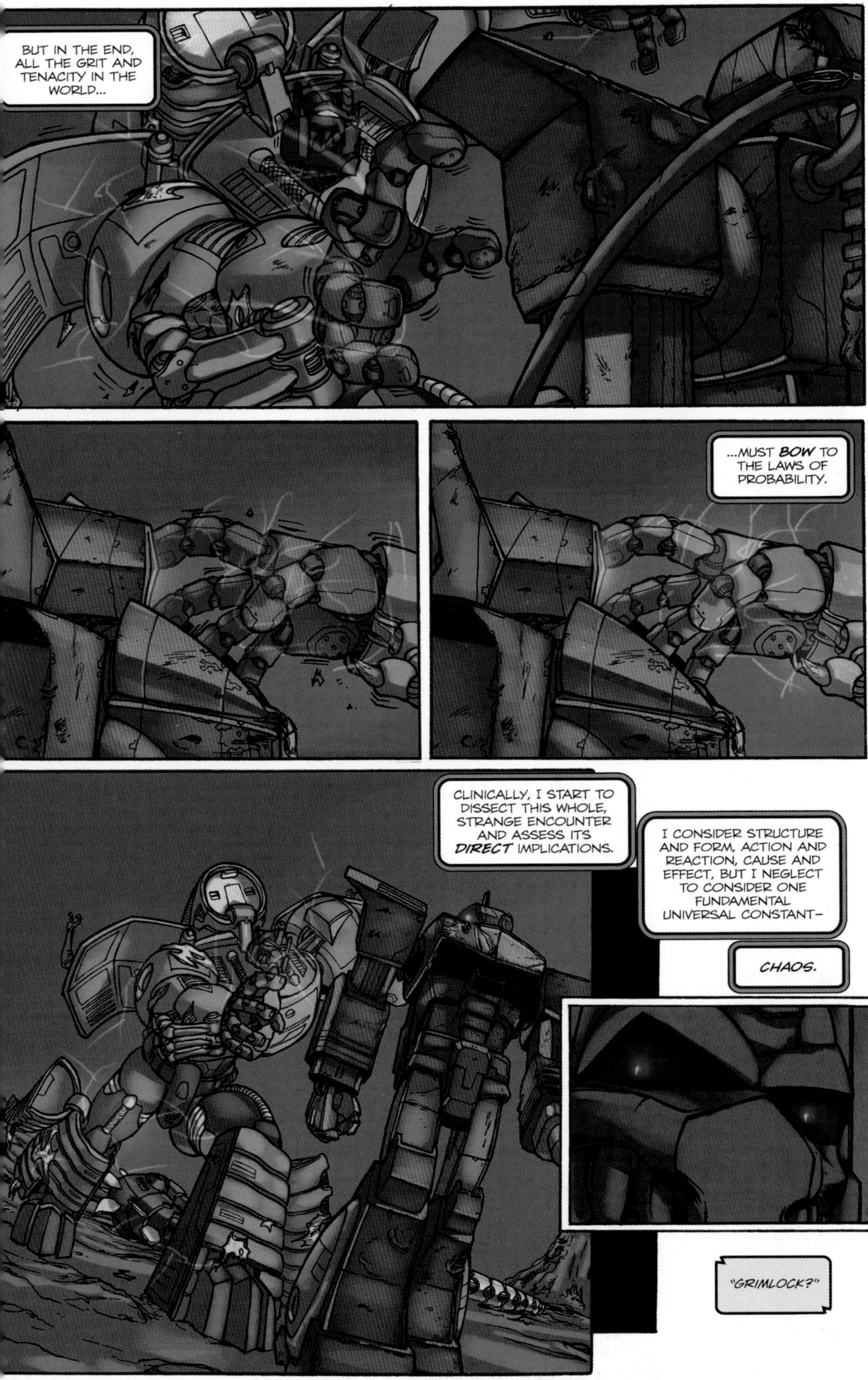
BUT IN THE END, ALL THE GRIT AND TENACITY IN THE WORLD...
...MUST BOW TO THE LAWS OF PROBABILITY.
CLINICALLY, I START TO DISSECT THIS WHOLE, STRANGE ENCOUNTER AND ASSESS ITS DIRECT IMPLICATIONS.
I CONSIDER STRUCTURE AND FORM, ACTION AND REACTION, CAUSE AND EFFECT, BUT I NEGLECT TO CONSIDER ONE FUNDAMENTAL UNIVERSAL CONSTANT–
CHAOS.
"GRIMLOCK?"

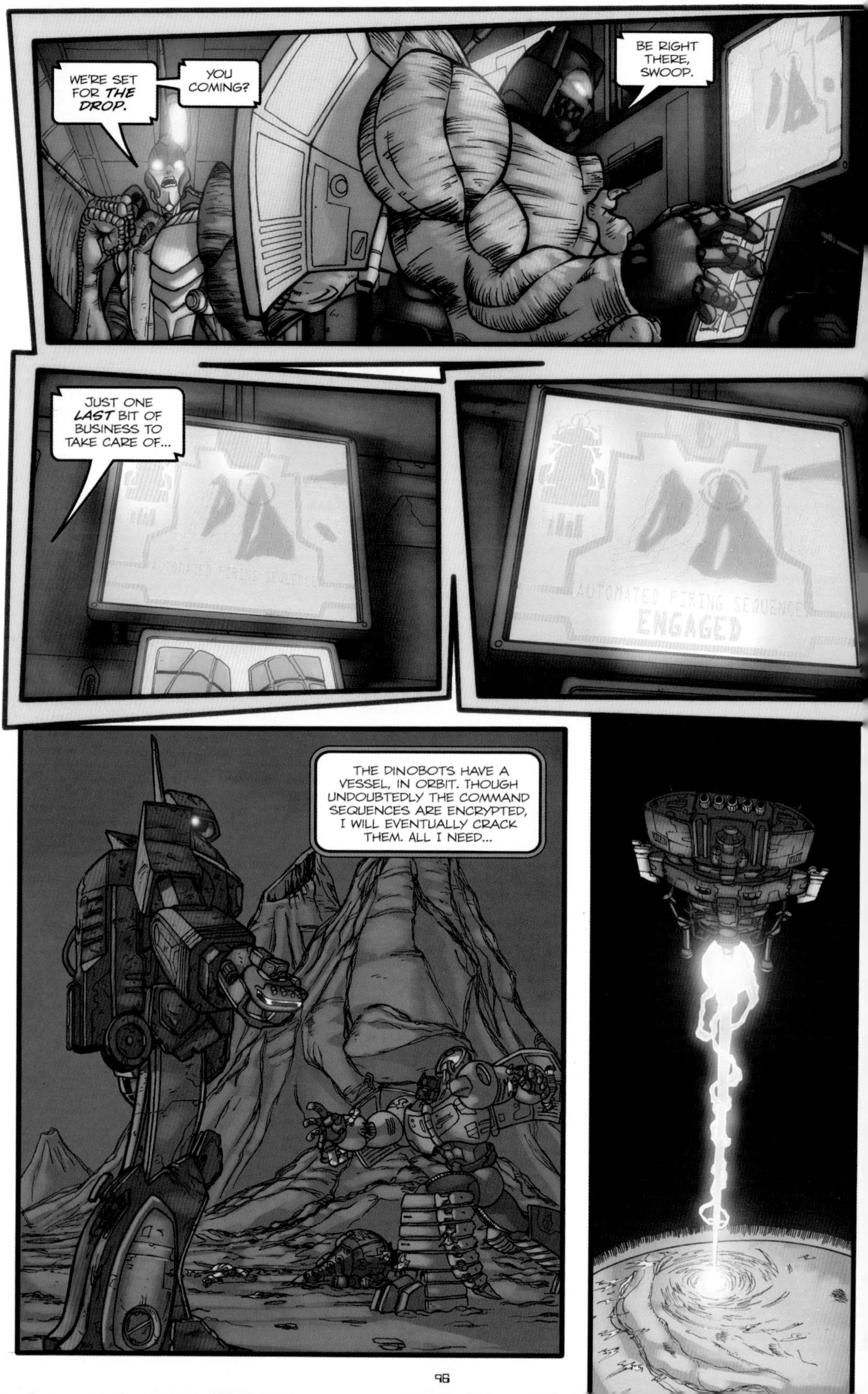
WE'RE SET FOR THE DROP.
YOU COMING?
BE RIGHT THERE, SWOOP.
JUST ONE LAST BIT OF BUSINESS TO TAKE CARE OF...
AUTOMATED FIRING SEQUENCE
AUTOMATED FIRING SEQUENCE ENGAGED
THE DINOBOTS HAVE A VESSEL, IN ORBIT. THOUGH UNDOUBTEDLY THE COMMAND SEQUENCES ARE ENCRYPTED, I WILL EVENTUALLY CRACK THEM. ALL I NEED...

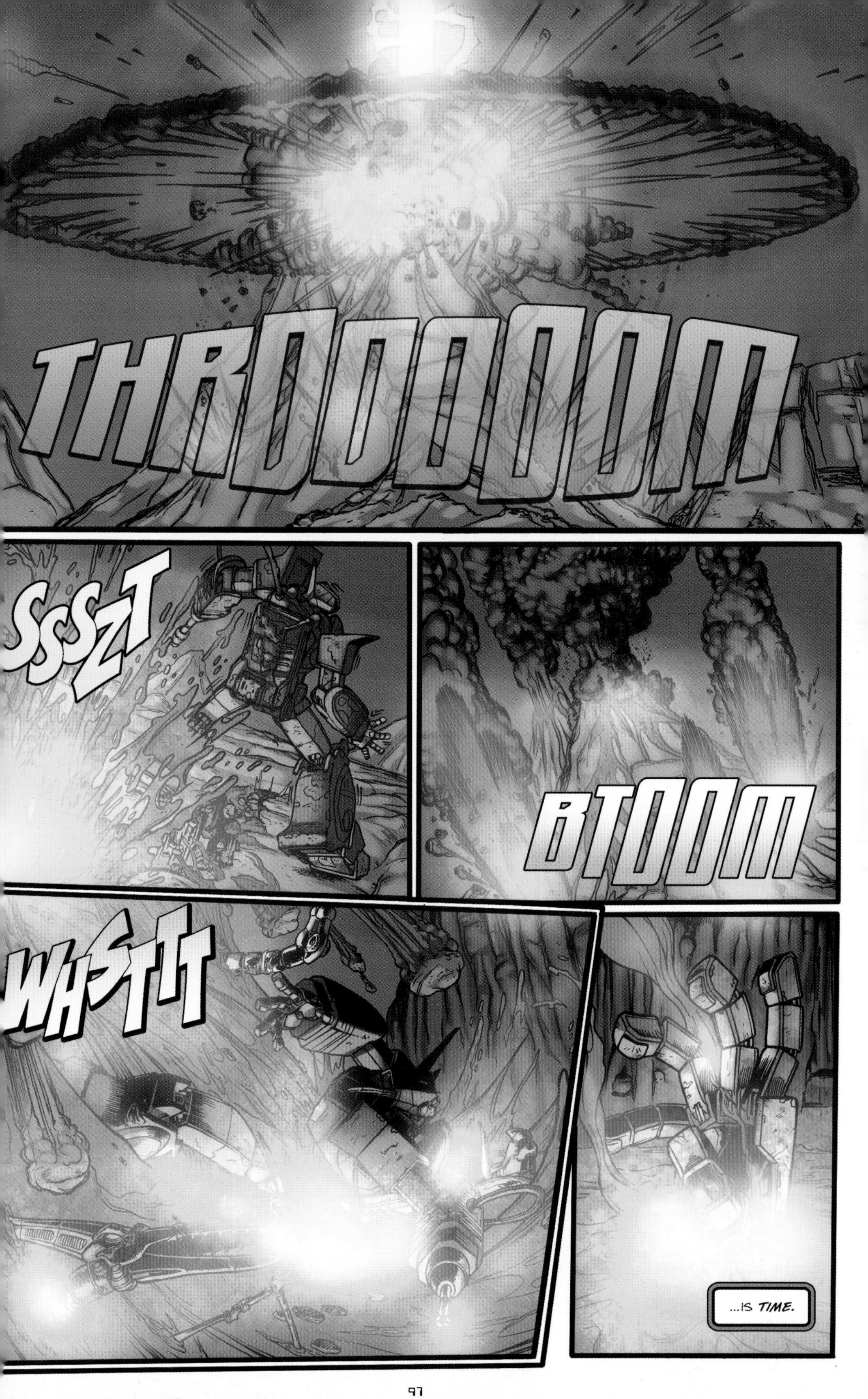
THROOOOOM
SSSZT
BTOOM
WHSTTT
...IS TIME.

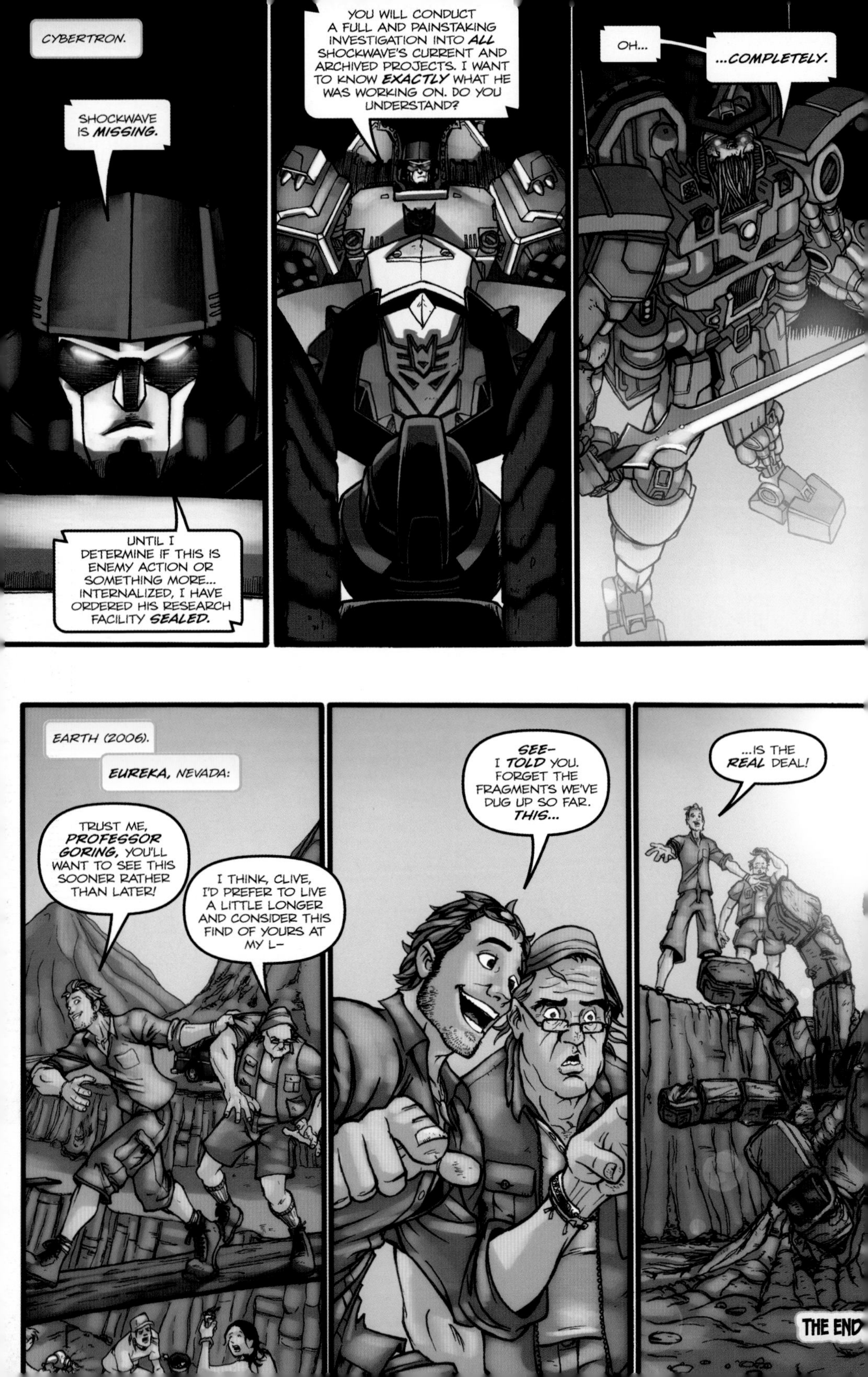

CYBERTRON.
SHOCKWAVE IS MISSING.
UNTIL I DETERMINE IF THIS IS ENEMY ACTION OR SOMETHING MORE... INTERNALIZED, I HAVE ORDERED HIS RESEARCH FACILITY SEALED.
YOU WILL CONDUCT A FULL AND PAINSTAKING INVESTIGATION INTO ALL SHOCKWAVE'S CURRENT AND ARCHIVED PROJECTS. I WANT TO KNOW EXACTLY WHAT HE WAS WORKING ON. DO YOU UNDERSTAND?
OH...
...COMPLETELY.
EARTH (2006).
EUREKA, NEVADA:
TRUST ME, PROFESSOR GORING, YOU'LL WANT TO SEE THIS SOONER RATHER THAN LATER!
I THINK, CLIVE, I'D PREFER TO LIVE A LITTLE LONGER AND CONSIDER THIS FIND OF YOURS AT MY L–
SEE– I TOLD YOU. FORGET THE FRAGMENTS WE'VE DUG UP SO FAR. THIS...
...IS THE REAL DEAL!
THE END

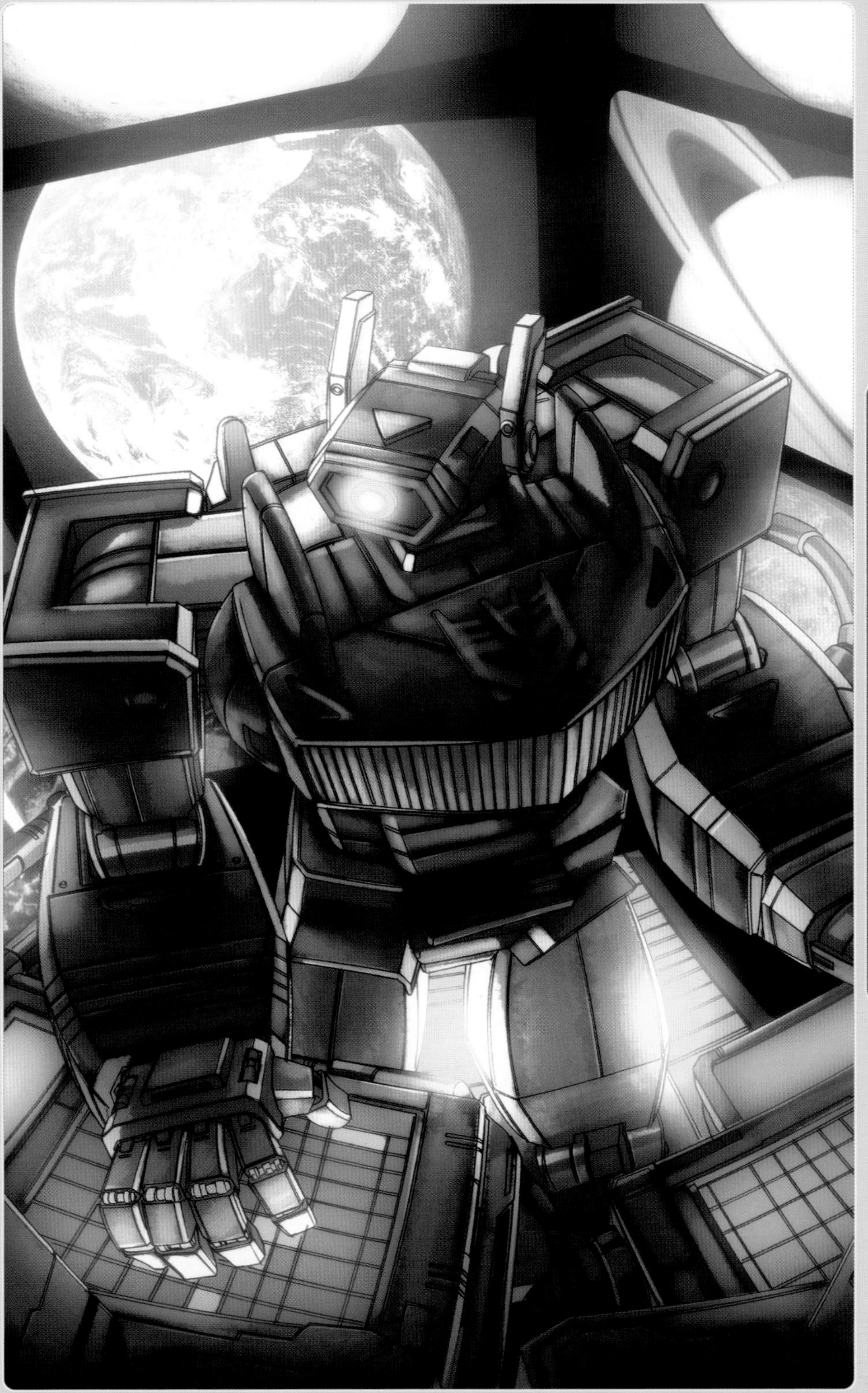

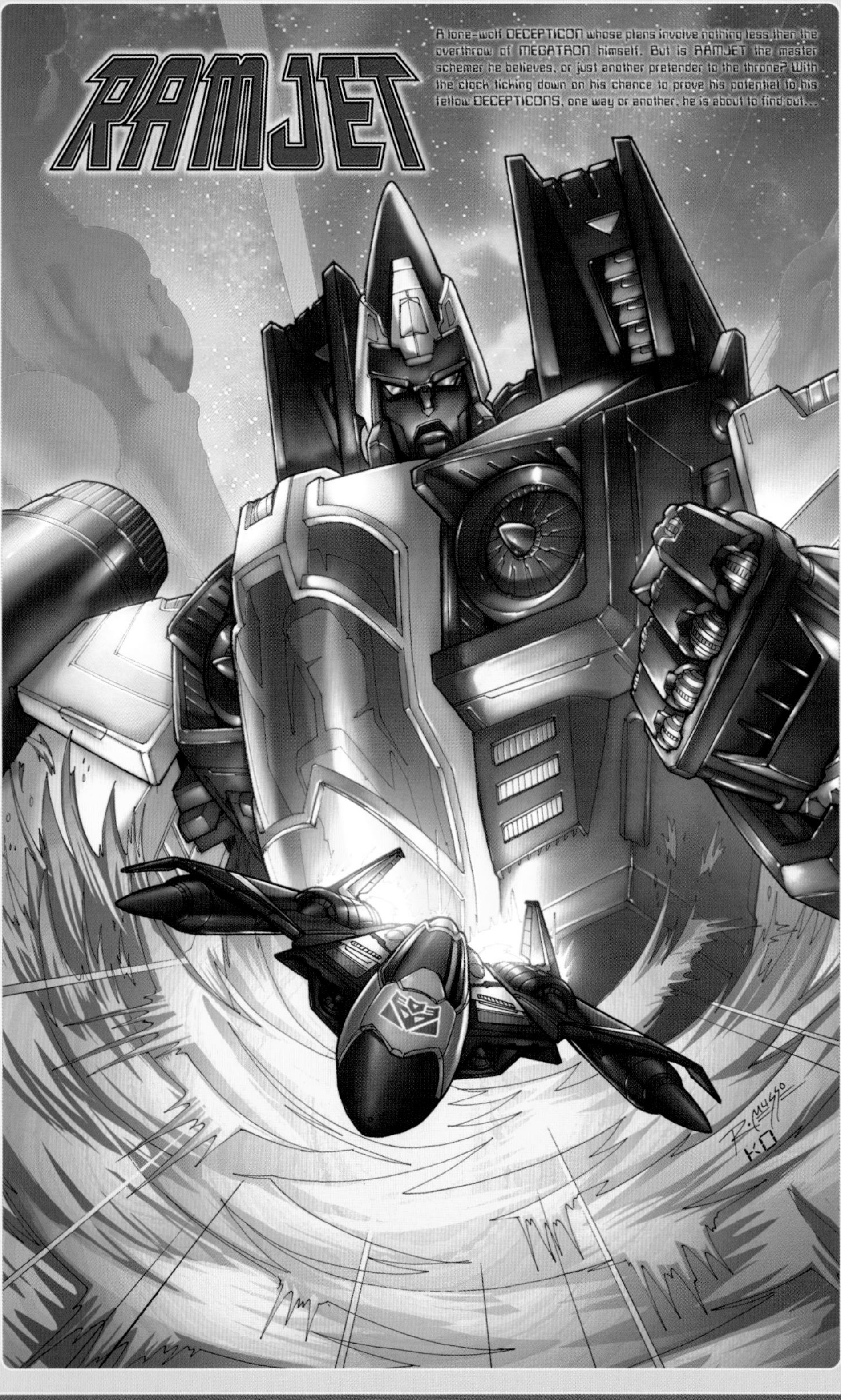
RAMJET
A lone-wolf DECEPTICON whose plans involve nothing less than the overthrow of MEGATRON himself. But is RAMJET the master schemer he believes, or just another pretender to the throne? With the clock ticking down on his chance to prove his potential to his fellow DECEPTICONS, one way or another, he is about to find out...
R. Musso
KO

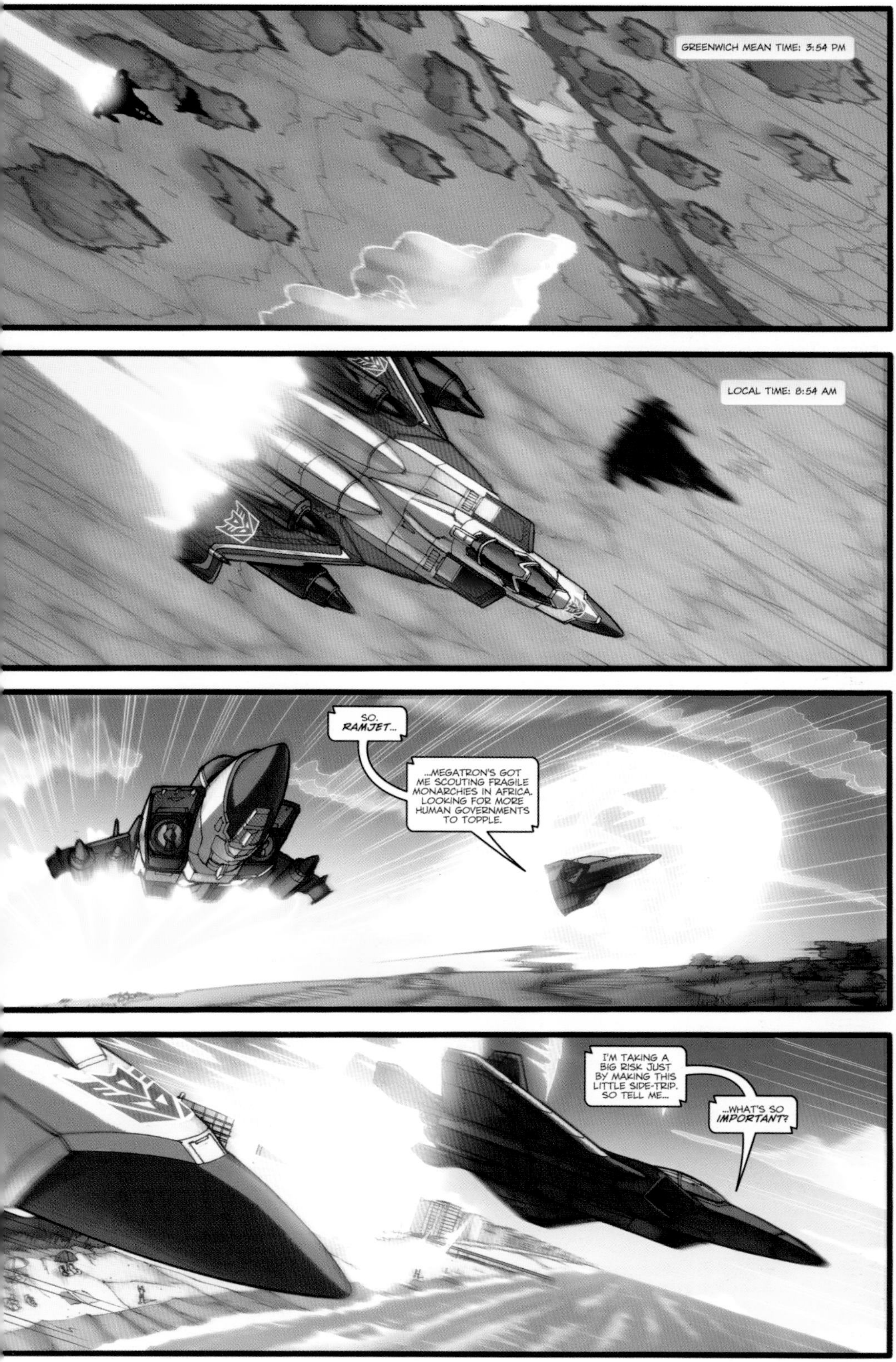
GREENWICH MEAN TIME: 3:54 PM
LOCAL TIME: 8:54 AM
SO. RAMJET...
...MEGATRON'S GOT ME SCOUTING FRAGILE MONARCHIES IN AFRICA. LOOKING FOR MORE HUMAN GOVERNMENTS TO TOPPLE.
I'M TAKING A BIG RISK JUST BY MAKING THIS LITTLE SIDE-TRIP. SO TELL ME...
...WHAT'S SO IMPORTANT?

HA!

FORGET ABOUT MEGATRON, SKYWARP.

HE'S YESTERDAY'S NEWSGRID.

TO *YOU*, MAYBE.

HE'S GOT NO USE FOR YOU EVER SINCE THAT BUSINESS IN—

I'VE GOT NO USE FOR HIM, EITHER.

AND SOON... HE WON'T EVEN MATTER.

WAIT A MINUTE. YOU'VE PULLED SOME CRAZY STUNTS BEFORE—

—BUT YOU'RE NOT THINKING OF GOING UP AGAINST *HIM*?

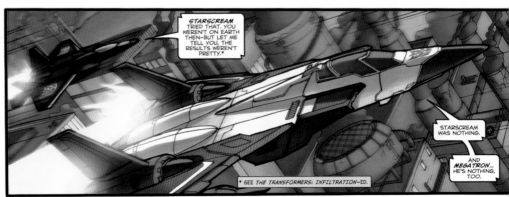

STARSCREAM TRIED THAT. YOU WEREN'T ON EARTH THEN—BUT LET ME TELL YOU, THE RESULTS WEREN'T PRETTY.*

STARSCREAM WAS NOTHING.

AND *MEGATRON*... HE'S NOTHING, TOO.

* SEE *THE TRANSFORMERS: INFILTRATION*—ED.

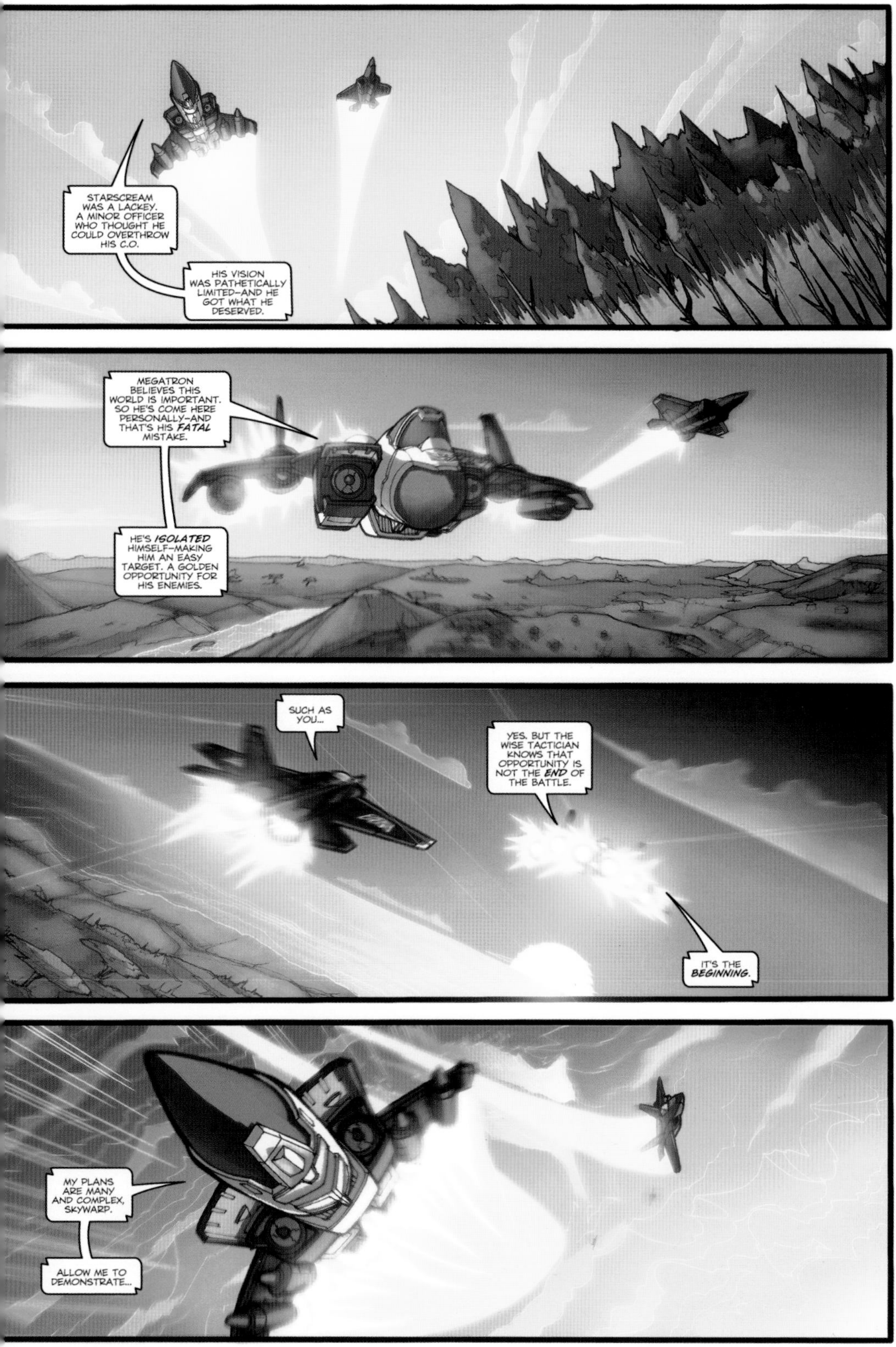
STARSCREAM WAS A LACKEY. A MINOR OFFICER WHO THOUGHT HE COULD OVERTHROW HIS C.O.
HIS VISION WAS PATHETICALLY LIMITED—AND HE GOT WHAT HE DESERVED.
MEGATRON BELIEVES THIS WORLD IS IMPORTANT. SO HE'S COME HERE PERSONALLY—AND THAT'S HIS *FATAL* MISTAKE.
HE'S *ISOLATED* HIMSELF—MAKING HIM AN EASY TARGET. A GOLDEN OPPORTUNITY FOR HIS ENEMIES.
SUCH AS YOU...
YES. BUT THE WISE TACTICIAN KNOWS THAT OPPORTUNITY IS NOT THE *END* OF THE BATTLE.
IT'S THE *BEGINNING*.
MY PLANS ARE MANY AND COMPLEX, SKYWARP.
ALLOW ME TO DEMONSTRATE...

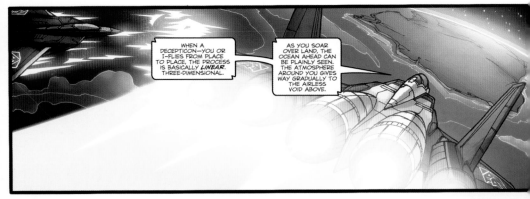

WHEN A DECEPTICON—YOU OR I—FLIES FROM PLACE TO PLACE, THE PROCESS IS BASICALLY *LINEAR.* THREE-DIMENSIONAL.

AS YOU SOAR OVER LAND, THE OCEAN AHEAD CAN BE PLAINLY SEEN. THE ATMOSPHERE AROUND YOU GIVES WAY GRADUALLY TO THE AIRLESS VOID ABOVE.

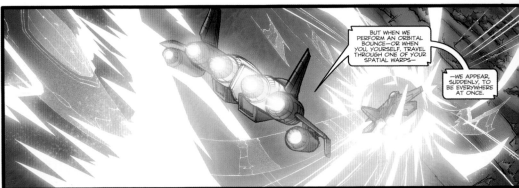

BUT WHEN WE PERFORM AN ORBITAL BOUNCE—OR WHEN YOU, YOURSELF, TRAVEL THROUGH ONE OF YOUR SPATIAL WARPS—

—WE APPEAR, SUDDENLY, TO BE EVERYWHERE AT ONCE.

MEGATRON'S PLANS, STARSCREAM'S—THOSE CONCEPTS ARE LIMITED AND THREE-DIMENSIONAL.

MINE ARE MUCH LARGER... MORE COMPLEX. LESS *LINEAR.*

THAT IS WHY, SKYWARP... I WILL ULTIMATELY TRIUMPH.

HA! YOU KNOW WHAT, RAMJET?

THAT'S THE BIGGEST BUNCH OF SLAG I'VE EVER HEARD.

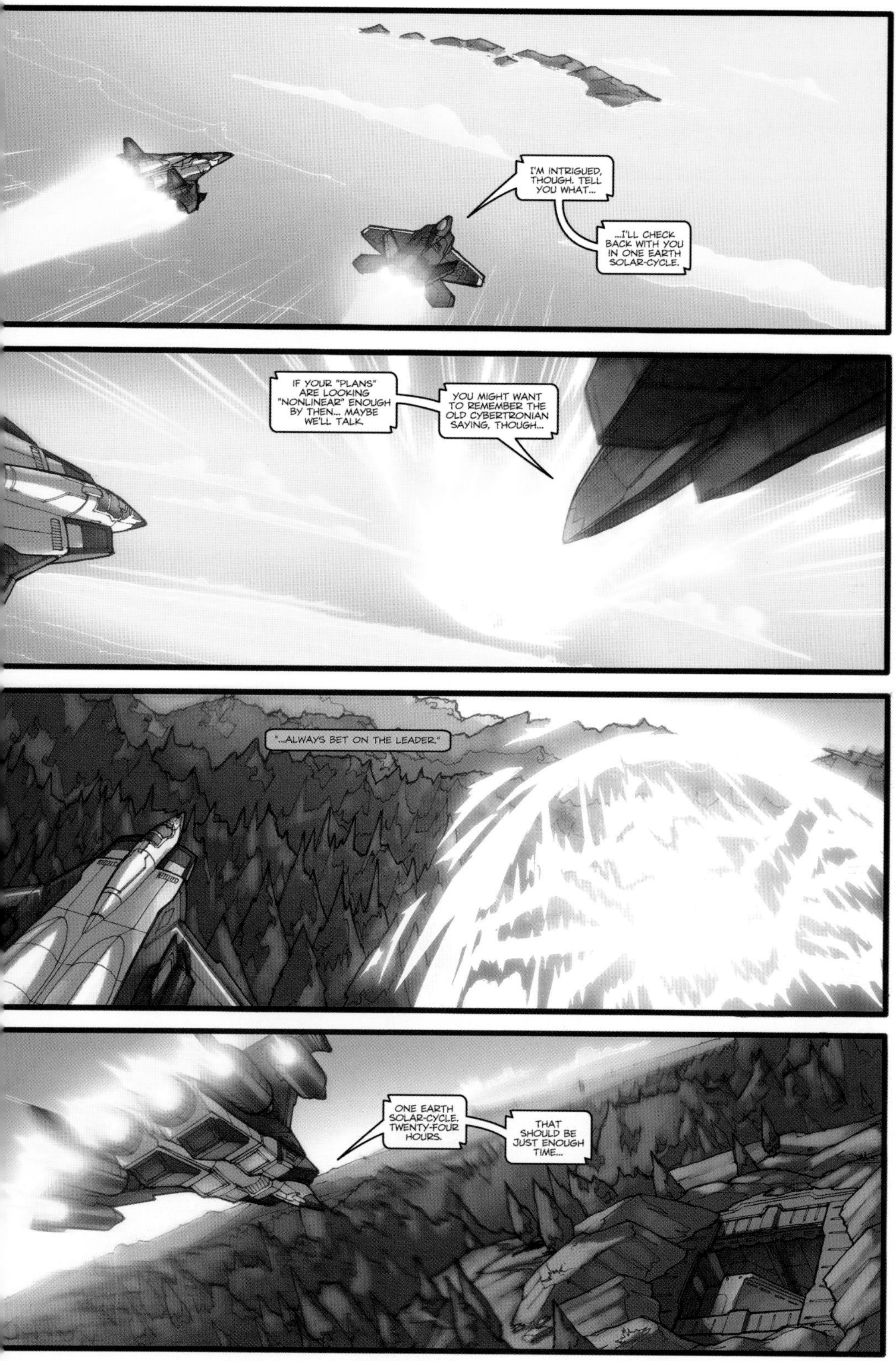
I'M INTRIGUED, THOUGH. TELL YOU WHAT...
...I'LL CHECK BACK WITH YOU IN ONE EARTH SOLAR-CYCLE.
IF YOUR "PLANS" ARE LOOKING "NONLINEAR" ENOUGH BY THEN... MAYBE WE'LL TALK.
YOU MIGHT WANT TO REMEMBER THE OLD CYBERTRONIAN SAYING, THOUGH...
"...ALWAYS BET ON THE LEADER."
ONE EARTH SOLAR-CYCLE. TWENTY-FOUR HOURS.
THAT SHOULD BE JUST ENOUGH TIME...

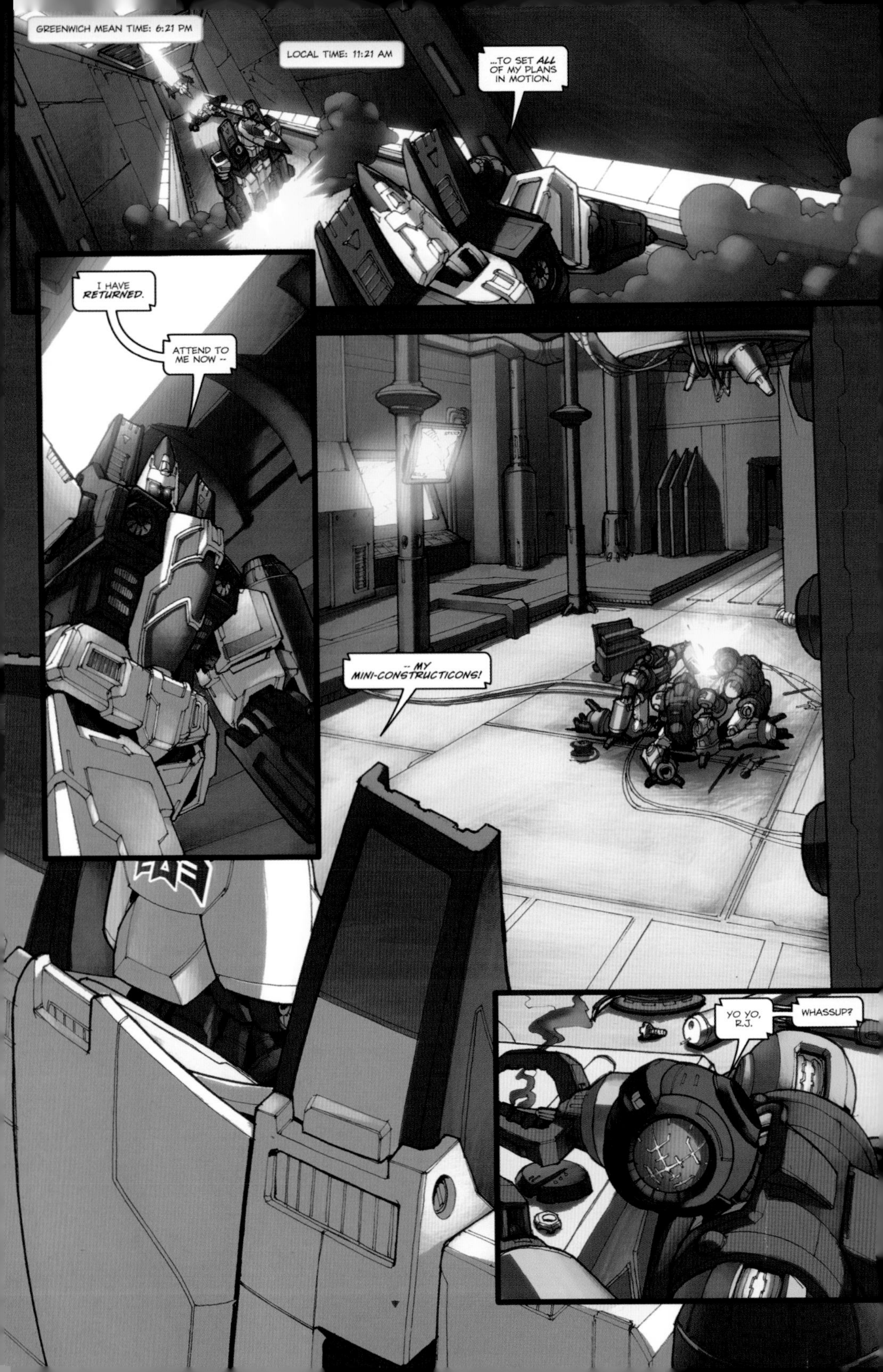
GREENWICH MEAN TIME: 6:21 PM
LOCAL TIME: 11:21 AM
...TO SET ALL OF MY PLANS IN MOTION.
I HAVE RETURNED.
ATTEND TO ME NOW --
-- MY MINI-CONSTRUCTICONS!
YO YO, R.J.
WHASSUP?

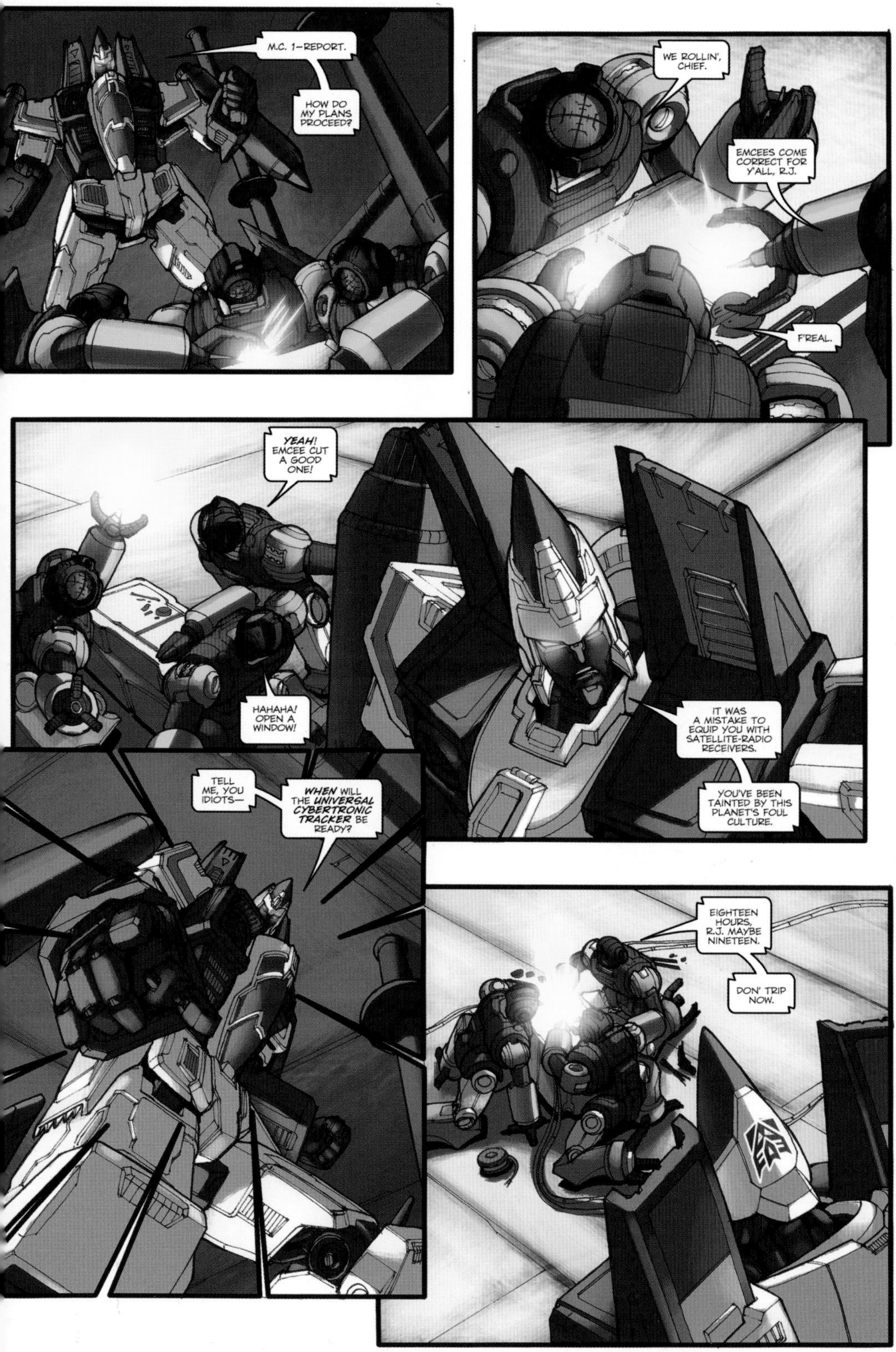
M.C. 1—REPORT.
HOW DO MY PLANS PROCEED?
WE ROLLIN', CHIEF.
EMCEES COME CORRECT FOR Y'ALL, R.J.
F'REAL.
YEAH! EMCEE CUT A GOOD ONE!
HAHAHA! OPEN A WINDOW!
IT WAS A MISTAKE TO EQUIP YOU WITH SATELLITE-RADIO RECEIVERS.
YOU'VE BEEN TAINTED BY THIS PLANET'S FOUL CULTURE.
TELL ME, YOU IDIOTS—
WHEN WILL THE UNIVERSAL CYBERTRONIC TRACKER BE READY?
EIGHTEEN HOURS, R.J. MAYBE NINETEEN.
DON' TRIP NOW.

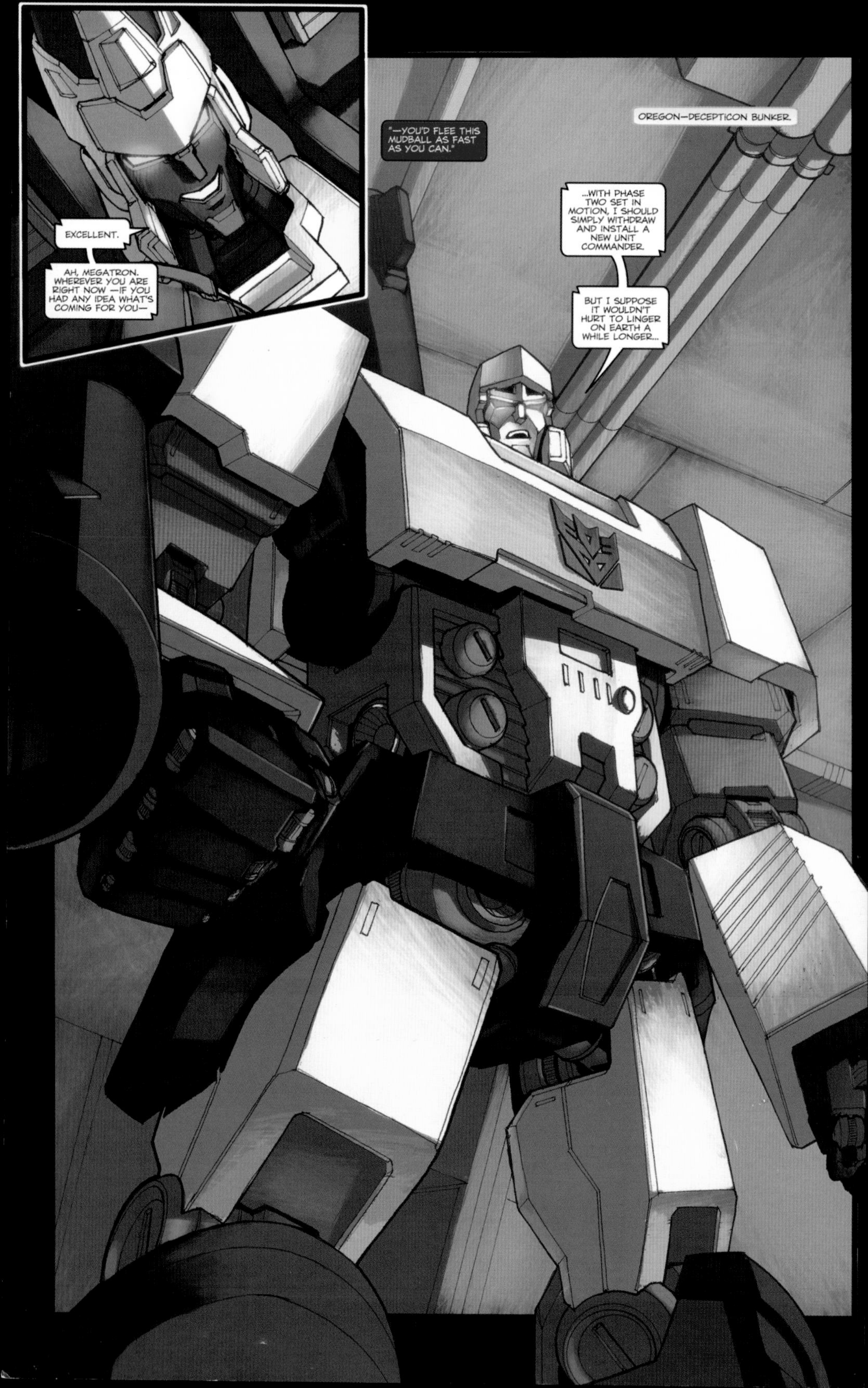
EXCELLENT.
AH, MEGATRON. WHEREVER YOU ARE RIGHT NOW —IF YOU HAD ANY IDEA WHAT'S COMING FOR YOU—
"—YOU'D FLEE THIS MUDBALL AS FAST AS YOU CAN."
OREGON—DECEPTICON BUNKER.
...WITH PHASE TWO SET IN MOTION, I SHOULD SIMPLY WITHDRAW AND INSTALL A NEW UNIT COMMANDER.
BUT I SUPPOSE IT WOULDN'T HURT TO LINGER ON EARTH A WHILE LONGER...

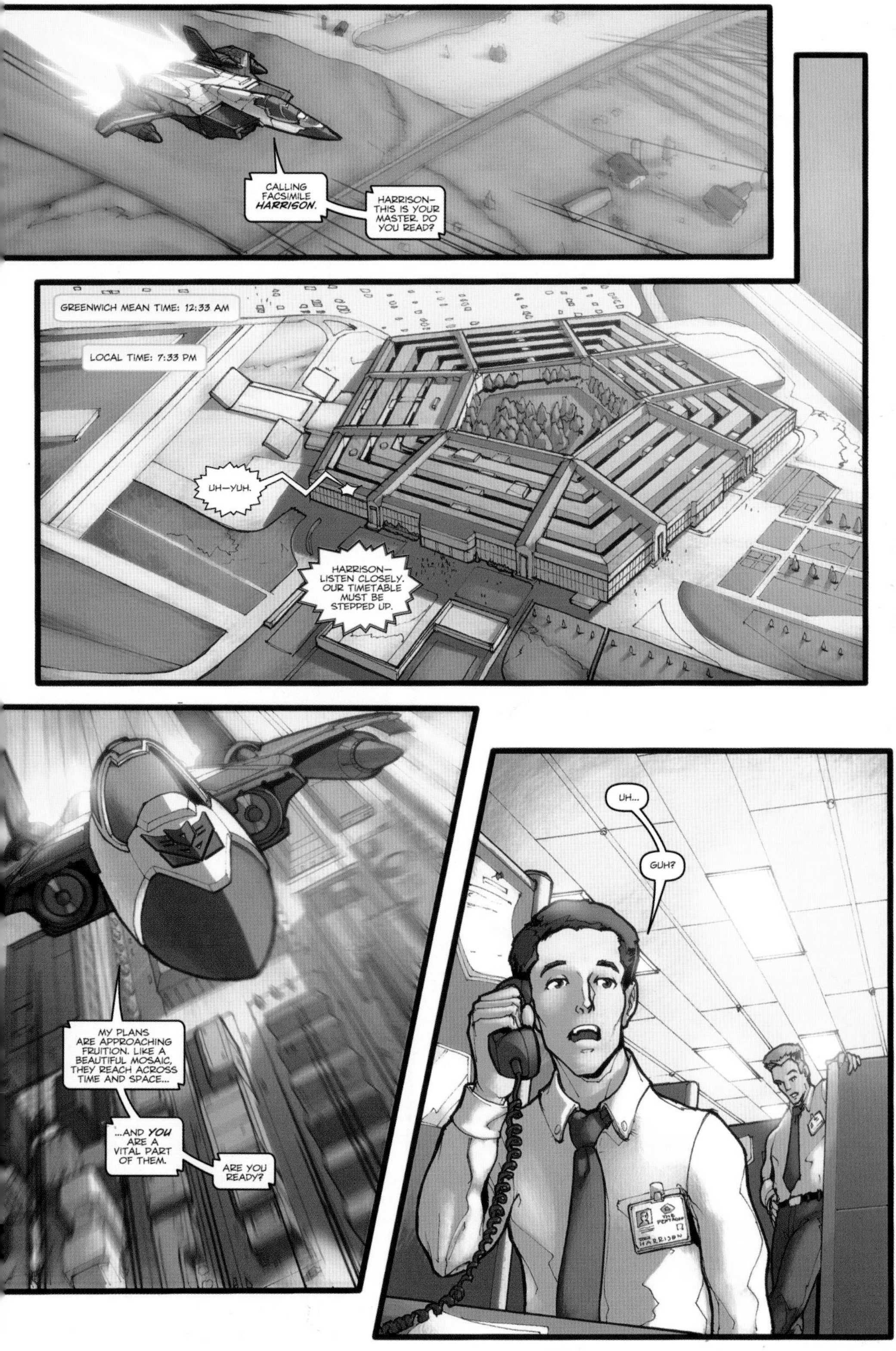
CALLING FACSIMILE *HARRISON*.
HARRISON— THIS IS YOUR MASTER. DO YOU READ?
GREENWICH MEAN TIME: 12:33 AM
LOCAL TIME: 7:33 PM
UH—YUH.
HARRISON— LISTEN CLOSELY. OUR TIMETABLE MUST BE STEPPED UP.
MY PLANS ARE APPROACHING FRUITION. LIKE A BEAUTIFUL MOSAIC, THEY REACH ACROSS TIME AND SPACE...
...AND *YOU* ARE A VITAL PART OF THEM.
ARE YOU READY?
UH...
GUH?

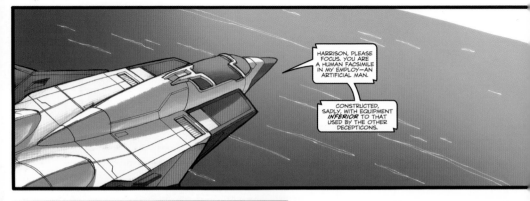

HARRISON, PLEASE FOCUS. YOU ARE A HUMAN FACSIMILE IN MY EMPLOY—AN ARTIFICIAL MAN.

CONSTRUCTED, SADLY, WITH EQUIPMENT *INFERIOR* TO THAT USED BY THE OTHER DECEPTICONS.

NEVERTHELESS, YOUR POSITION ON THE PENTAGON'S CLERICAL STAFF IS CRUCIAL TO MY PLANS.

YUH?

WHAT'S WITH *THAT GUY?*

I HEAR HE'S A NEW HIRE. HOLLYWOOD UNIVERSITY.

AH.

WHEN I GIVE THE WORD—I NEED YOU TO MEET ME AT THE PRE-ARRANGED LOCATION—

—WITH THE REMOTE MISSILE-LAUNCHER CODES YOU ACQUIRED LAST WEEK.

HARRISON: *CAN YOU DO THAT?*

UH...

YUH.

I CAN DO IT.

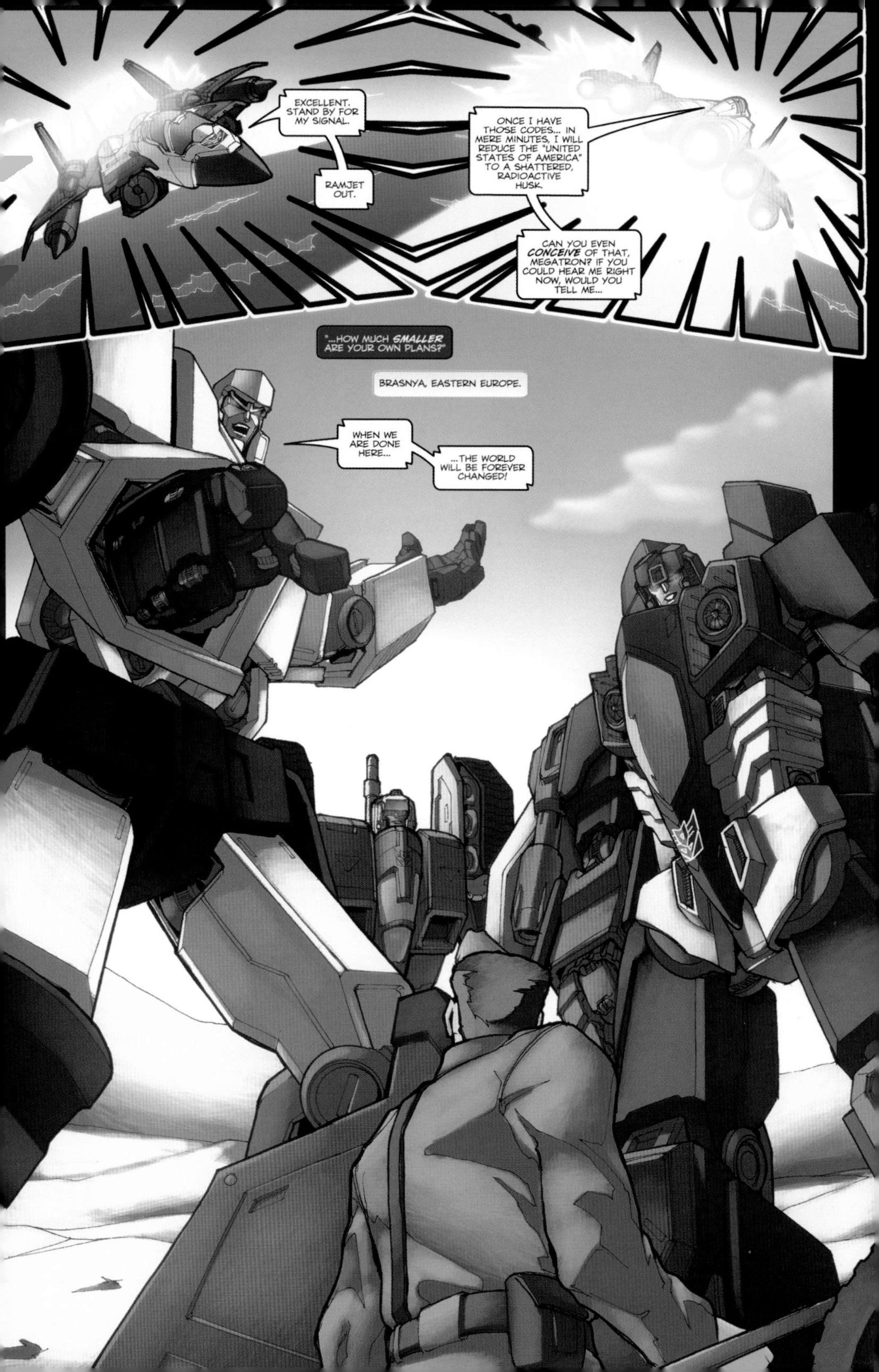
EXCELLENT. STAND BY FOR MY SIGNAL.
RAMJET OUT.
ONCE I HAVE THOSE CODES... IN MERE MINUTES, I WILL REDUCE THE "UNITED STATES OF AMERICA" TO A SHATTERED, RADIOACTIVE HUSK.
CAN YOU EVEN CONCEIVE OF THAT, MEGATRON? IF YOU COULD HEAR ME RIGHT NOW, WOULD YOU TELL ME...
"...HOW MUCH SMALLER ARE YOUR OWN PLANS?"
BRASNYA, EASTERN EUROPE.
WHEN WE ARE DONE HERE...
...THE WORLD WILL BE FOREVER CHANGED!

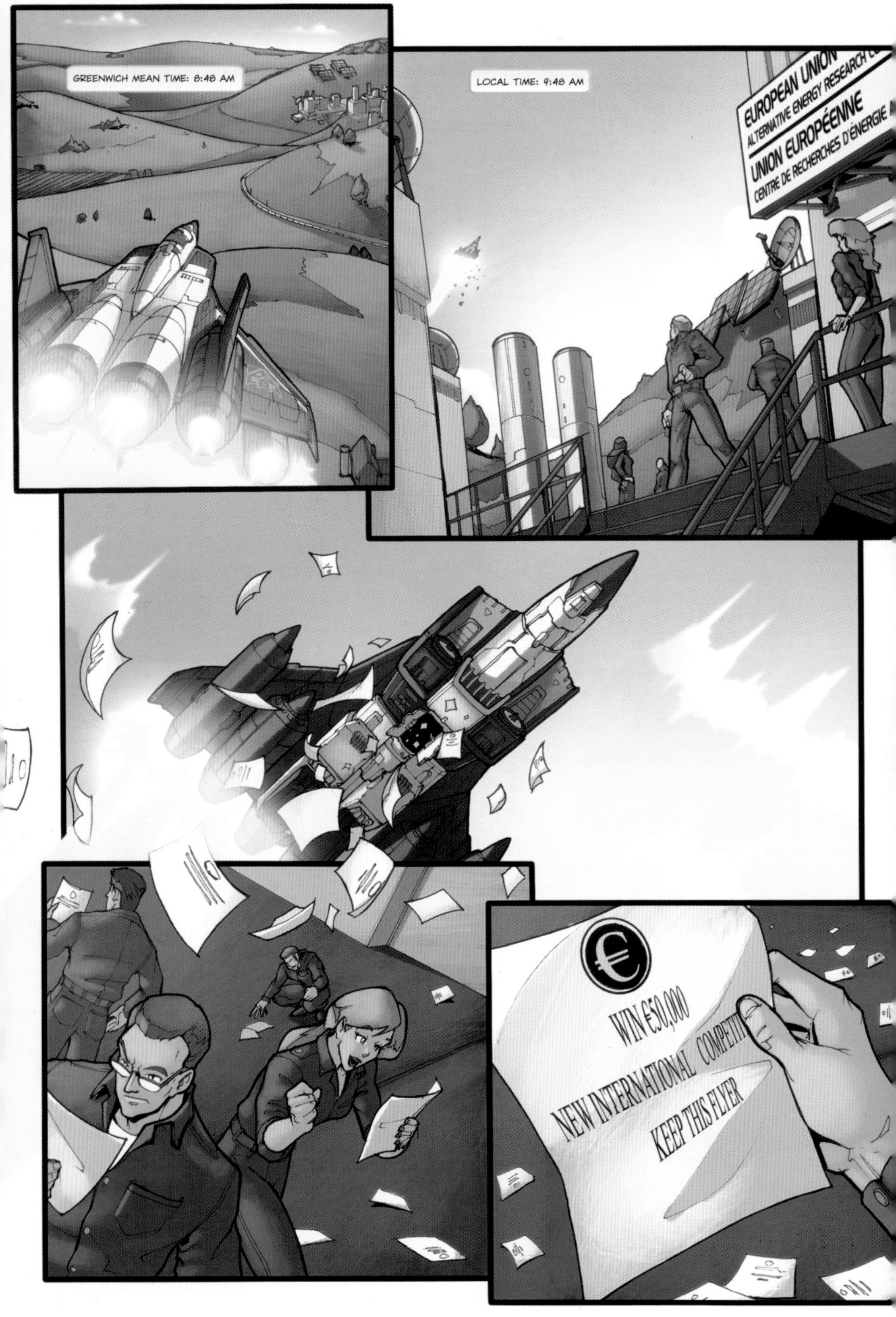

GREENWICH MEAN TIME: 8:48 AM
LOCAL TIME: 9:48 AM
EUROPEAN UNION
ALTERNATIVE ENERGY RESEARCH
UNION EUROPÉENNE
CENTRE DE RECHERCHES D'ÉNERGIE
WIN €50,000
NEW INTERNATIONAL COMPETITI
KEEP THIS FLYER

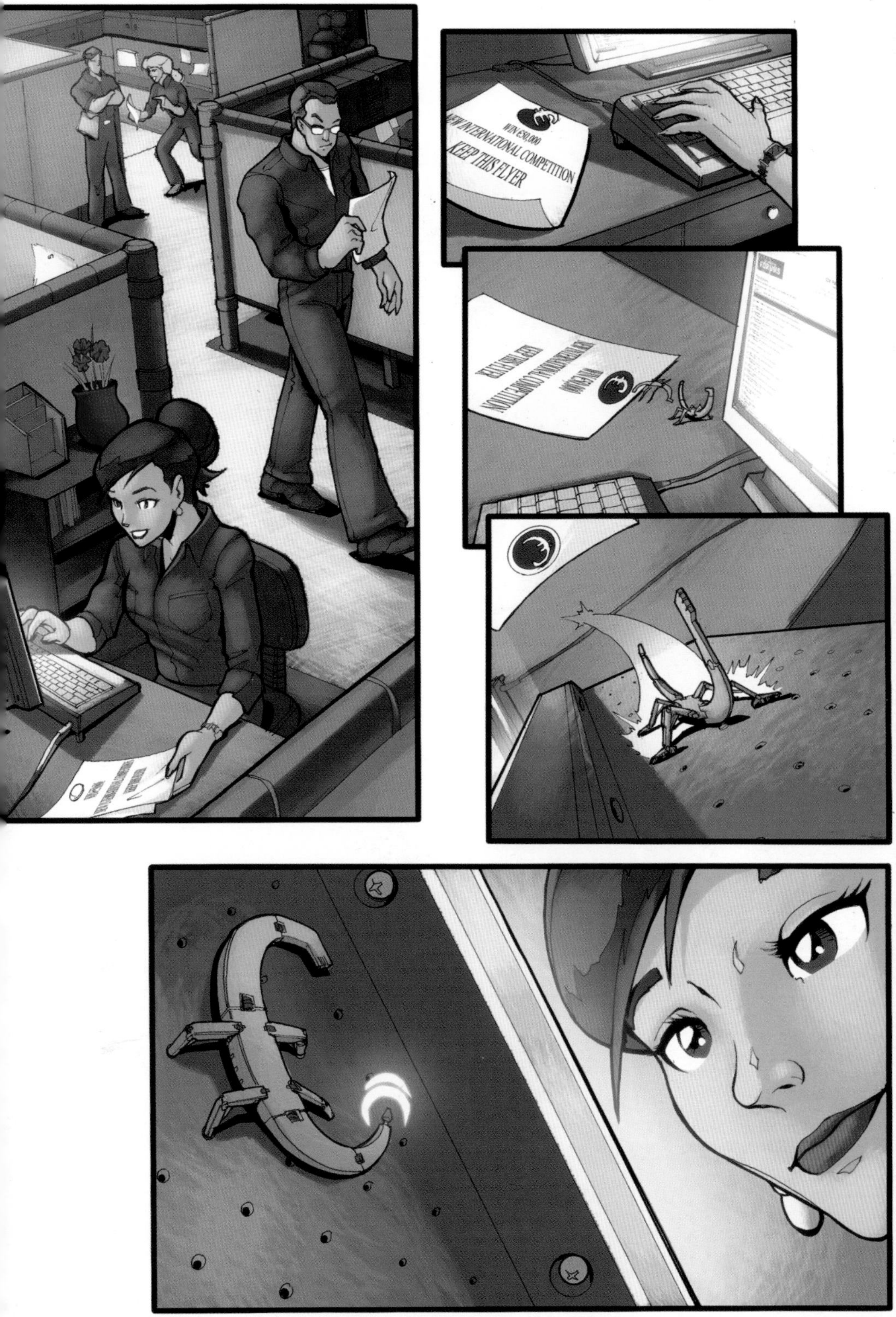
WIN €50,000
NEW INTERNATIONAL COMPETITION
KEEP THIS FLYER

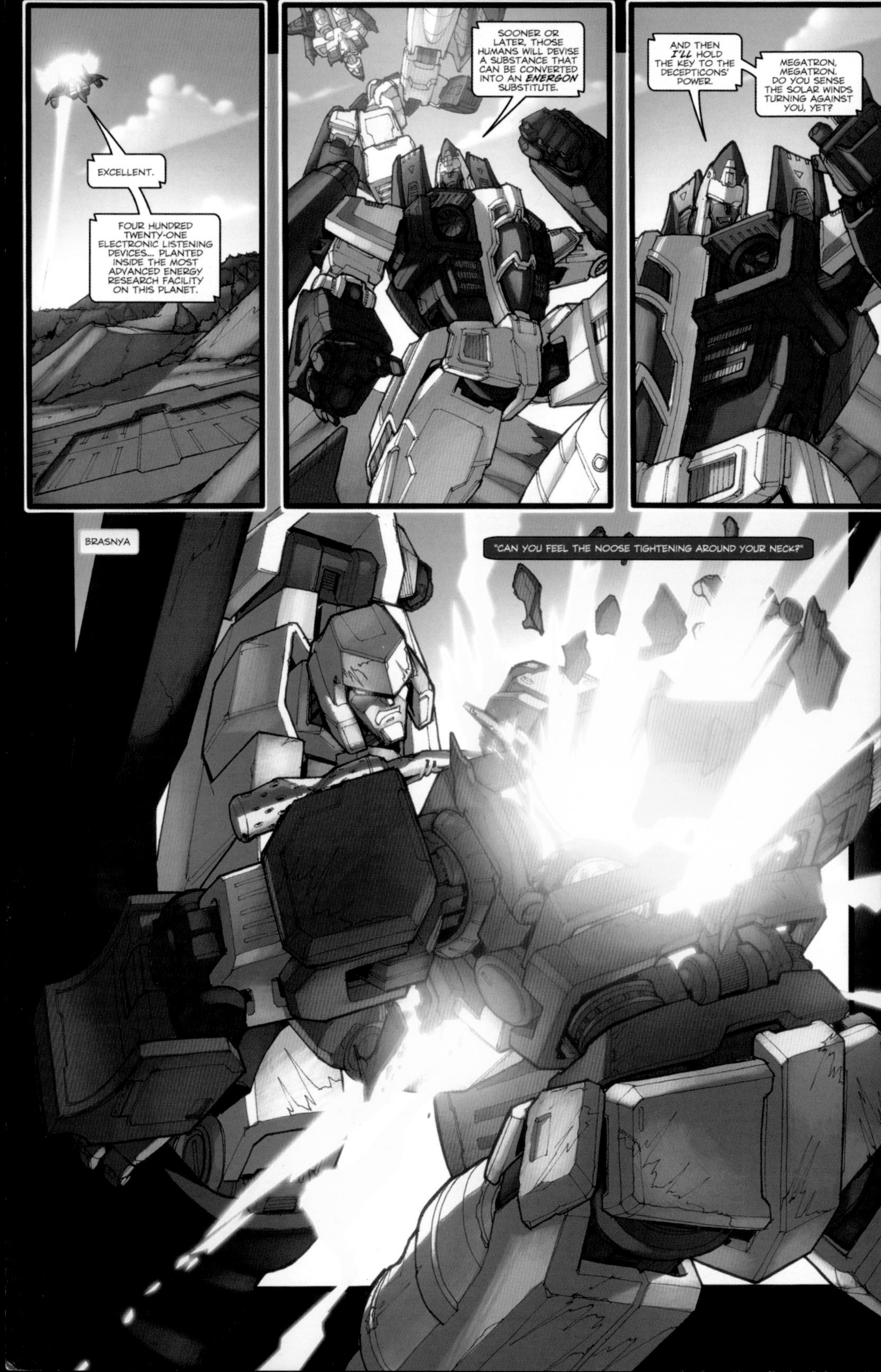
EXCELLENT.
FOUR HUNDRED TWENTY-ONE ELECTRONIC LISTENING DEVICES... PLANTED INSIDE THE MOST ADVANCED ENERGY RESEARCH FACILITY ON THIS PLANET.
SOONER OR LATER, THOSE HUMANS WILL DEVISE A SUBSTANCE THAT CAN BE CONVERTED INTO AN ENERGON SUBSTITUTE.
AND THEN I'LL HOLD THE KEY TO THE DECEPTICONS' POWER.
MEGATRON, MEGATRON. DO YOU SENSE THE SOLAR WINDS TURNING AGAINST YOU, YET?
BRASNYA
"CAN YOU FEEL THE NOOSE TIGHTENING AROUND YOUR NECK?"

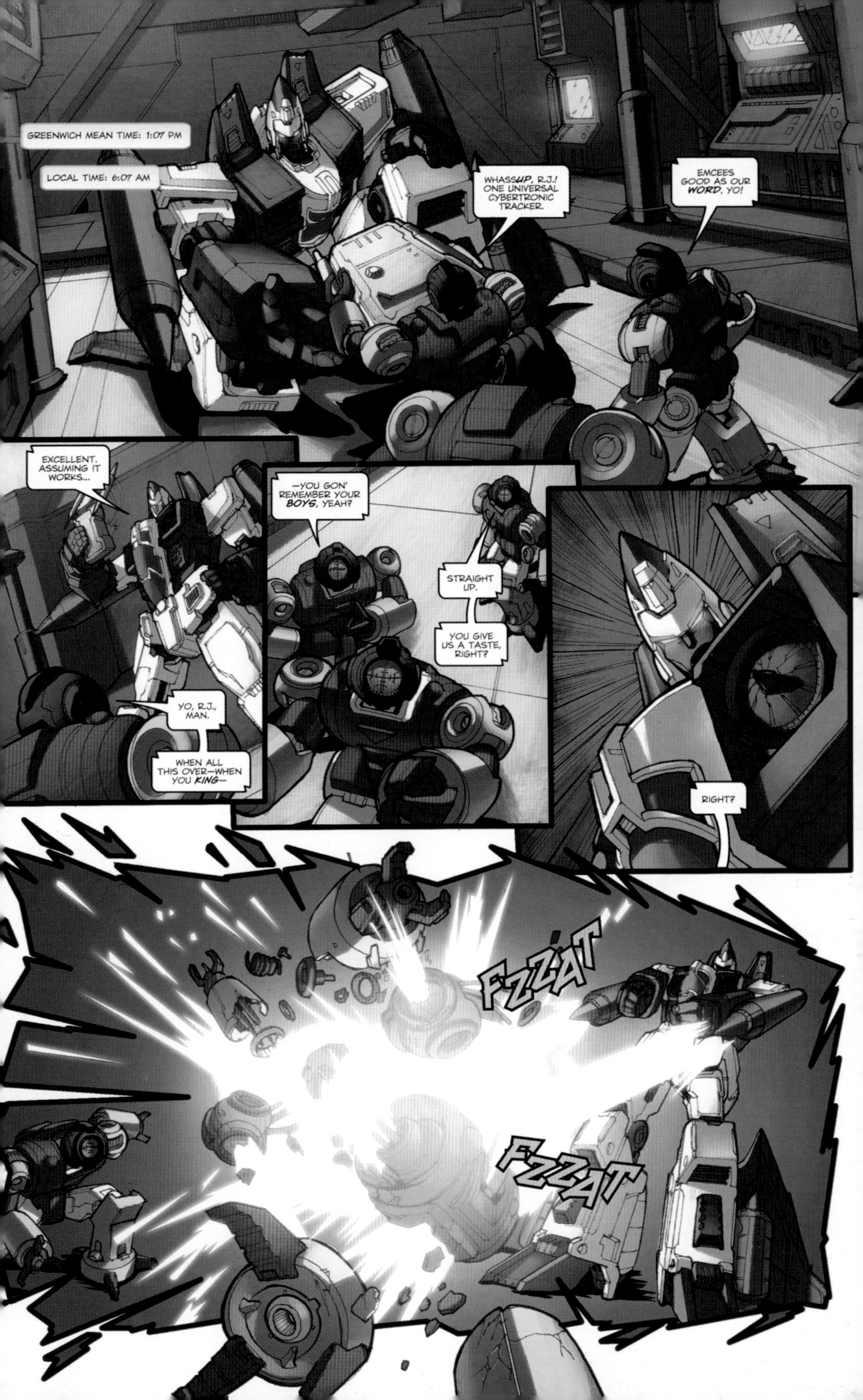
GREENWICH MEAN TIME: 1:07 PM
LOCAL TIME: 6:07 AM
WHASSUP, R.J.! ONE UNIVERSAL CYBERTRONIC TRACKER.
EMCEES GOOD AS OUR WORD, YO!
EXCELLENT. ASSUMING IT WORKS...
YO, R.J., MAN.
WHEN ALL THIS OVER—WHEN YOU KING—
—YOU GON' REMEMBER YOUR BOYS, YEAH?
STRAIGHT UP.
YOU GIVE US A TASTE, RIGHT?
RIGHT?
FZZAT
FZZAT

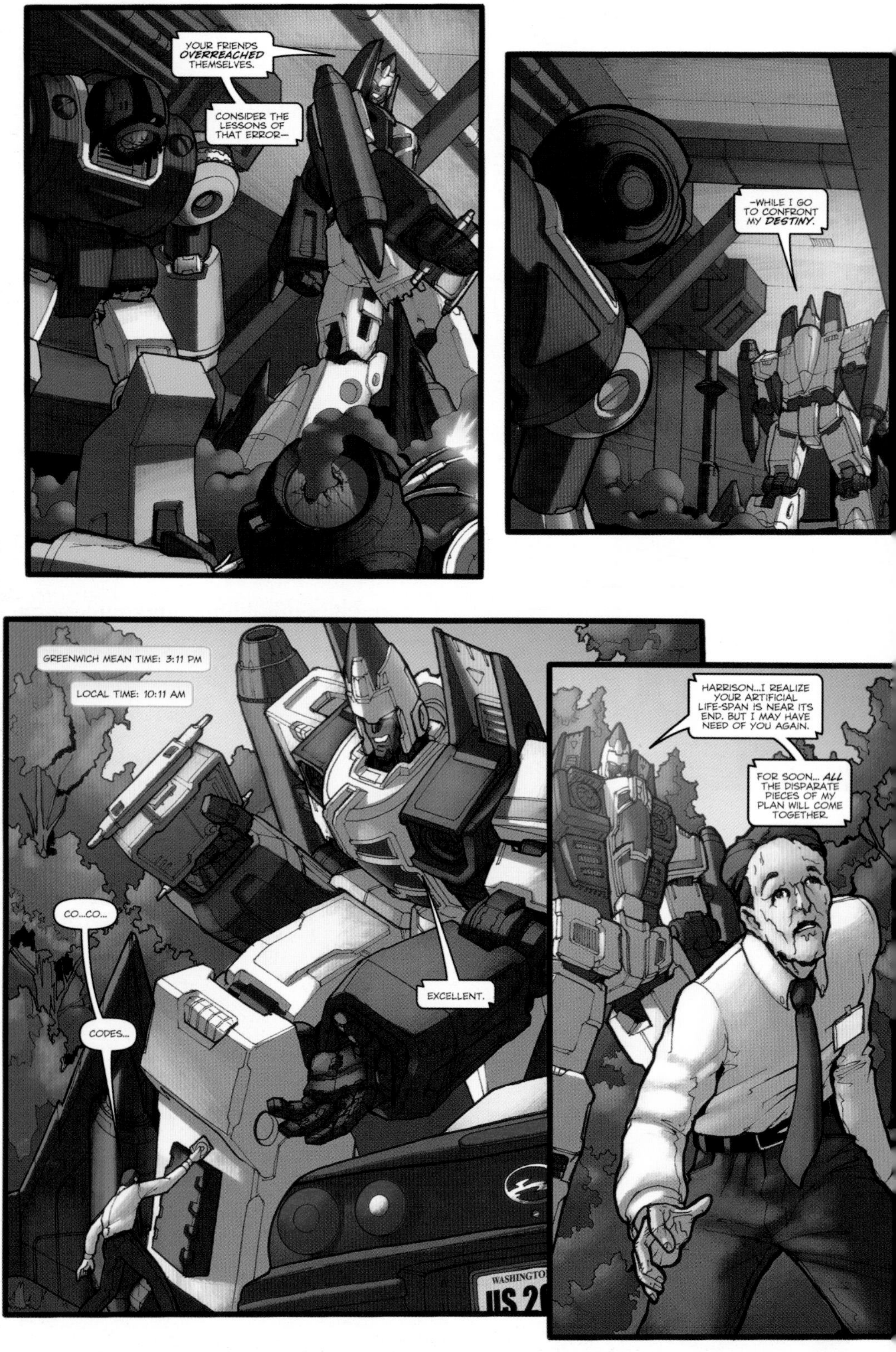
YOUR FRIENDS OVERREACHED THEMSELVES.
CONSIDER THE LESSONS OF THAT ERROR—
—WHILE I GO TO CONFRONT MY DESTINY.
GREENWICH MEAN TIME: 3:11 PM
LOCAL TIME: 10:11 AM
CO...CO...
CODES...
EXCELLENT.
WASHINGTON
HARRISON...I REALIZE YOUR ARTIFICIAL LIFE-SPAN IS NEAR ITS END. BUT I MAY HAVE NEED OF YOU AGAIN.
FOR SOON... ALL THE DISPARATE PIECES OF MY PLAN WILL COME TOGETHER.

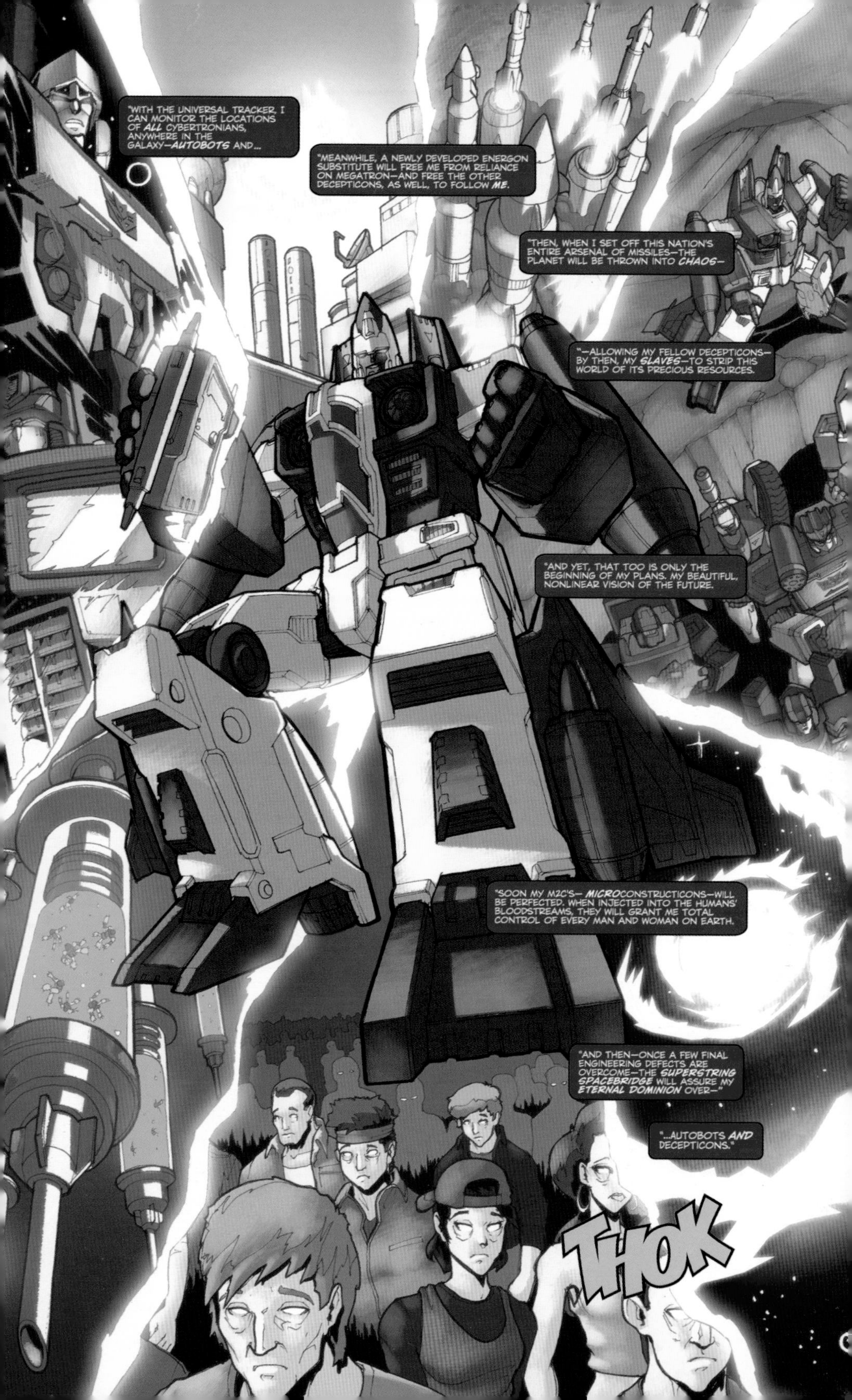
"WITH THE UNIVERSAL TRACKER, I CAN MONITOR THE LOCATIONS OF ALL CYBERTRONIANS, ANYWHERE IN THE GALAXY—AUTOBOTS AND...
"MEANWHILE, A NEWLY DEVELOPED ENERGON SUBSTITUTE WILL FREE ME FROM RELIANCE ON MEGATRON—AND FREE THE OTHER DECEPTICONS, AS WELL, TO FOLLOW ME.
"THEN, WHEN I SET OFF THIS NATION'S ENTIRE ARSENAL OF MISSILES—THE PLANET WILL BE THROWN INTO CHAOS—
"—ALLOWING MY FELLOW DECEPTICONS—BY THEN, MY SLAVES—TO STRIP THIS WORLD OF ITS PRECIOUS RESOURCES.
"AND YET, THAT TOO IS ONLY THE BEGINNING OF MY PLANS. MY BEAUTIFUL, NONLINEAR VISION OF THE FUTURE.
"SOON MY M2C'S— MICROCONSTRUCTICONS—WILL BE PERFECTED. WHEN INJECTED INTO THE HUMANS' BLOODSTREAMS, THEY WILL GRANT ME TOTAL CONTROL OF EVERY MAN AND WOMAN ON EARTH.
"AND THEN—ONCE A FEW FINAL ENGINEERING DEFECTS ARE OVERCOME—THE SUPERSTRING SPACEBRIDGE WILL ASSURE MY ETERNAL DOMINION OVER—"
"...AUTOBOTS AND DECEPTICONS."
THOK

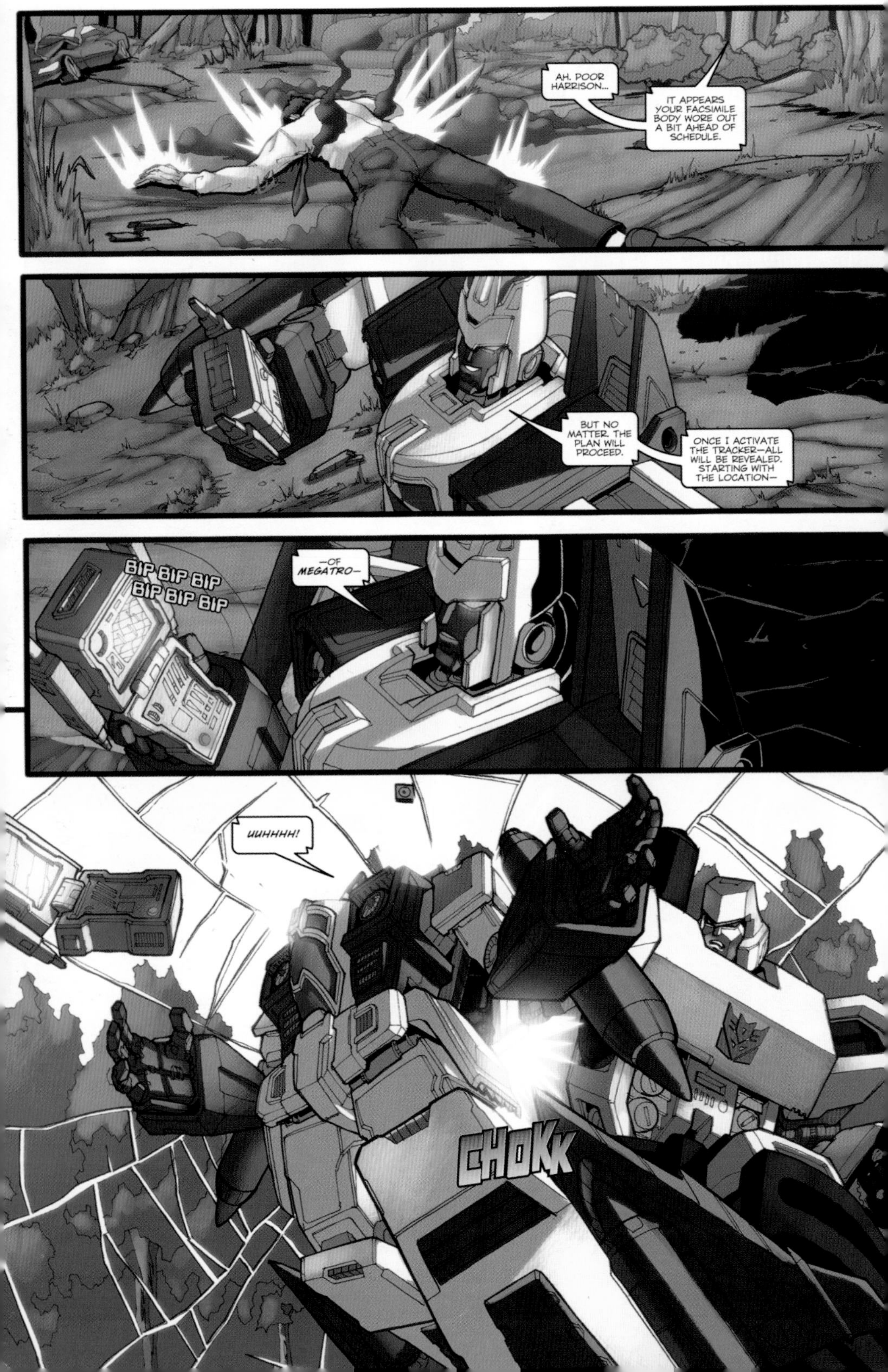
AH. POOR HARRISON...
IT APPEARS YOUR FACSIMILE BODY WORE OUT A BIT AHEAD OF SCHEDULE.
BUT NO MATTER. THE PLAN WILL PROCEED.
ONCE I ACTIVATE THE TRACKER—ALL WILL BE REVEALED. STARTING WITH THE LOCATION—
BIP BIP BIP BIP BIP BIP
—OF MEGATRO—
UUHHHH!
CHOKK

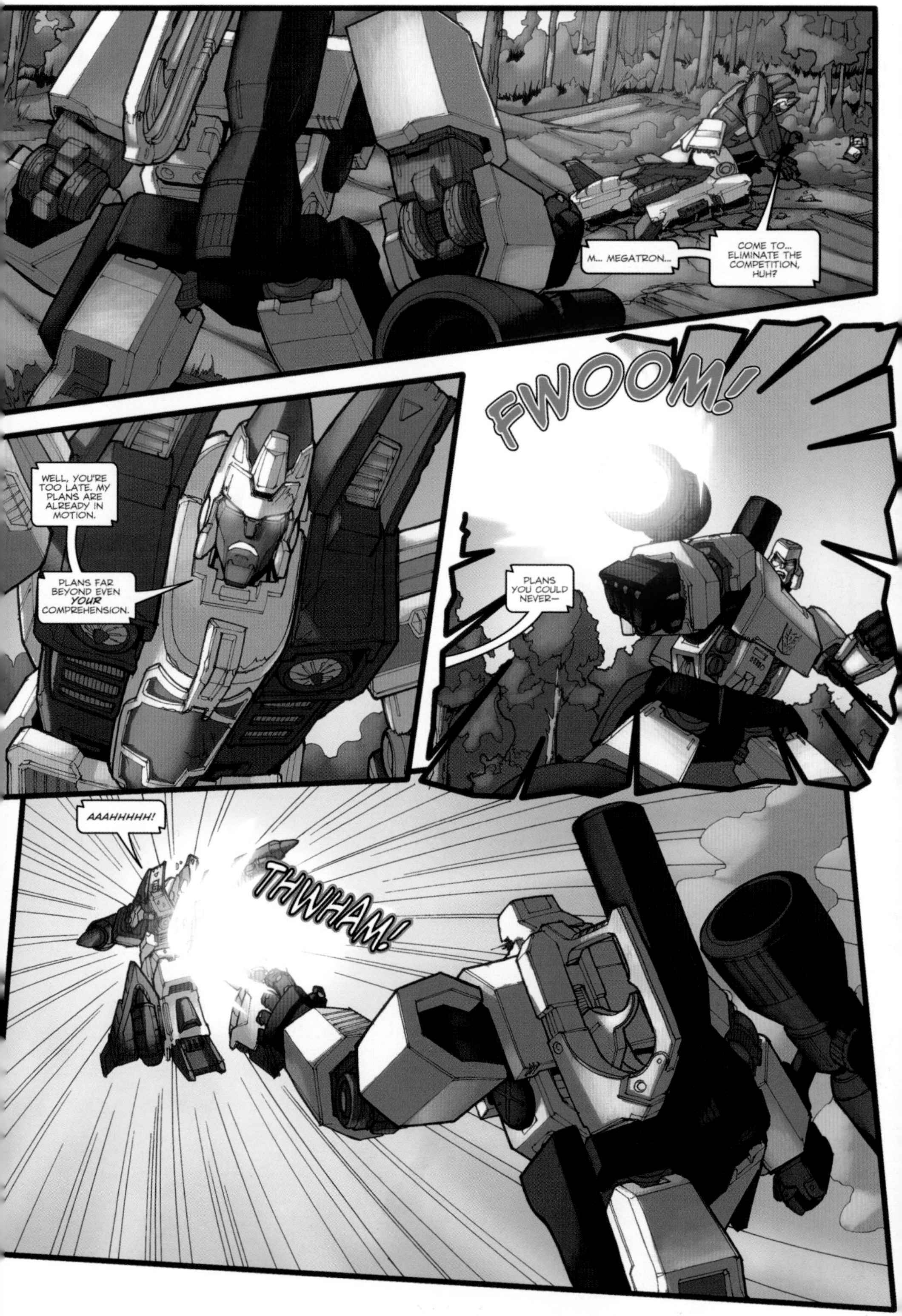
M... MEGATRON...
COME TO... ELIMINATE THE COMPETITION, HUH?
WELL, YOU'RE TOO LATE. MY PLANS ARE ALREADY IN MOTION.
PLANS FAR BEYOND EVEN *YOUR* COMPREHENSION.
FWOOM!
PLANS YOU COULD NEVER—
AAAHHHHH!
THWHAM!

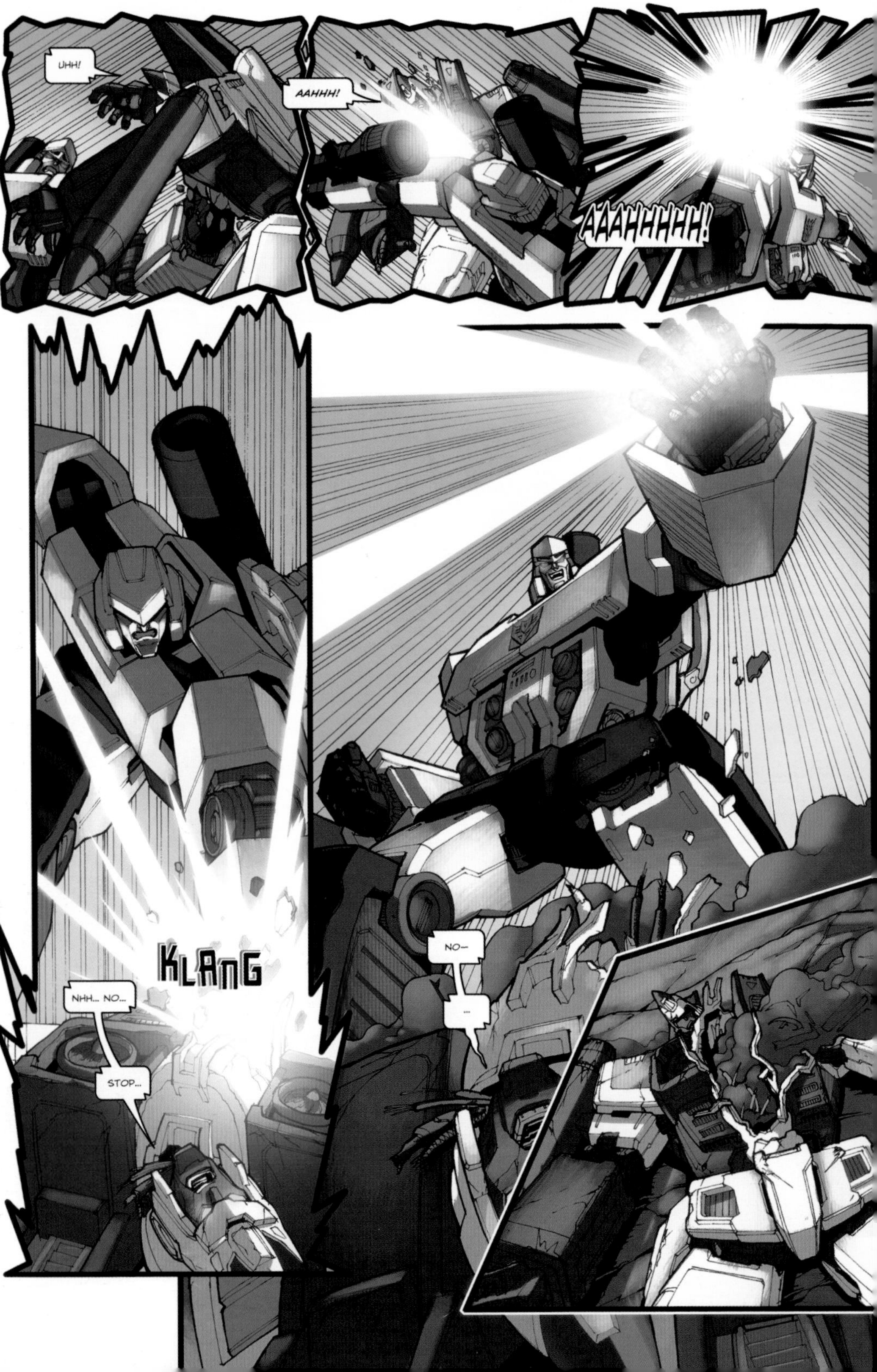
UHH!
AAHHH!
AAAHHHHH!
KLANG
NHH... NO...
STOP...
NO—
...

GREENWICH MEAN TIME: 5:32 PM

LOCAL TIME: 12:32 PM

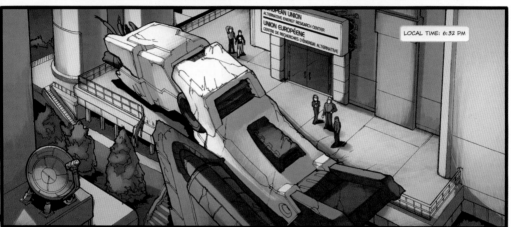

EUROPEAN UNION
ALTERNATIVE ENERGY RESEARCH CENTER
UNION EUROPÉENE
CENTRE DE RECHERCHES D'ÉNERGIE ALTERNATIVE

LOCAL TIME: 6:32 PM

LOCAL TIME: 10:32 AM

HARSH.

"PLANS ARE GREAT. LINEAR, NONLINEAR... FACSIMILES, ENERGON, STARBRIDGES...

"BUT NO MATTER HOW MUCH YOU PLAN, THE OLD SAYING'S STILL TRUE..."

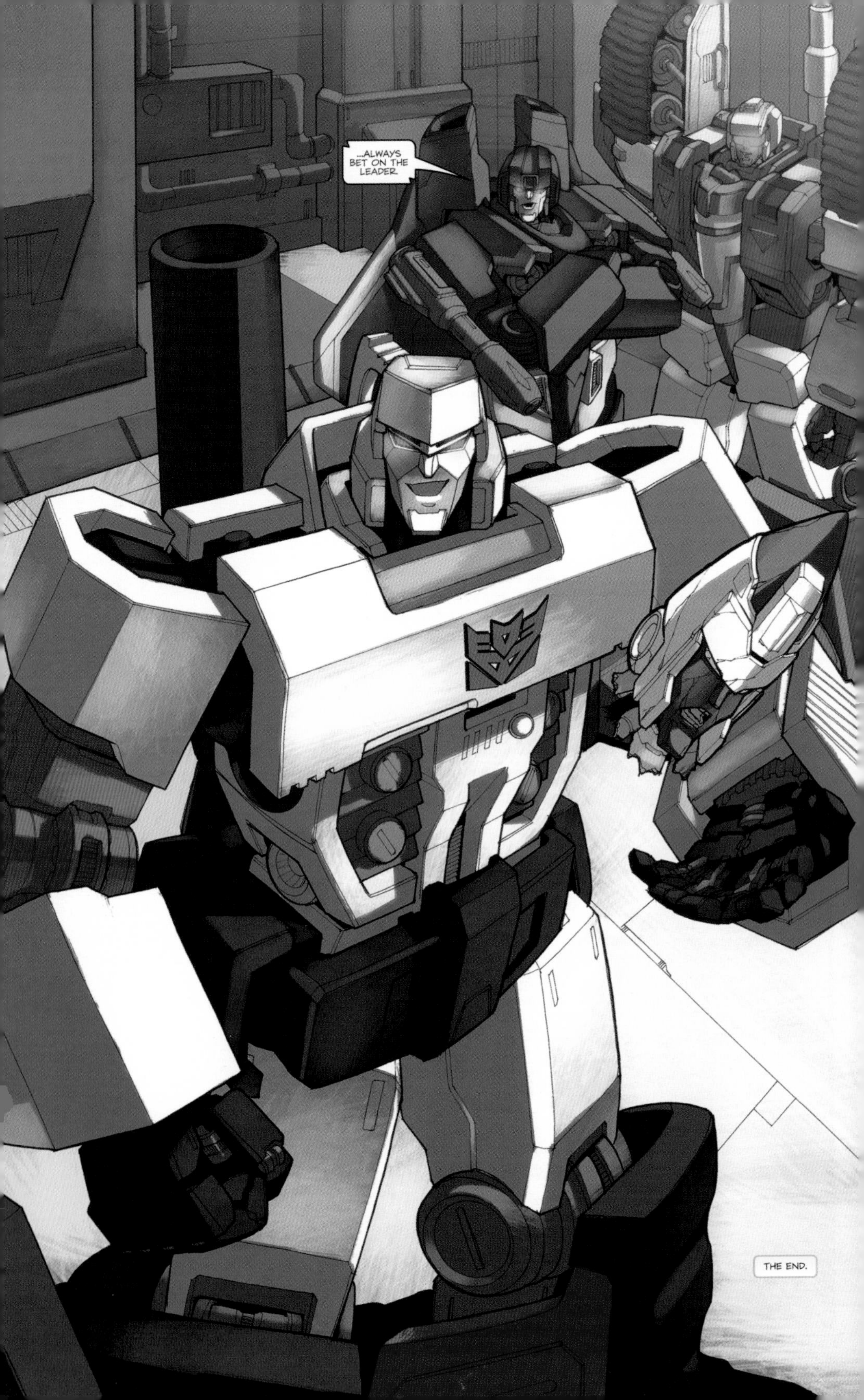
...ALWAYS BET ON THE LEADER.
THE END.

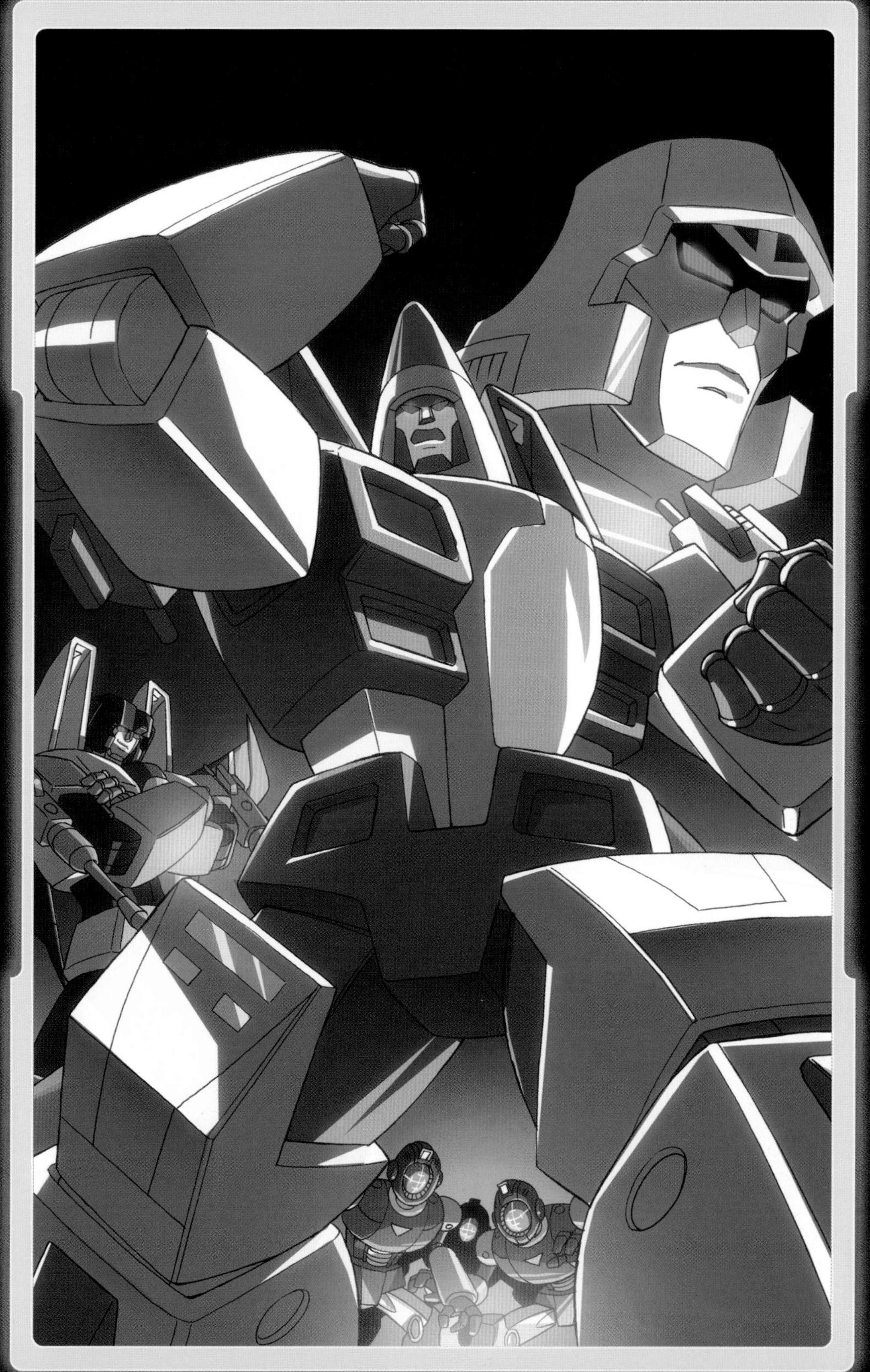

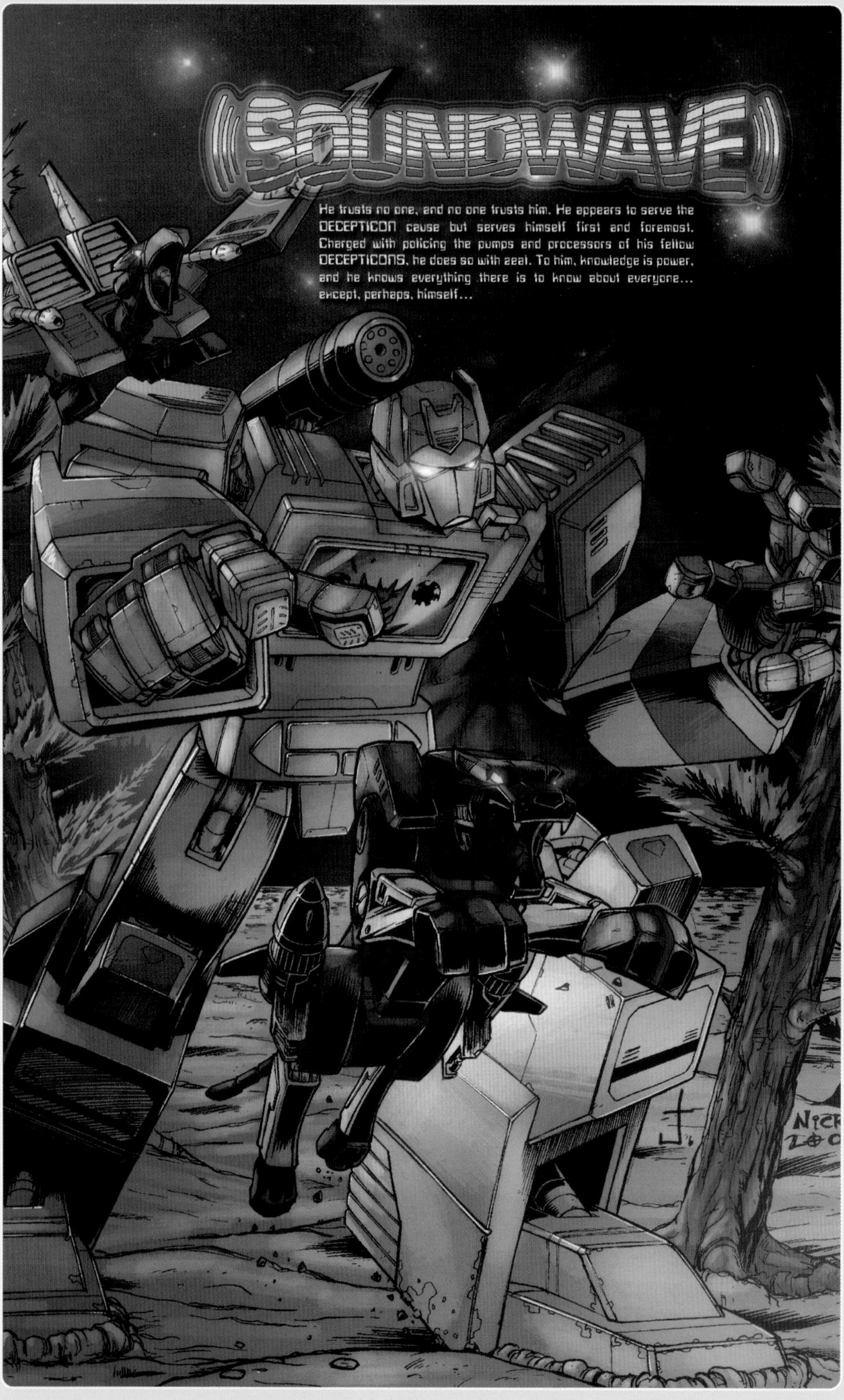
SOUNDWAVE
He trusts no one, and no one trusts him. He appears to serve the DECEPTICON cause but serves himself first and foremost. Charged with policing the pumps and processors of his fellow DECEPTICONS, he does so with zeal. To him, knowledge is power, and he knows everything there is to know about everyone... except, perhaps, himself...

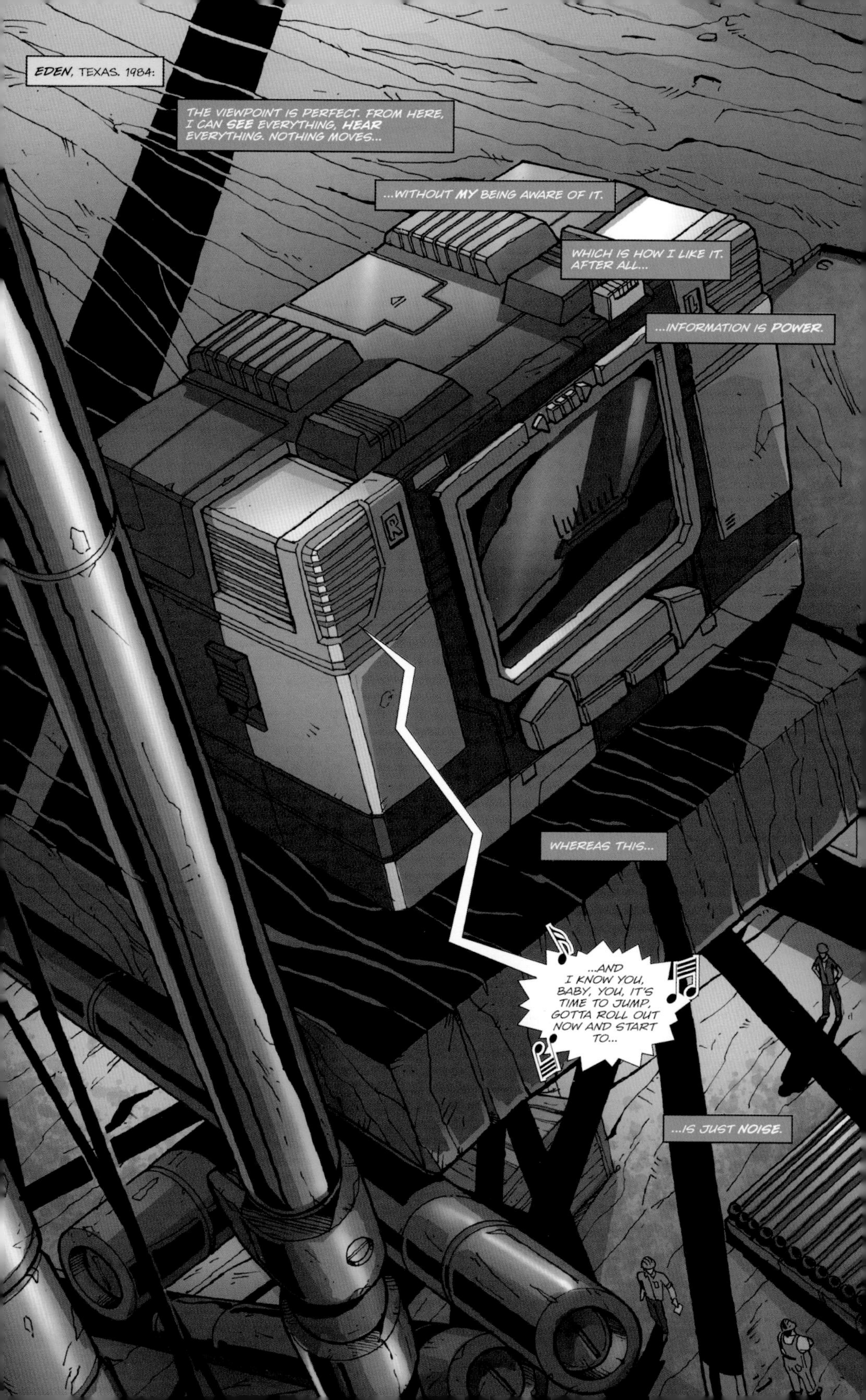
EDEN, TEXAS. 1984:
THE VIEWPOINT IS PERFECT. FROM HERE, I CAN SEE EVERYTHING, HEAR EVERYTHING. NOTHING MOVES...
...WITHOUT MY BEING AWARE OF IT.
WHICH IS HOW I LIKE IT. AFTER ALL...
...INFORMATION IS POWER.
WHEREAS THIS...
...AND I KNOW YOU, BABY, YOU, IT'S TIME TO JUMP, GOTTA ROLL OUT NOW AND START TO...
...IS JUST NOISE.

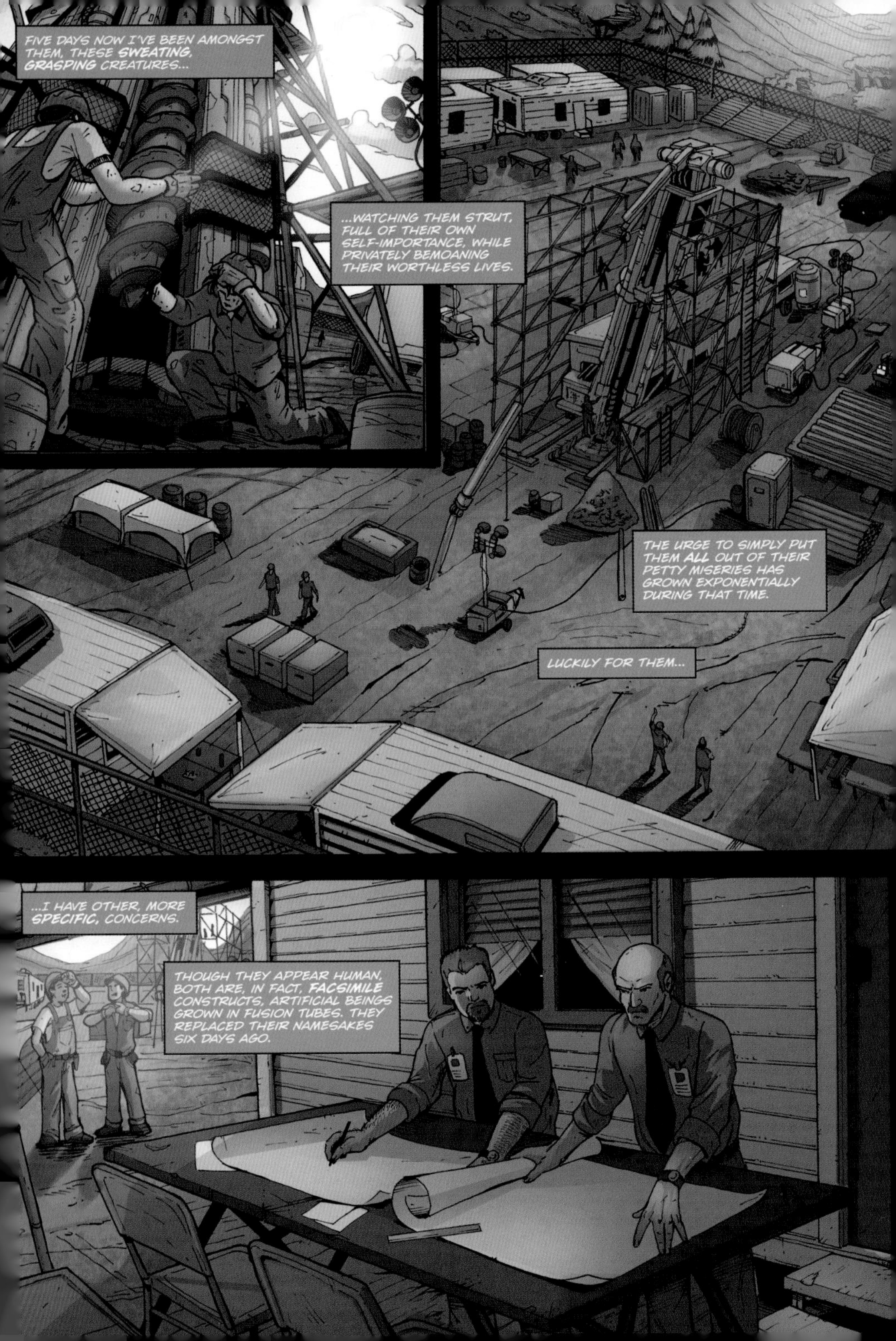
FIVE DAYS NOW I'VE BEEN AMONGST THEM, THESE SWEATING, GRASPING CREATURES...
...WATCHING THEM STRUT, FULL OF THEIR OWN SELF-IMPORTANCE, WHILE PRIVATELY BEMOANING THEIR WORTHLESS LIVES.
THE URGE TO SIMPLY PUT THEM ALL OUT OF THEIR PETTY MISERIES HAS GROWN EXPONENTIALLY DURING THAT TIME.
LUCKILY FOR THEM...
...I HAVE OTHER, MORE SPECIFIC, CONCERNS.
THOUGH THEY APPEAR HUMAN, BOTH ARE, IN FACT, FACSIMILE CONSTRUCTS, ARTIFICIAL BEINGS GROWN IN FUSION TUBES. THEY REPLACED THEIR NAMESAKES SIX DAYS AGO.

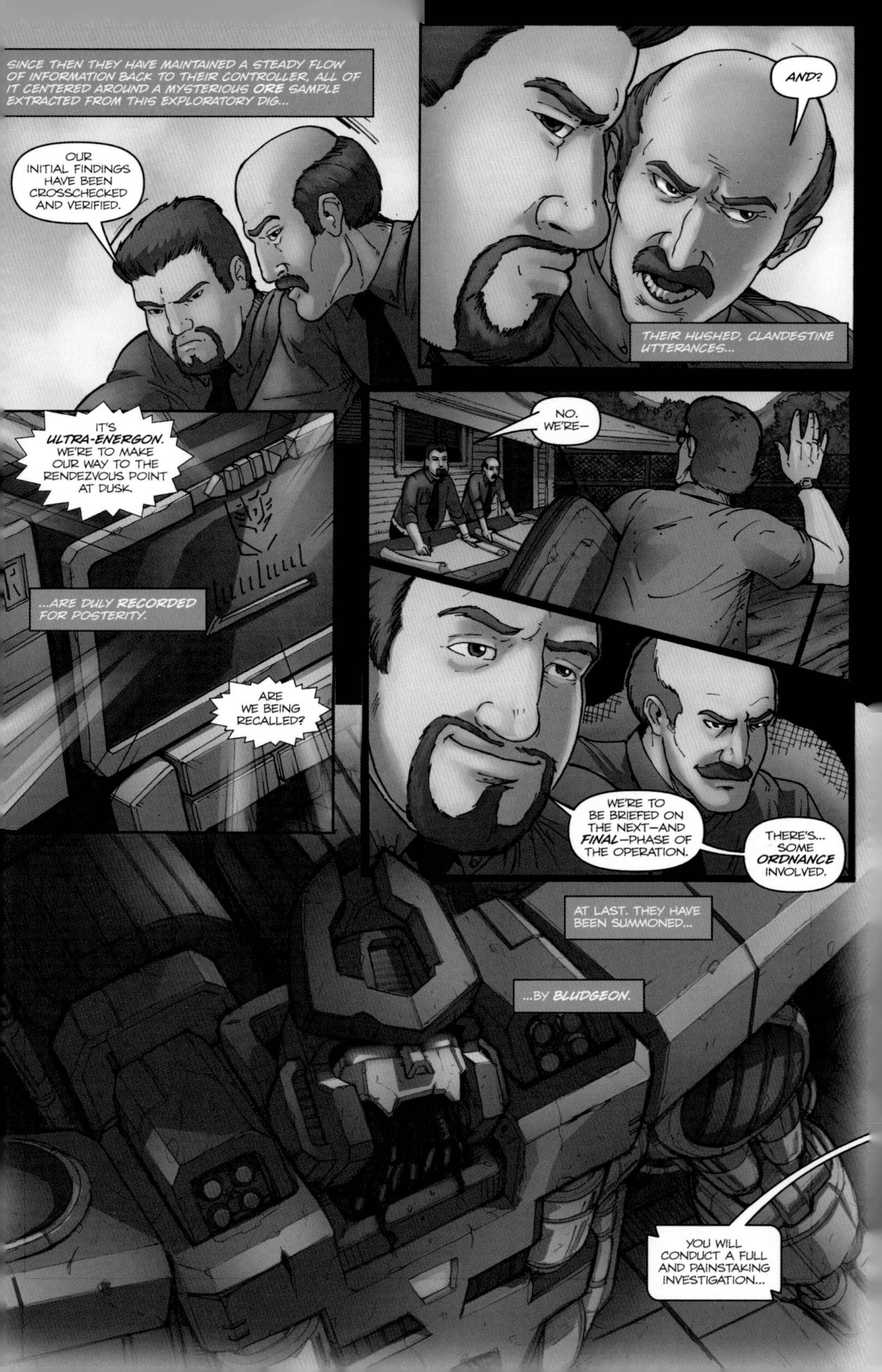
SINCE THEN THEY HAVE MAINTAINED A STEADY FLOW OF INFORMATION BACK TO THEIR CONTROLLER, ALL OF IT CENTERED AROUND A MYSTERIOUS ORE SAMPLE EXTRACTED FROM THIS EXPLORATORY DIG...
OUR INITIAL FINDINGS HAVE BEEN CROSSCHECKED AND VERIFIED.
AND?
THEIR HUSHED, CLANDESTINE UTTERANCES...
IT'S ULTRA-ENERGON. WE'RE TO MAKE OUR WAY TO THE RENDEZVOUS POINT AT DUSK.
...ARE DULY RECORDED FOR POSTERITY.
ARE WE BEING RECALLED?
NO. WE'RE—
WE'RE TO BE BRIEFED ON THE NEXT—AND FINAL—PHASE OF THE OPERATION.
THERE'S... SOME ORDNANCE INVOLVED.
AT LAST. THEY HAVE BEEN SUMMONED...
...BY BLUDGEON.
YOU WILL CONDUCT A FULL AND PAINSTAKING INVESTIGATION...

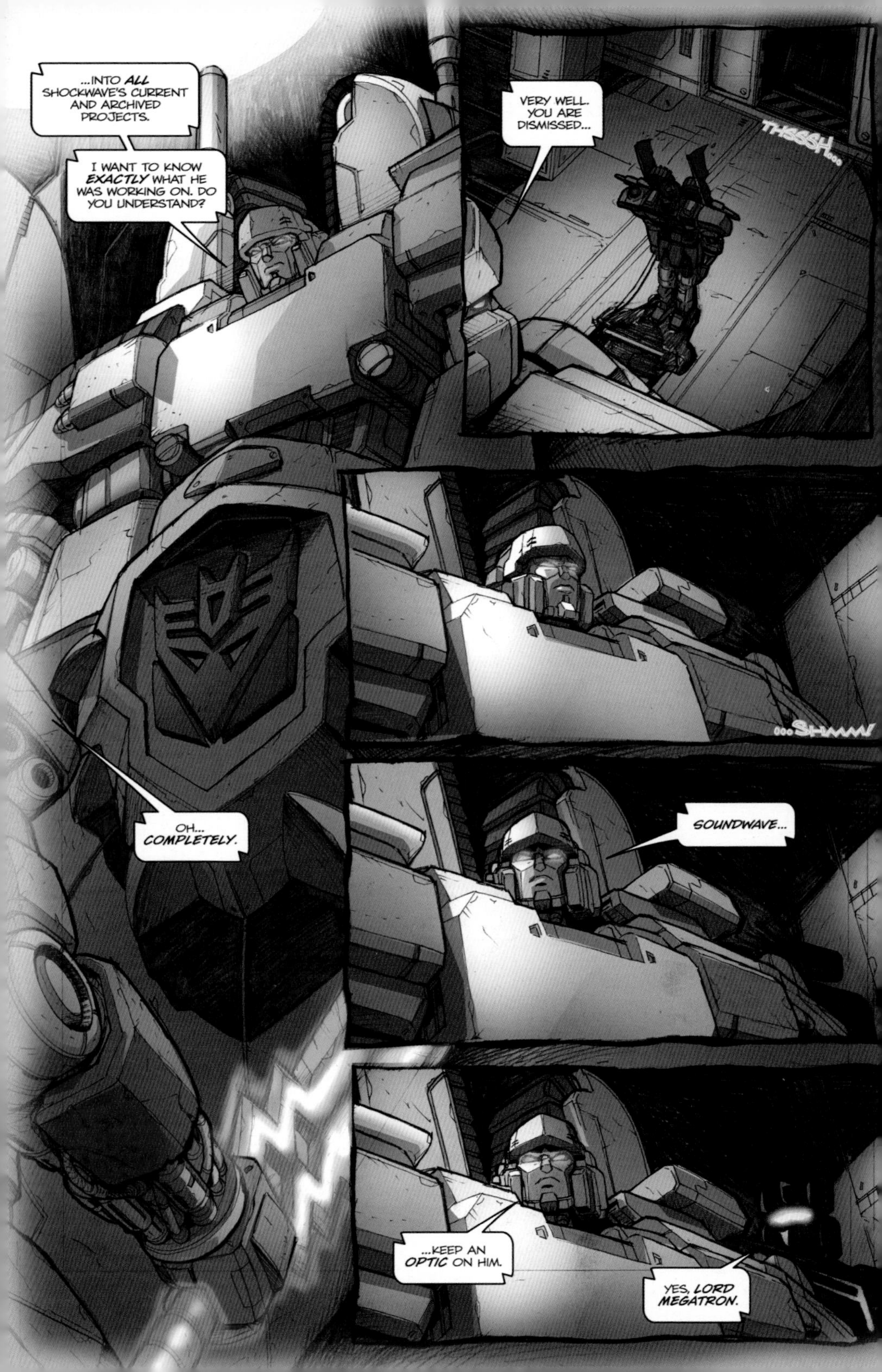

...INTO ALL SHOCKWAVE'S CURRENT AND ARCHIVED PROJECTS.
I WANT TO KNOW EXACTLY WHAT HE WAS WORKING ON. DO YOU UNDERSTAND?
OH... COMPLETELY.
VERY WELL. YOU ARE DISMISSED...
THSSSH...
...SHMM!
SOUNDWAVE...
...KEEP AN OPTIC ON HIM.
YES, LORD MEGATRON.

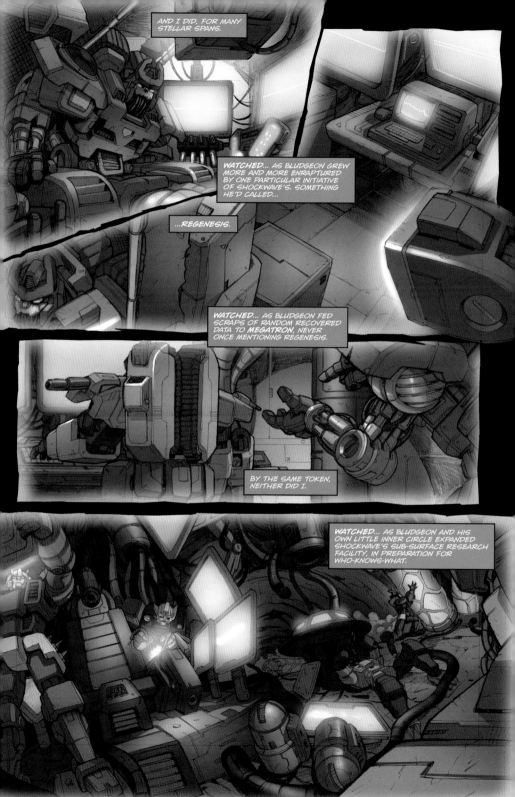

AND I DID, FOR MANY STELLAR SPANS.

WATCHED... AS BLUDGEON GREW MORE AND MORE ENRAPTURED BY ONE PARTICULAR INITIATIVE OF SHOCKWAVE'S. SOMETHING HE'D CALLED...

...REGENESIS.

WATCHED... AS BLUDGEON FED SCRAPS OF RANDOM RECOVERED DATA TO *MEGATRON*, NEVER ONCE MENTIONING REGENESIS.

BY THE SAME TOKEN, NEITHER DID I.

WATCHED... AS BLUDGEON AND HIS OWN LITTLE INNER CIRCLE EXPANDED SHOCKWAVE'S SUB-SURFACE RESEARCH FACILITY, IN PREPARATION FOR WHO-KNOWS-WHAT.

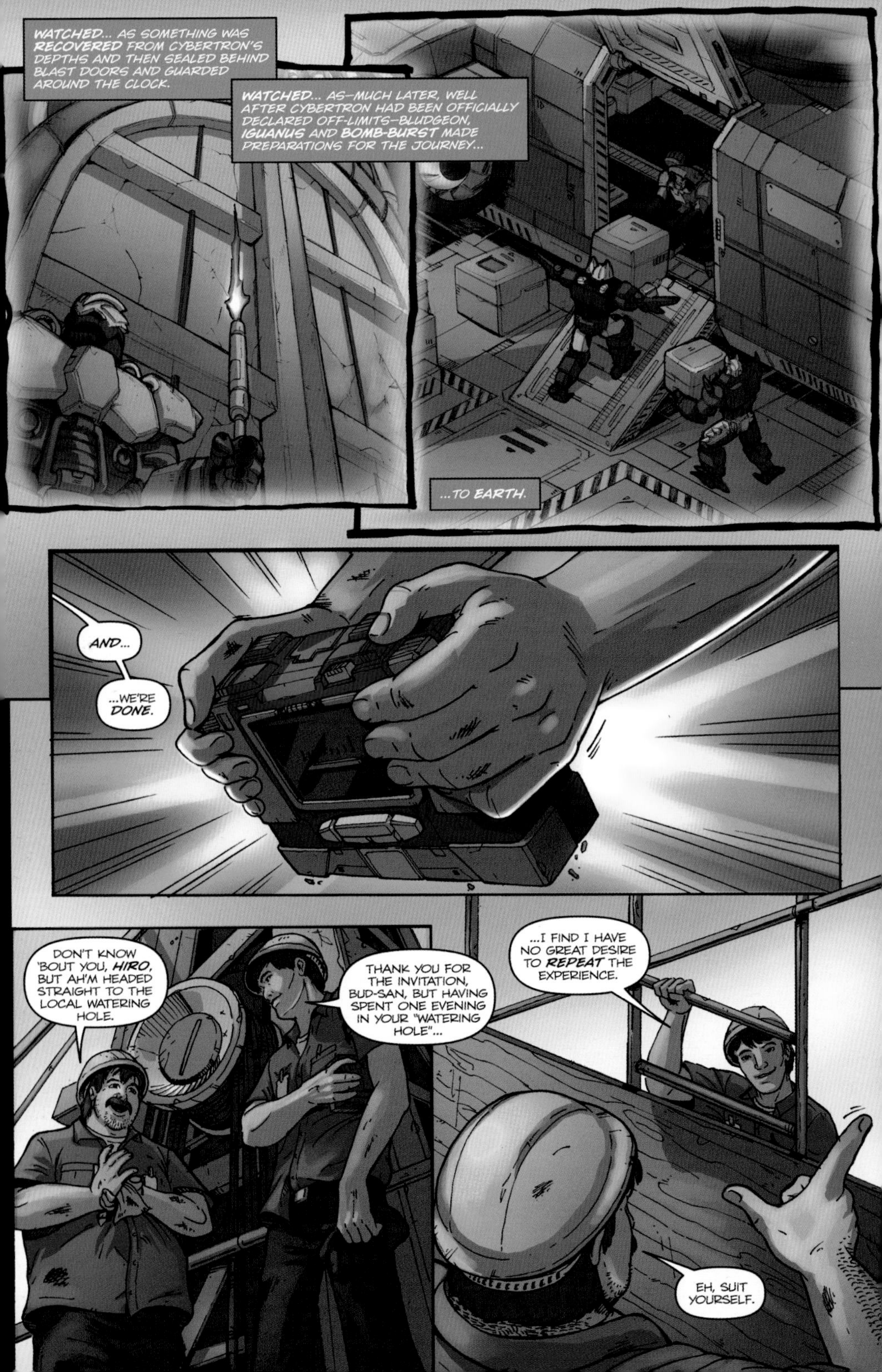
WATCHED... AS SOMETHING WAS RECOVERED FROM CYBERTRON'S DEPTHS AND THEN SEALED BEHIND BLAST DOORS AND GUARDED AROUND THE CLOCK.
WATCHED... AS—MUCH LATER, WELL AFTER CYBERTRON HAD BEEN OFFICIALLY DECLARED OFF-LIMITS—BLUDGEON, IGUANUS AND BOMB-BURST MADE PREPARATIONS FOR THE JOURNEY...
...TO EARTH.
AND...
...WE'RE DONE.
DON'T KNOW 'BOUT YOU, HIRO, BUT AH'M HEADED STRAIGHT TO THE LOCAL WATERING HOLE.
THANK YOU FOR THE INVITATION, BUD-SAN, BUT HAVING SPENT ONE EVENING IN YOUR "WATERING HOLE"...
...I FIND I HAVE NO GREAT DESIRE TO REPEAT THE EXPERIENCE.
EH, SUIT YOURSELF.

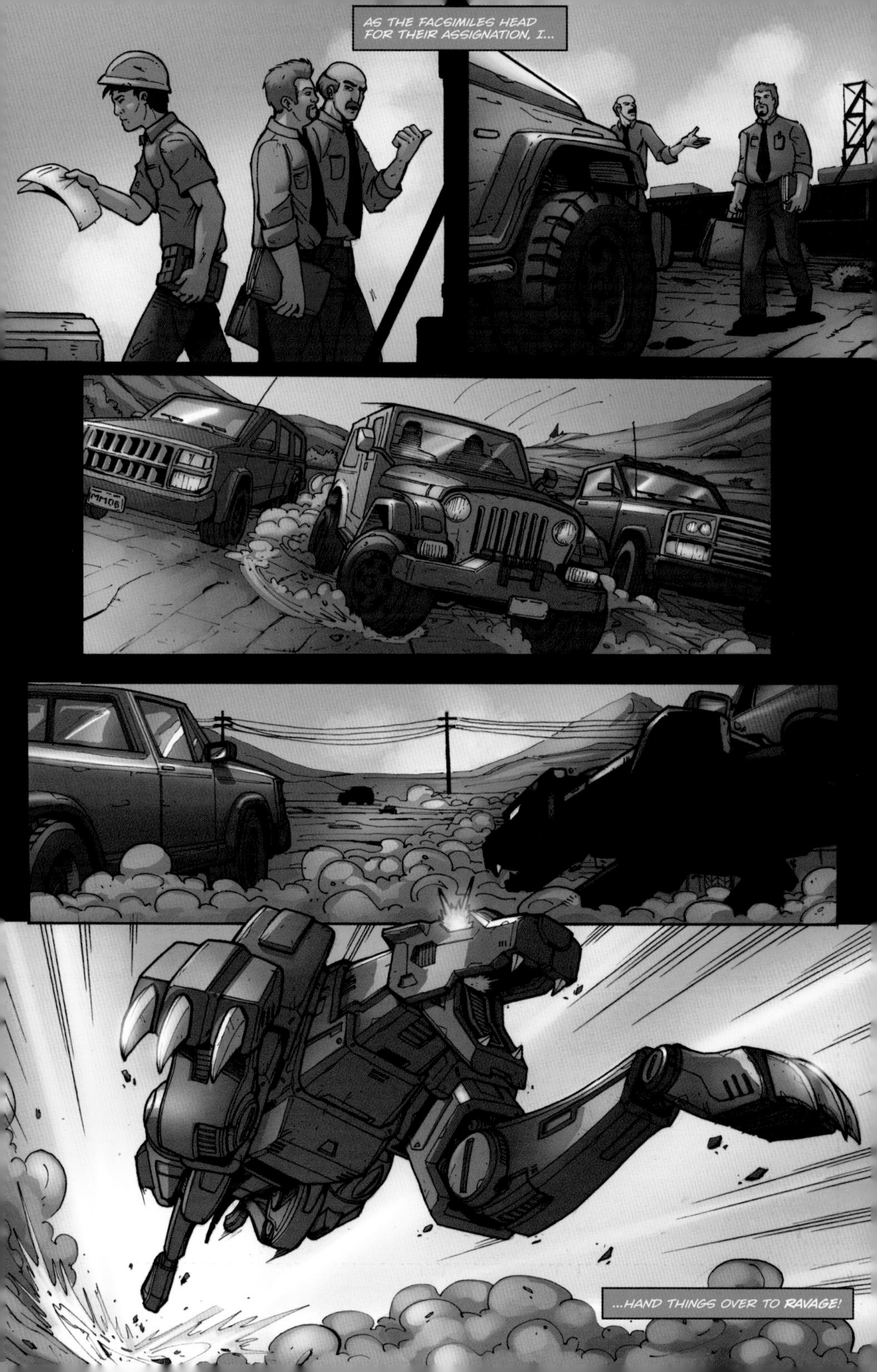
AS THE FACSIMILES HEAD FOR THEIR ASSIGNATION, I...
MM06
...HAND THINGS OVER TO RAVAGE!

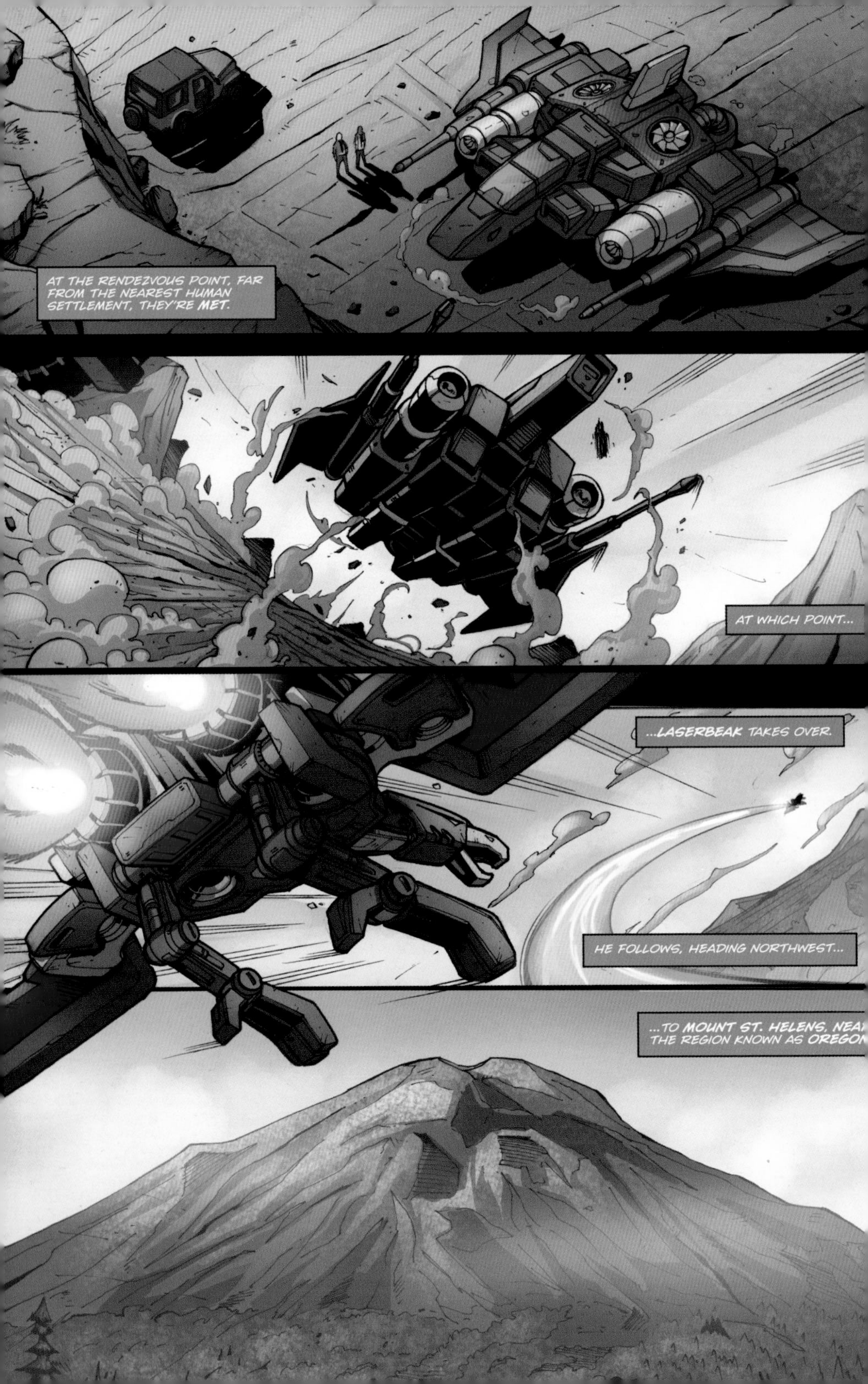
AT THE RENDEZVOUS POINT, FAR FROM THE NEAREST HUMAN SETTLEMENT, THEY'RE MET.
AT WHICH POINT...
...LASERBEAK TAKES OVER.
HE FOLLOWS, HEADING NORTHWEST...
...TO MOUNT ST. HELENS, NEA
THE REGION KNOWN AS OREGON

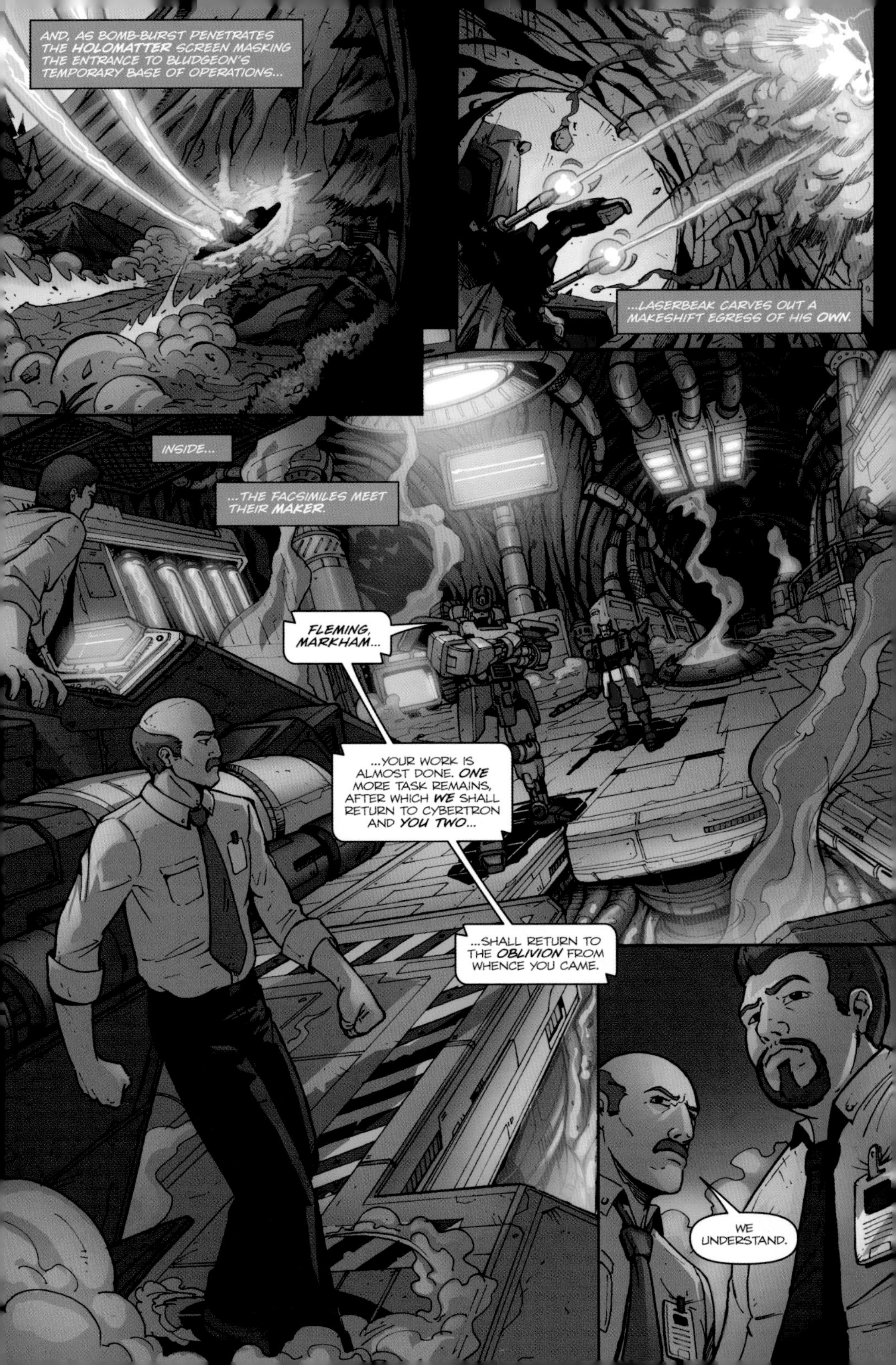
AND, AS BOMB-BURST PENETRATES THE HOLOMATTER SCREEN MASKING THE ENTRANCE TO BLUDGEON'S TEMPORARY BASE OF OPERATIONS...
...LASERBEAK CARVES OUT A MAKESHIFT EGRESS OF HIS OWN.
INSIDE...
...THE FACSIMILES MEET THEIR MAKER.
FLEMING, MARKHAM...
...YOUR WORK IS ALMOST DONE. ONE MORE TASK REMAINS, AFTER WHICH WE SHALL RETURN TO CYBERTRON AND YOU TWO...
...SHALL RETURN TO THE OBLIVION FROM WHENCE YOU CAME.
WE UNDERSTAND.

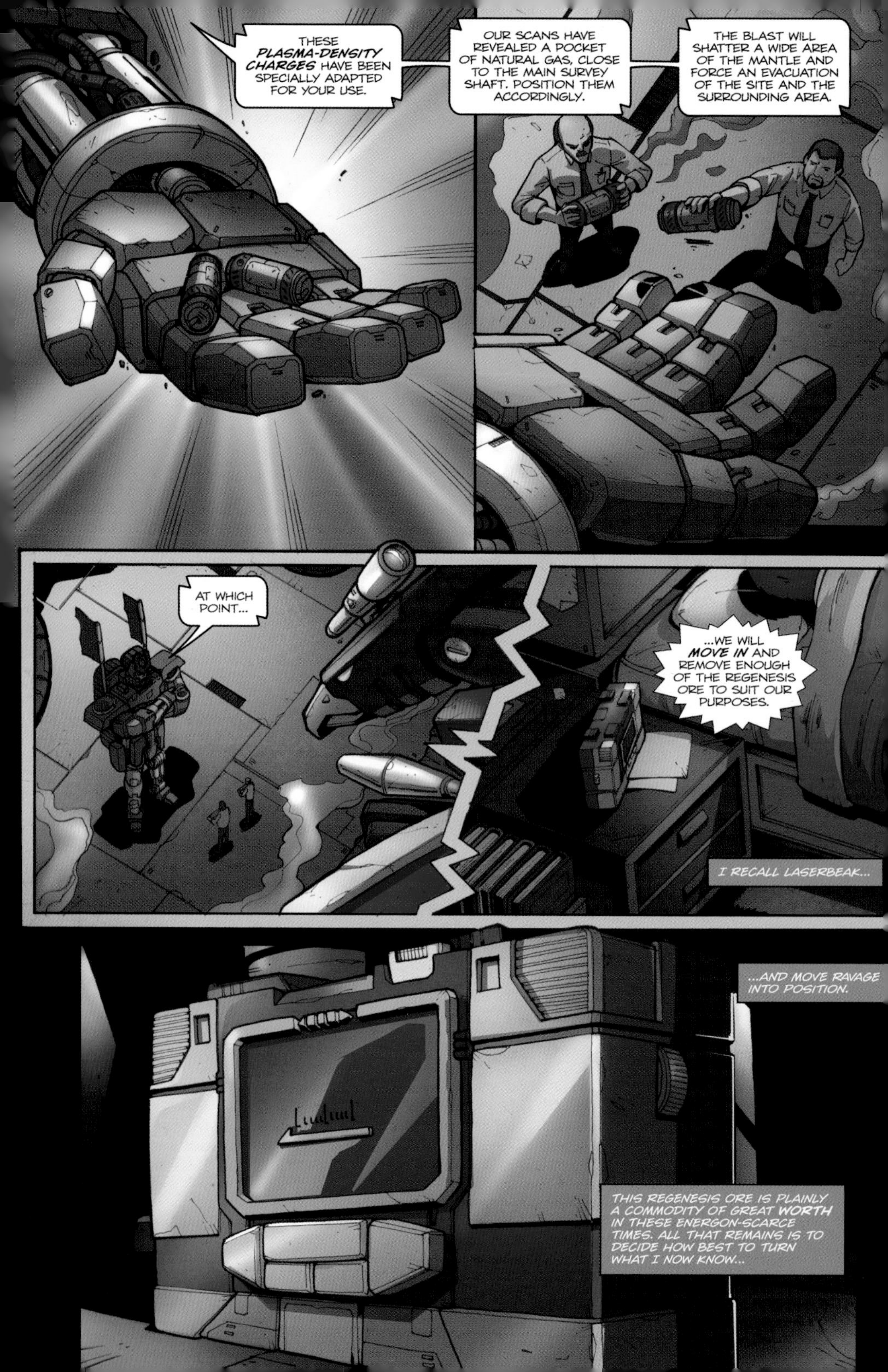
THESE PLASMA-DENSITY CHARGES HAVE BEEN SPECIALLY ADAPTED FOR YOUR USE.
OUR SCANS HAVE REVEALED A POCKET OF NATURAL GAS, CLOSE TO THE MAIN SURVEY SHAFT. POSITION THEM ACCORDINGLY.
THE BLAST WILL SHATTER A WIDE AREA OF THE MANTLE AND FORCE AN EVACUATION OF THE SITE AND THE SURROUNDING AREA.
AT WHICH POINT...
...WE WILL MOVE IN AND REMOVE ENOUGH OF THE REGENESIS ORE TO SUIT OUR PURPOSES.
I RECALL LASERBEAK...
...AND MOVE RAVAGE INTO POSITION.
THIS REGENESIS ORE IS PLAINLY A COMMODITY OF GREAT WORTH IN THESE ENERGON-SCARCE TIMES. ALL THAT REMAINS IS TO DECIDE HOW BEST TO TURN WHAT I NOW KNOW...

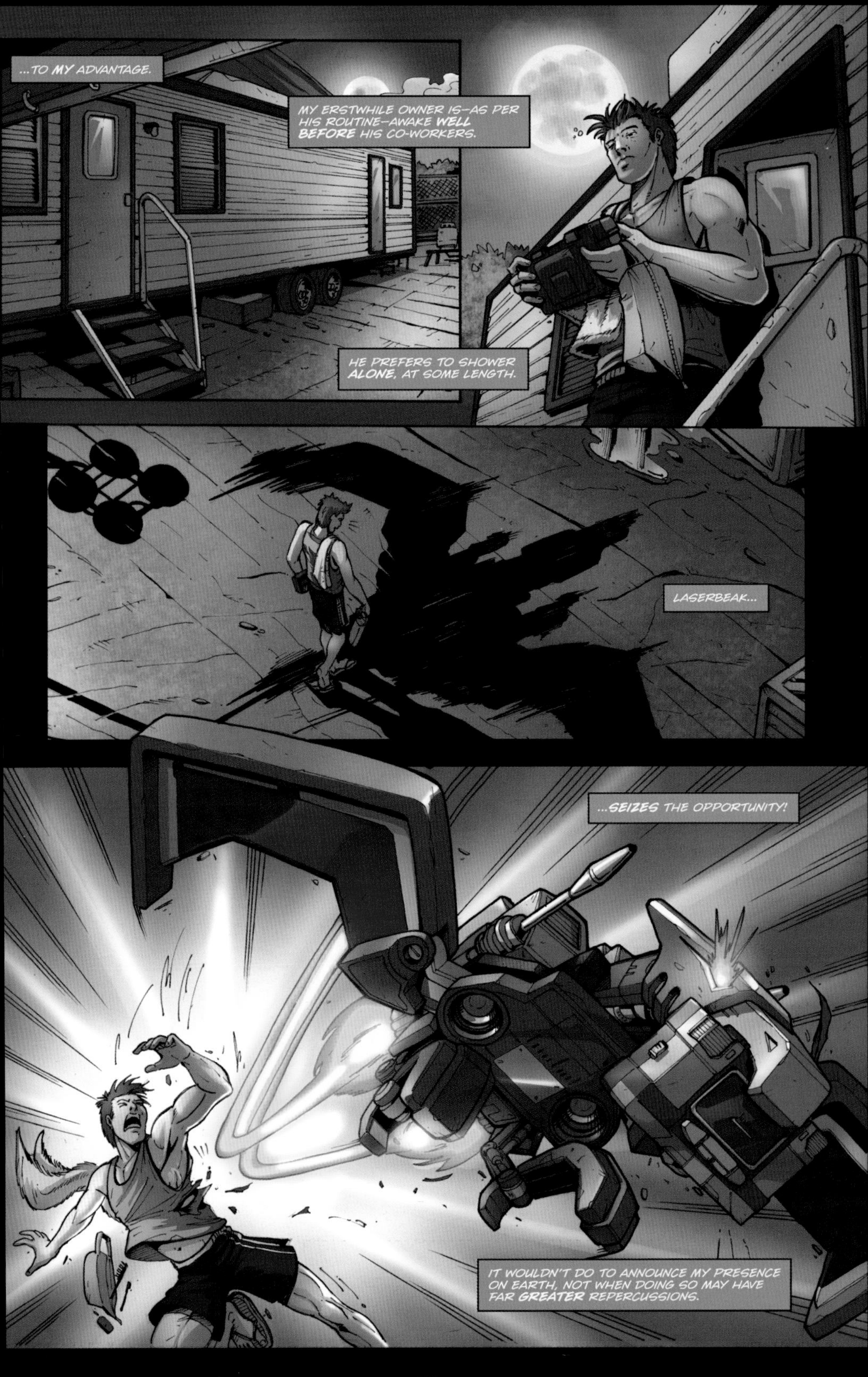
...TO MY ADVANTAGE.
MY ERSTWHILE OWNER IS—AS PER HIS ROUTINE—AWAKE WELL BEFORE HIS CO-WORKERS.
HE PREFERS TO SHOWER ALONE, AT SOME LENGTH.
LASERBEAK...
...SEIZES THE OPPORTUNITY!
IT WOULDN'T DO TO ANNOUNCE MY PRESENCE ON EARTH, NOT WHEN DOING SO MAY HAVE FAR GREATER REPERCUSSIONS.

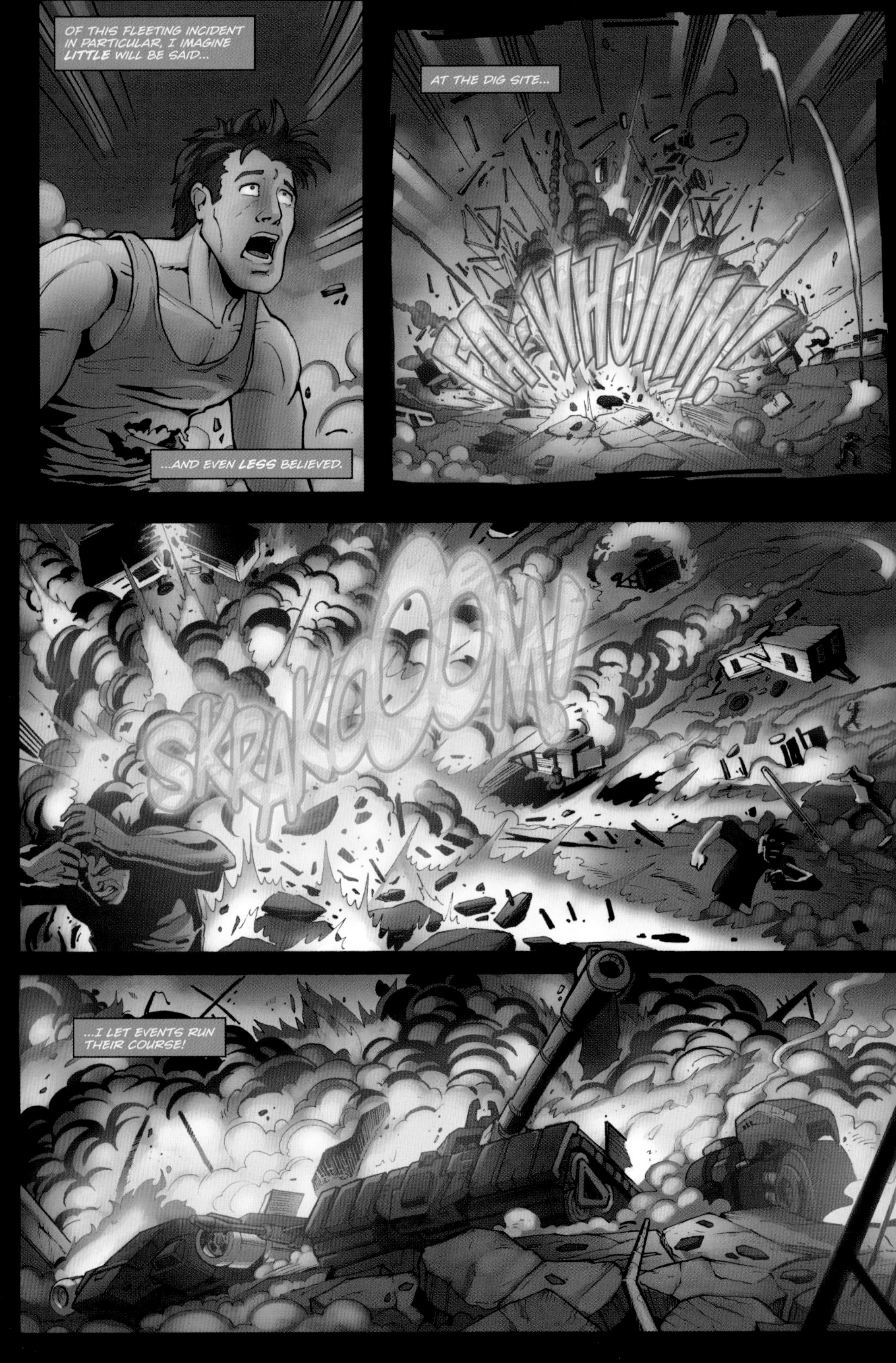
OF THIS FLEETING INCIDENT IN PARTICULAR, I IMAGINE LITTLE WILL BE SAID...
...AND EVEN LESS BELIEVED.
AT THE DIG SITE...
CH-WHUMM!
SKRAKOOOM!
...I LET EVENTS RUN THEIR COURSE!

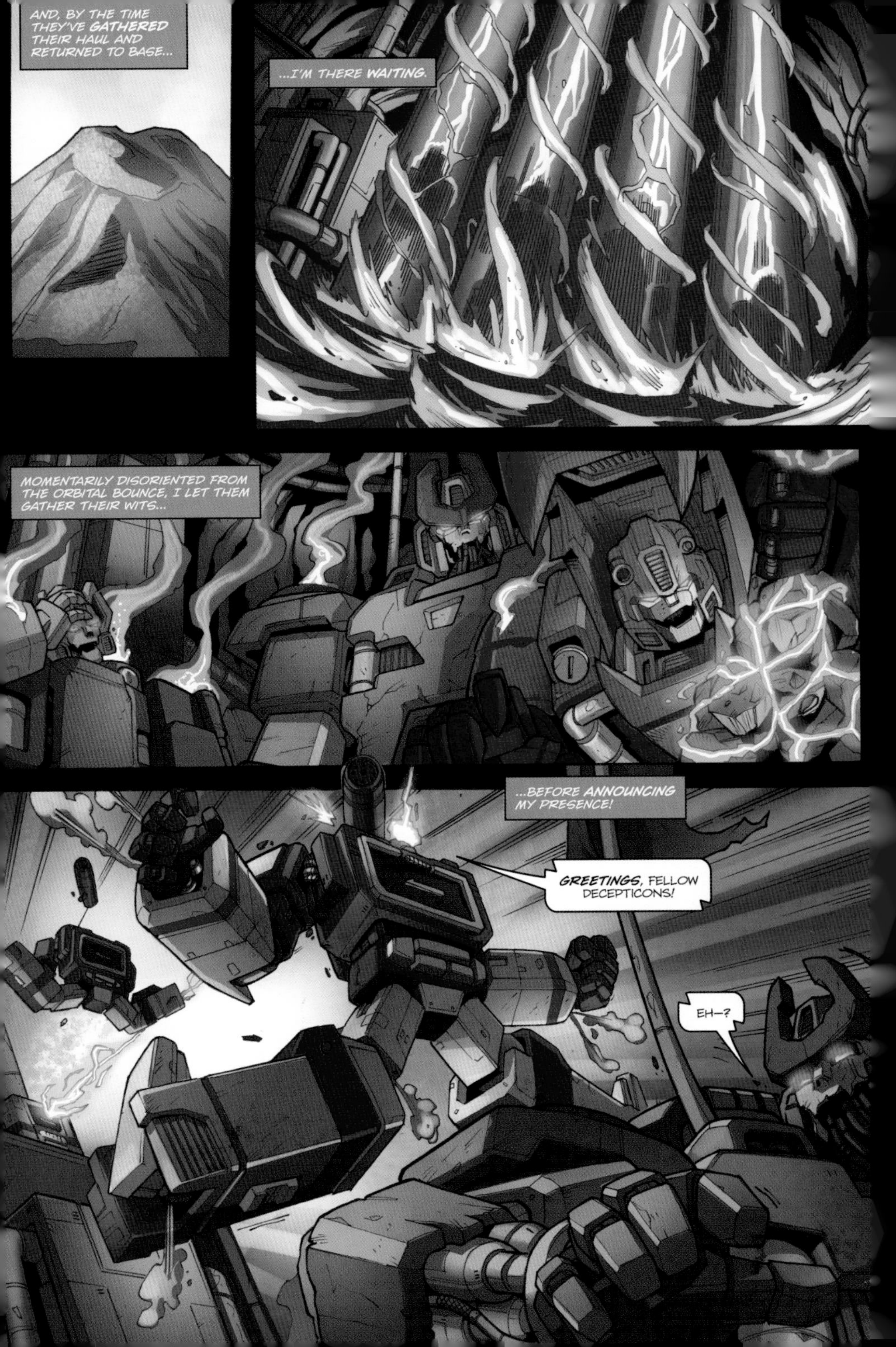
AND, BY THE TIME THEY'VE GATHERED THEIR HAUL AND RETURNED TO BASE...
...I'M THERE WAITING.
MOMENTARILY DISORIENTED FROM THE ORBITAL BOUNCE, I LET THEM GATHER THEIR WITS...
...BEFORE ANNOUNCING MY PRESENCE!
GREETINGS, FELLOW DECEPTICONS!
EH—?

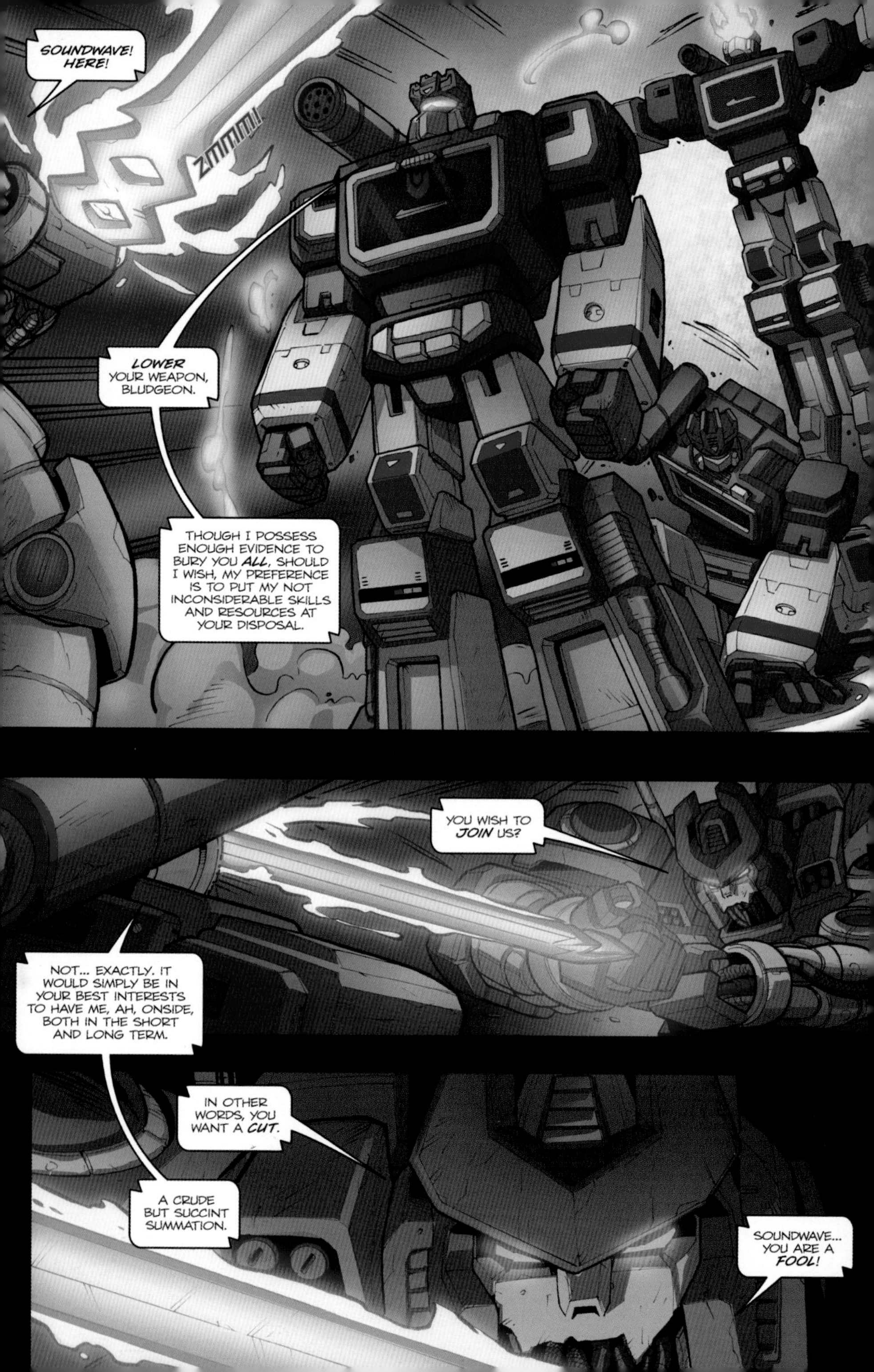
SOUNDWAVE! HERE!
ZMMM!
LOWER YOUR WEAPON, BLUDGEON.
THOUGH I POSSESS ENOUGH EVIDENCE TO BURY YOU ALL, SHOULD I WISH, MY PREFERENCE IS TO PUT MY NOT INCONSIDERABLE SKILLS AND RESOURCES AT YOUR DISPOSAL.
YOU WISH TO JOIN US?
NOT... EXACTLY. IT WOULD SIMPLY BE IN YOUR BEST INTERESTS TO HAVE ME, AH, ONSIDE, BOTH IN THE SHORT AND LONG TERM.
IN OTHER WORDS, YOU WANT A CUT.
A CRUDE BUT SUCCINT SUMMATION.
SOUNDWAVE... YOU ARE A FOOL!

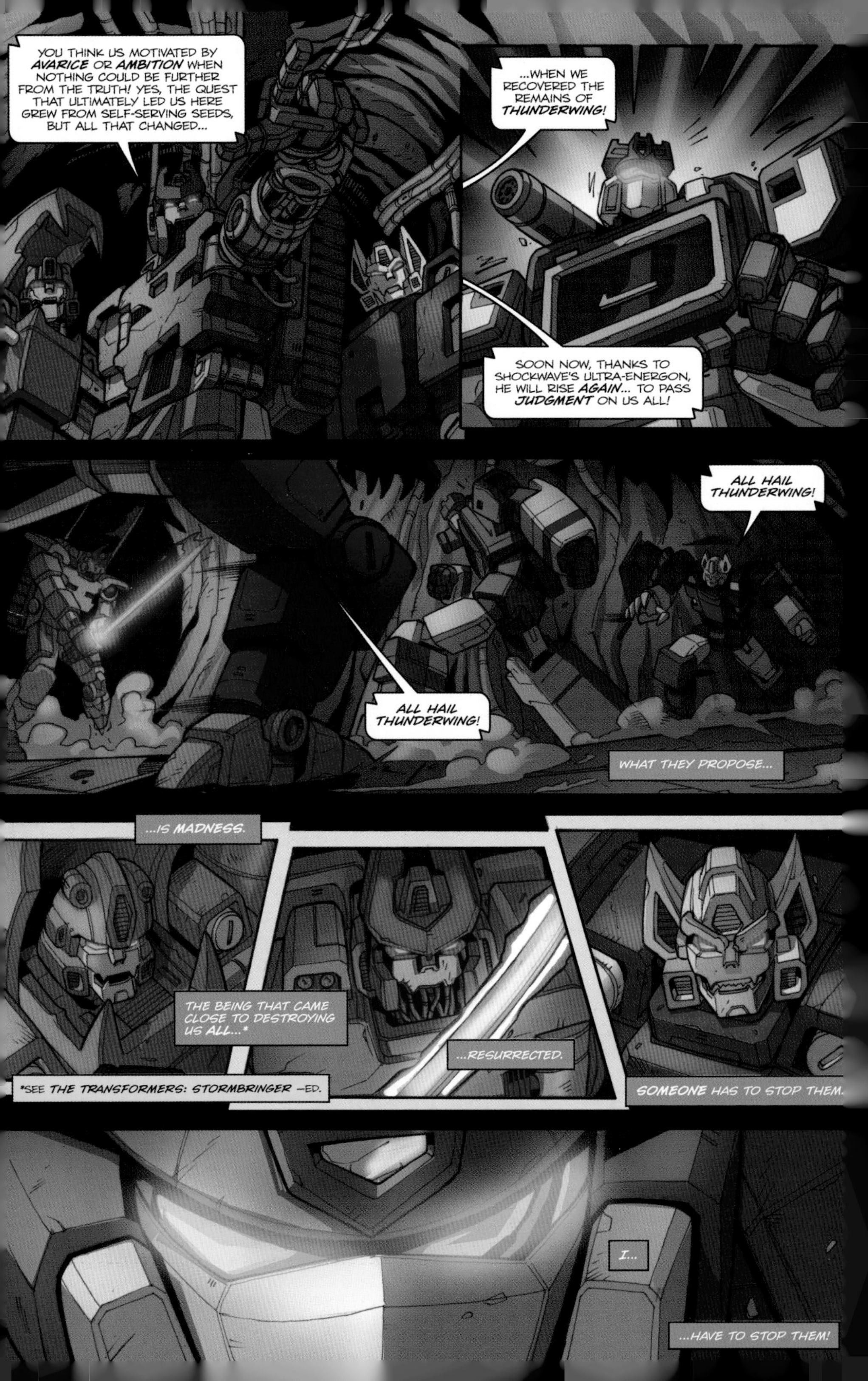
YOU THINK US MOTIVATED BY AVARICE OR AMBITION WHEN NOTHING COULD BE FURTHER FROM THE TRUTH! YES, THE QUEST THAT ULTIMATELY LED US HERE GREW FROM SELF-SERVING SEEDS, BUT ALL THAT CHANGED...
...WHEN WE RECOVERED THE REMAINS OF THUNDERWING!
SOON NOW, THANKS TO SHOCKWAVE'S ULTRA-ENERGON, HE WILL RISE AGAIN... TO PASS JUDGMENT ON US ALL!
ALL HAIL THUNDERWING!
ALL HAIL THUNDERWING!
WHAT THEY PROPOSE...
...IS MADNESS.
THE BEING THAT CAME CLOSE TO DESTROYING US ALL...*
*SEE THE TRANSFORMERS: STORMBRINGER —ED.
...RESURRECTED.
SOMEONE HAS TO STOP THEM.
I...
...HAVE TO STOP THEM!

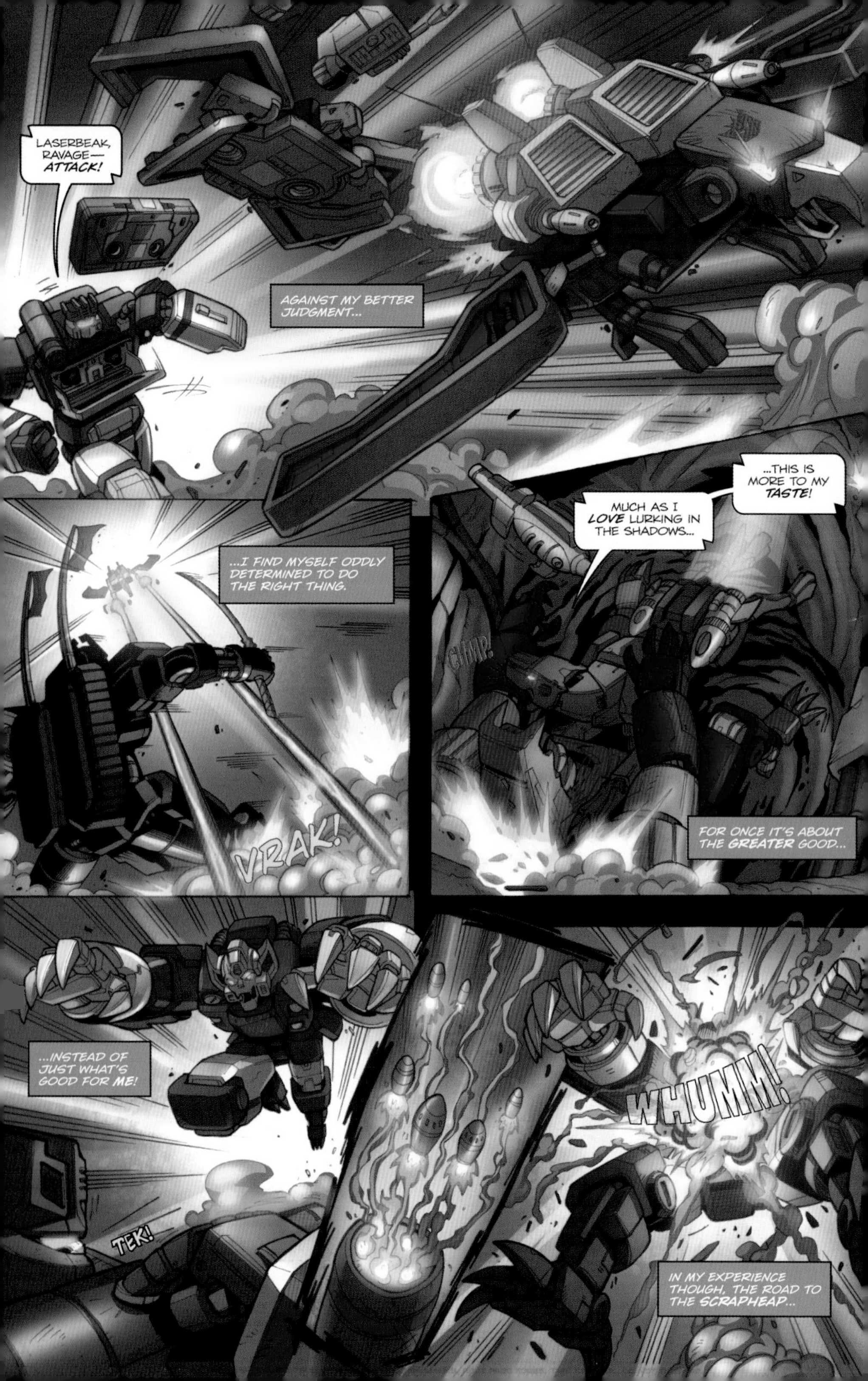
LASERBEAK, RAVAGE—ATTACK!
AGAINST MY BETTER JUDGMENT...
...I FIND MYSELF ODDLY DETERMINED TO DO THE RIGHT THING.
VRAK!
MUCH AS I LOVE LURKING IN THE SHADOWS...
...THIS IS MORE TO MY TASTE!
CHMP!
FOR ONCE IT'S ABOUT THE GREATER GOOD...
...INSTEAD OF JUST WHAT'S GOOD FOR ME!
TEK!
WHUMM!
IN MY EXPERIENCE THOUGH, THE ROAD TO THE SCRAPHEAP...

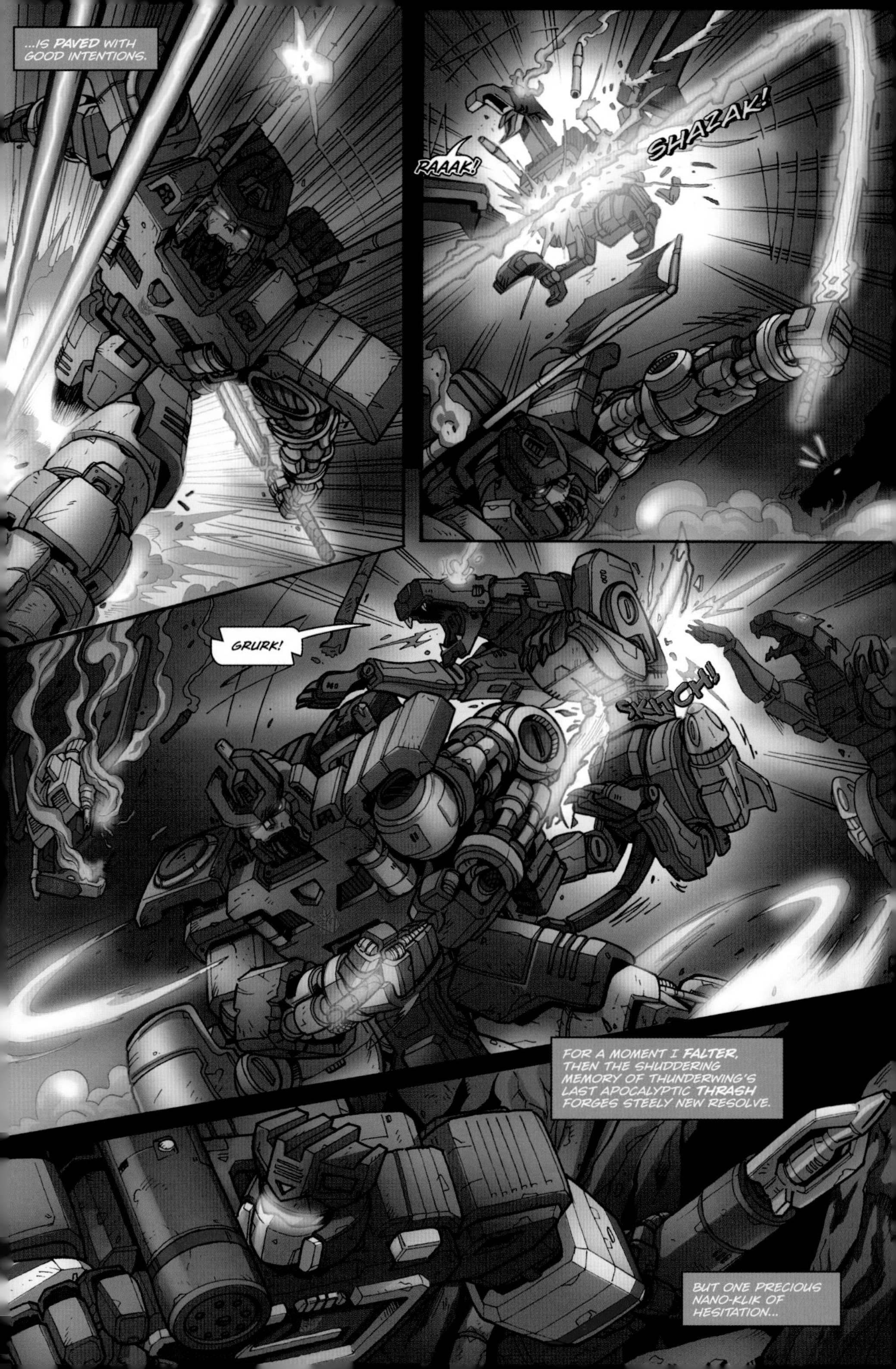
...IS PAVED WITH GOOD INTENTIONS.
RAAAK!
SHAZAK!
GRURK!
SKITCH!
FOR A MOMENT I FALTER, THEN THE SHUDDERING MEMORY OF THUNDERWING'S LAST APOCALYPTIC THRASH FORGES STEELY NEW RESOLVE.
BUT ONE PRECIOUS NANO-KLIK OF HESITATION...

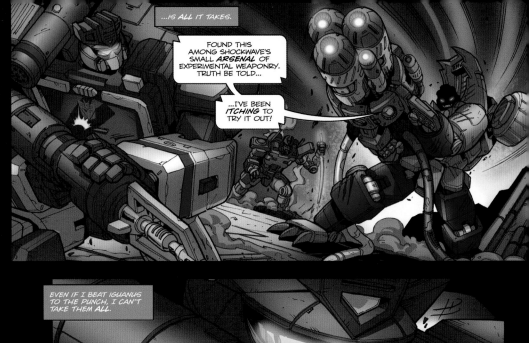

...IS *ALL* IT TAKES.

FOUND THIS AMONG SHOCKWAVE'S SMALL *ARSENAL* OF EXPERIMENTAL WEAPONRY. TRUTH BE TOLD...

...I'VE BEEN *ITCHING* TO TRY IT OUT!

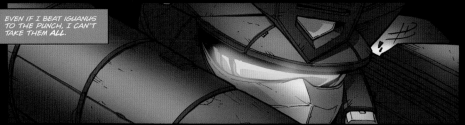

EVEN IF I BEAT IGUANUS TO THE PUNCH, I CAN'T TAKE THEM *ALL*.

SO...

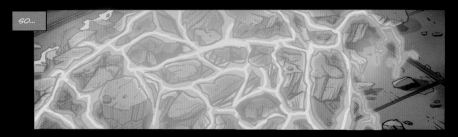

GRNN-OW!

RIIIZZRT!

AS WE UNDERSTAND IT, THE WEAPON *OVERRIDES* YOUR PRIMARY TRANSFORMATION COG...

UH-UH-UH—

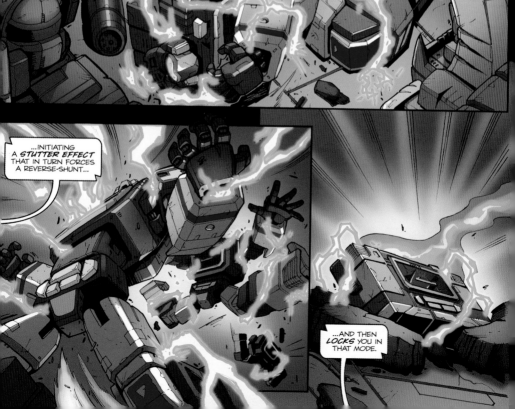

...INITIATING A *STUTTER EFFECT* THAT IN TURN FORCES A REVERSE-SHUNT...

...AND THEN *LOCKS* YOU IN THAT MODE.

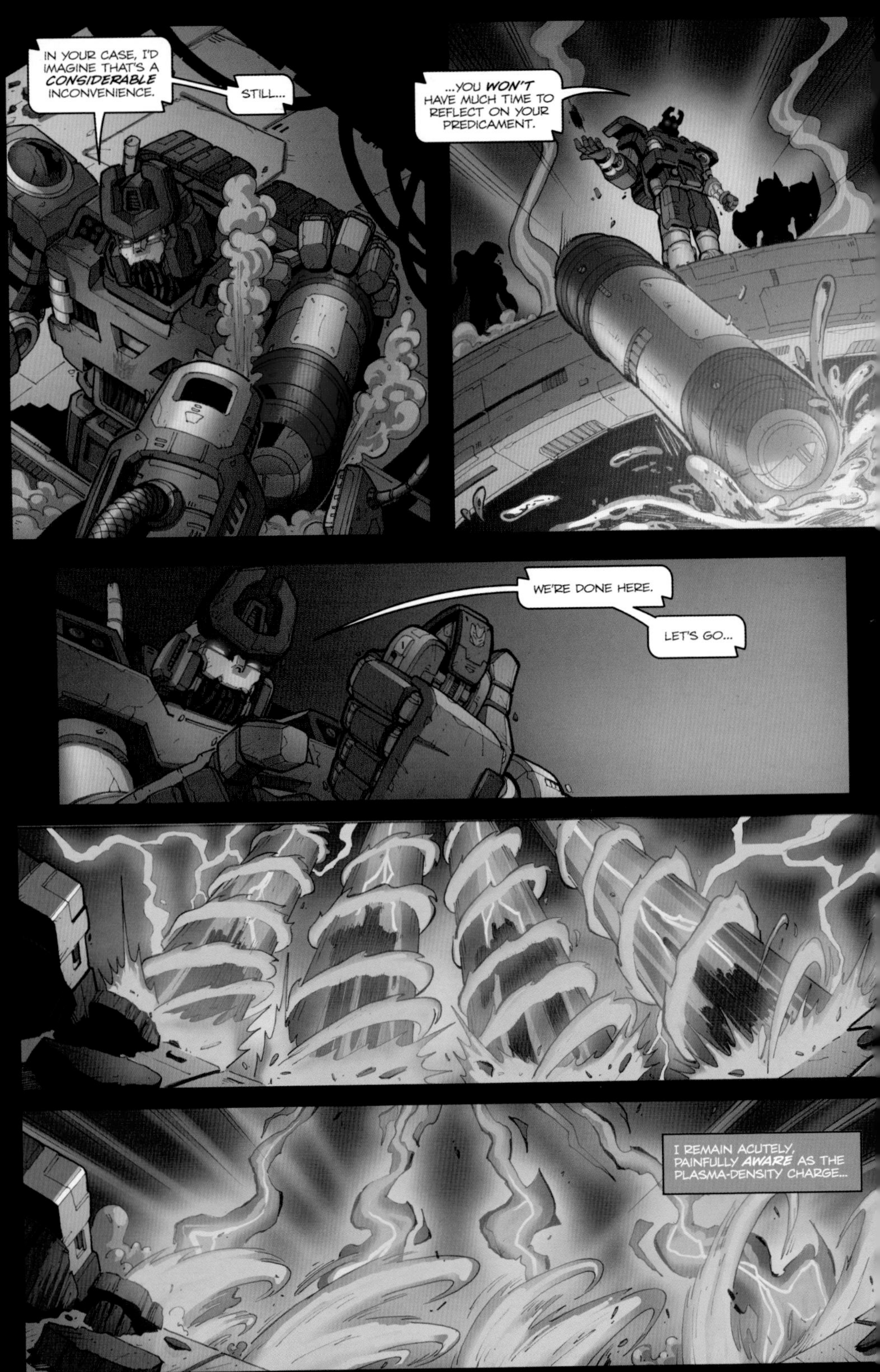
IN YOUR CASE, I'D IMAGINE THAT'S A CONSIDERABLE INCONVENIENCE.
STILL...
...YOU WON'T HAVE MUCH TIME TO REFLECT ON YOUR PREDICAMENT.
WE'RE DONE HERE.
LET'S GO...
I REMAIN ACUTELY, PAINFULLY AWARE AS THE PLASMA-DENSITY CHARGE...

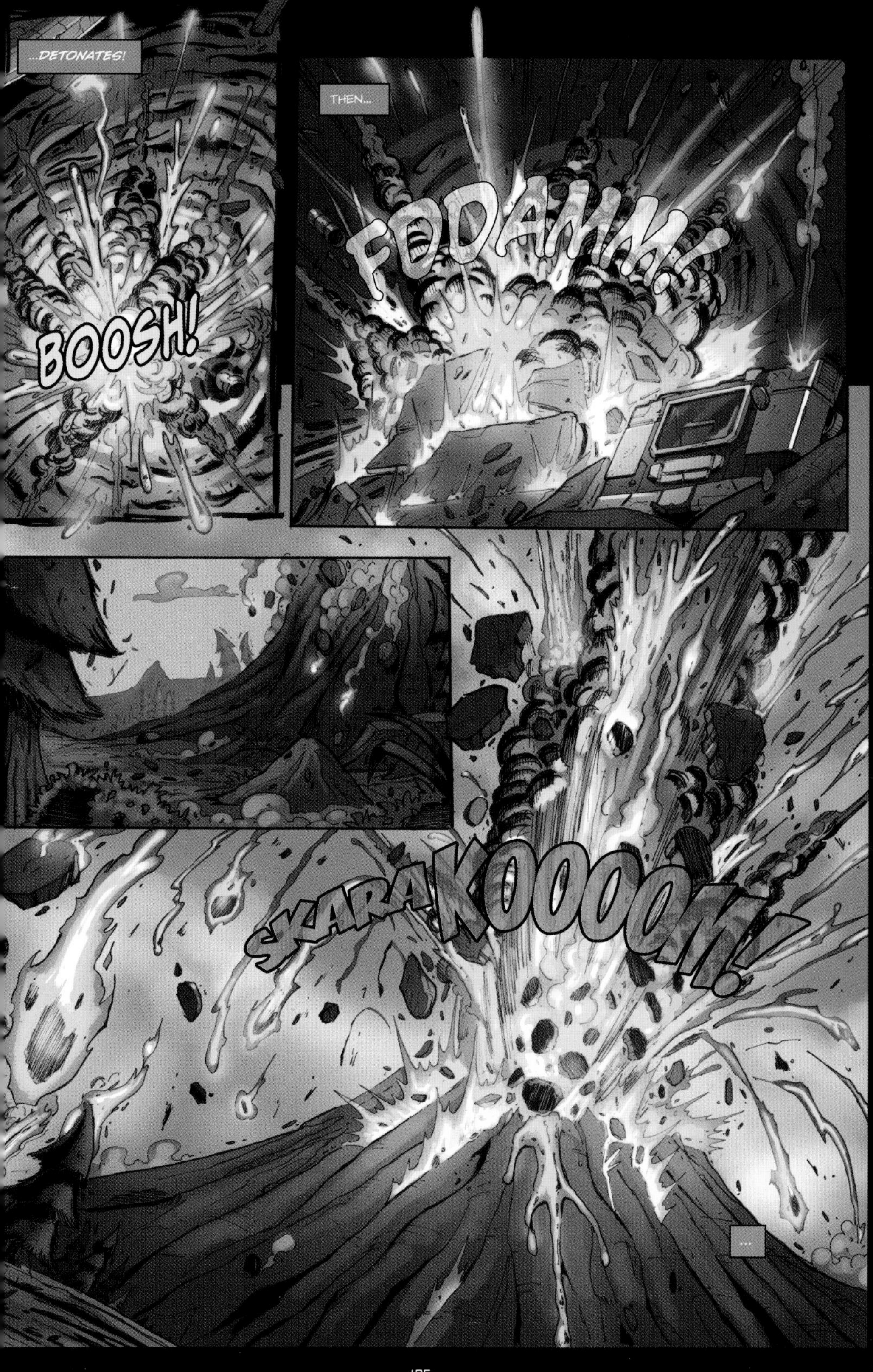

...DETONATES!
BOOSH!
THEN...
FDDAMM!!
SKARAKOOOOM!
...

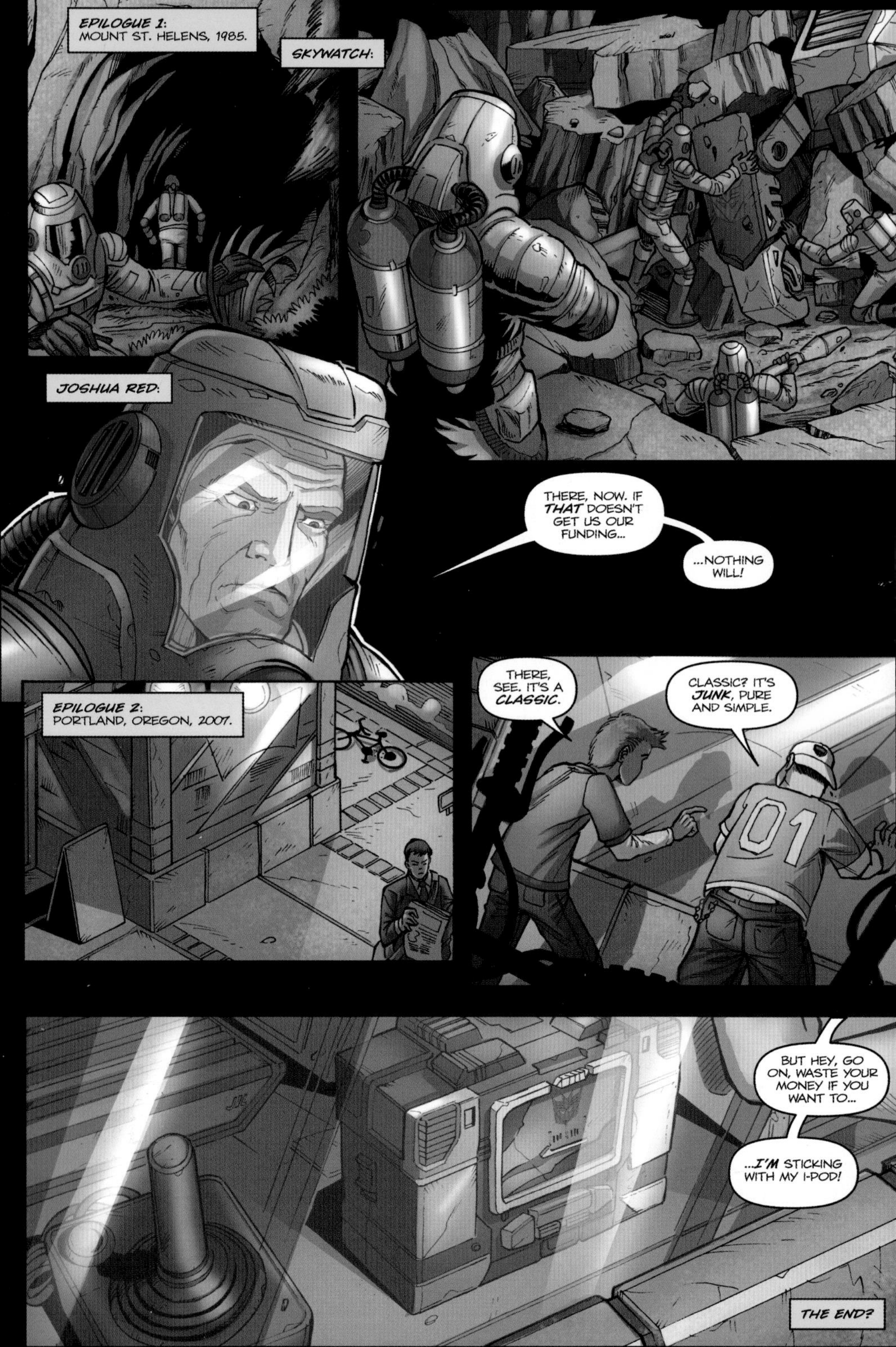
EPILOGUE 1: MOUNT ST. HELENS, 1985.
SKYWATCH:
JOSHUA RED:
THERE, NOW. IF THAT DOESN'T GET US OUR FUNDING...
...NOTHING WILL!
EPILOGUE 2: PORTLAND, OREGON, 2007.
THERE, SEE. IT'S A CLASSIC.
CLASSIC? IT'S JUNK, PURE AND SIMPLE.
01
BUT HEY, GO ON, WASTE YOUR MONEY IF YOU WANT TO...
...I'M STICKING WITH MY I-POD!
THE END?

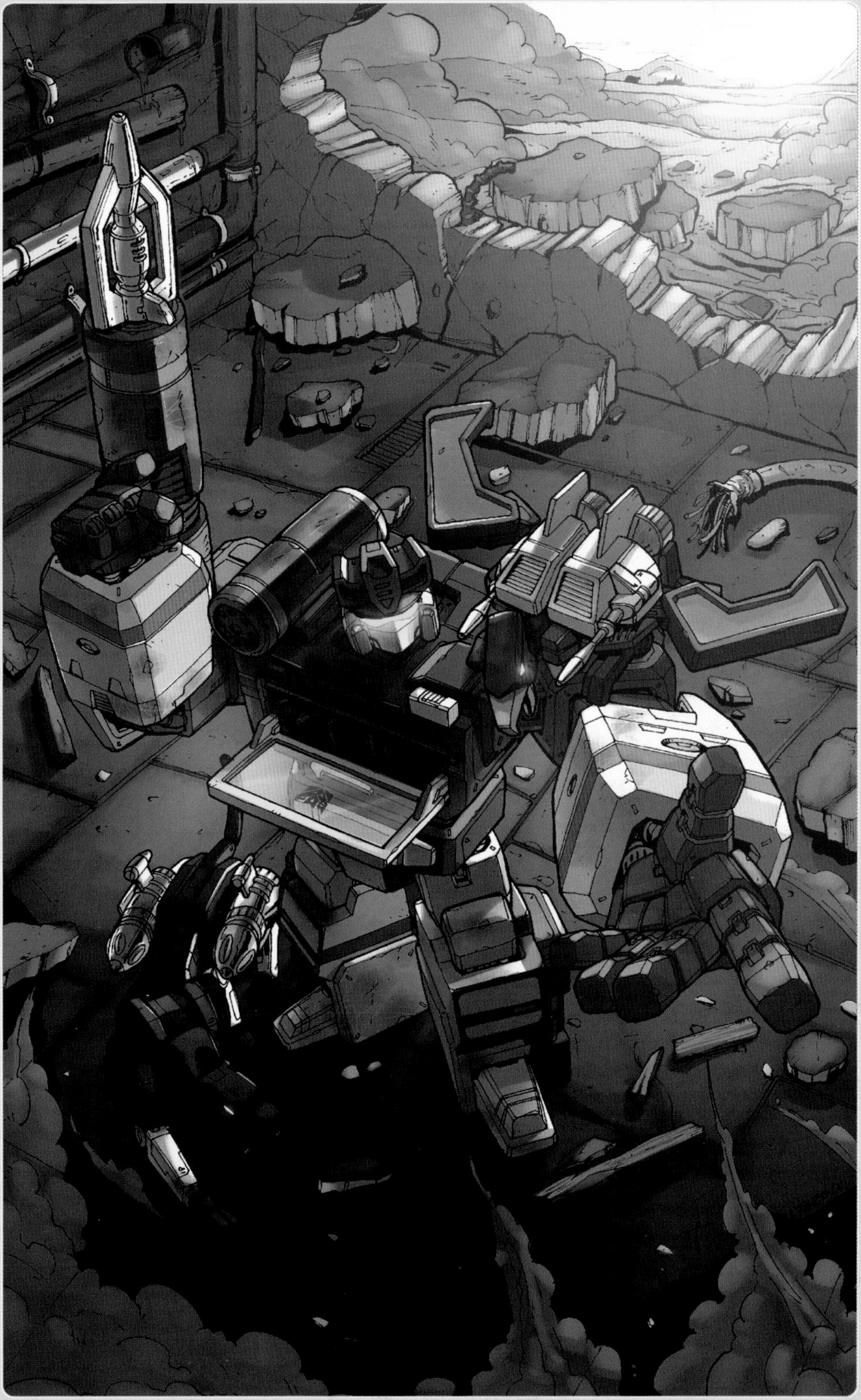

THE TRANSFORMERS

HEROES & VILLAINS

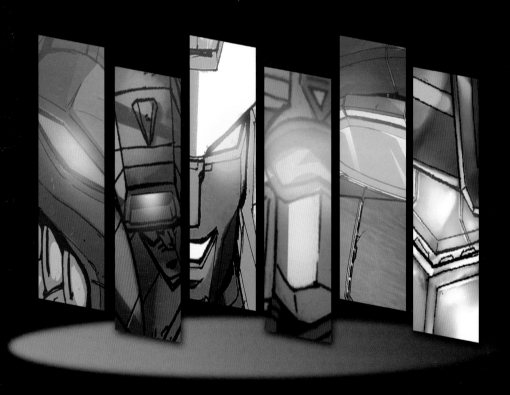